HONEYMOON
with My Brother

HONEYMOON
with My Brother

A Memoir

FRANZ WISNER

St. Martin's Griffin ☙ New York

www.stmartins.com

Maps by Jeffrey L. Ward

Library of Congress Cataloging-in-Publication Data

Wisner, Franz.
    Honeymoon with my brother : a memoir / Franz Wisner.
       p. cm.
    ISBN 0-312-32090-6 (hc)
    ISBN 0-312-34084-2 (pbk)
    EAN 978-0-312-34084-1
    1. Wisner, Franz—Travel.   2. Wisner, Kurt Oscar—Travel.   3. Brothers—United States—Biography.   4. Travelers—United States—Biography.   5. Betrothal—United States.   6. Man-woman relationships—United States.   I. Title.

CT275.W58479A3 2005
910.4—dc22
                                          2004056655

First Edition: February 2006

10 9 8 7 6 5 4 3 2 1

For
LARUE BOCARDE DAULTON
1902–2002

and

KURT OSCAR WISNER
my brother, my hero, my new best friend

ACKNOWLEDGMENTS

From the time I was dumped at the altar, this has been a female-dominated project. Thank God.

Justine Amodeo, the multitalented editor of *Coast Magazine,* inspired the title of this book and the decision to do it. Throughout the writing process, Alix Clyburn both pushed me to dig deeper and reined in my rambles, even while on her way to the hospital to give birth. Martha Adams served as cheerleader and facilitator extraordinaire, putting us in touch with the right people throughout the process. Huge thanks to them and their husbands, Chris, Jeff, and Alex (aka Al One through Al Four), respectively.

Kris Dahl and Catherine Brackey at International Creative Management were the first agents to embrace the story. They, along with Jud Laghi, guided us with wise counsel and patient replies to our rookie questions ("You mean we can't just send publishers a couple columns?"). Their colleagues Josie Freedman, Pamela Bruce, Michael McCarthy, Brian Sher, and Jon Huddle continued the ICM TLC.

None of this would have been possible had Diane Reverand of St. Martin's Press not taken a chance on a couple vagabond brothers with an unusual tale. For her conviction, savvy edits, love and laughs, and foreign film recommendations, we remain enormously thankful. Thanks as well to John Murphy, publicity king, Gina Scarpa, Steve Snider, Susan Yang, Jim DiMiero, Gregg Sullivan, and the entire St. Martin's team for their support.

Paul Campos, friend since Davis Parent Nursery School and premier arbiter of world football, *Spinal Tap* dialogue, and JT-isms, made many of our trips enjoyable and meaningful. Ben Johnson, who has helped me in countless situations before and since, hatched the idea of a brideless wedding and bailed me out at a time when I needed a bucket. The *Orange County Register*'s Amy Wilson swapped e-mails with us for months in order to tell this story with her elegant prose. Rick Reiff of the *Orange County Business Journal,* John Flynn of the *San Francisco Chronicle,* and Craig Reem and Steve Churm of *OC Metro* all published my far-flung road missives and deserve our gratitude and a couple cold beers.

For their inspiration, more than they'll ever know or admit, *muchos, muchos gracias* to Larry Thomas, Jo Ann Taylor, Deborah, Lisa England, Lisa P., Angela D., and Celeste Signorino. For opening their homes and sharing their lives, tons o' thanks to John and Lena Dawkins, Jonathan Terra, Iveta, Irina, the Mancera family, Charlotte, Ytzel Ponte, Tom Schaffer, Emma and Alejandro, Douglas (of course), the de Sá family of Rio, Rita, Pete, Seth, Liezl, Givenchy, Guta, the legendary Tom Knox, Alex and Ana Ana Ana Ana Ana (see, I told you I would). For privacy purposes, I've changed some names in the text.

For nourishment, both edible and spiritual, and a hand along the way, hats off to Yuca's, Il Cappriccio, Jim Sachs and Puroast Coffee, DCide Records, Jesse Raben, Scott Garrison, Paul Kranhold, Loominocity, the Olsens, the celebrated Sea Ranch Crew and those there in spirit(s), Matt Welch (Wiz Three) and the closers at Carter VW/Saab, Natasha Schumacher, Big D, Jessica Johnson, Marla Miller, Mirka Jamniczky, Charmaine Craig, Renee Croce, Jennifer Temple, Michael Franti, Terry Heagney, the Benners, the Fureys, Saba Malak, Greg and Donna Lucas, the Badenhausens, Karen Portik, Ed Ross, Jeff Kubiak, Jennifer Parker and Rudy Van Zyl, Eric Lochner, the Palmers, the Youngs, Libby Spears, Erin Mitchell, TIC, Governor Pete Wilson, Bob White and the Wilson Administration(s), Tom Tucker and the New Majority, Walkie Ray, Jason Luther, Debra Saunders, and my writing partner, Fritz.

Toward the end of the honeymoon, we were spoiled by the gracious hospitality of Patty Harper and the five-star staff at several Orient Express properties, including the Copacabana Palace, Westcliff Hotel in Johannesburg, Mount Nelson in Cape Town and their jaw-dropping safari camps in Botswana. Visit them all. Sincere thanks as well to Teddi Anderson and her colleagues at The Limtiaco Company for unveiling the island gems of Palau and Yap. Go there, too.

While we met them after the honeymoon, thanks to: Ayla, Kim, Laura and the ladies of Laura Davidson Public Relations, Larry Leamer, Marina Albert, and the vivacious Gina Greblo.

For adopting our baby and ushering it to the silver screen, *obrigado* to: Jimmy Miller, Julie Darmody, and George Gatins at Mosaic; Kevin Bisch; and Rachel O'Connor, Doug Belgrad, Jonathan Kadin, and folks at Sony Pictures.

For making life bloom, a special thank you to Tracy Middendorf.

Last on our list, huge in our hearts, is our immediate family—Joyce and Bob Wisner, Doug and Lisa Menzmer, and our nieces, Elizabeth and Ellie. Here's to many more DEAs ahead.

HONEYMOON
with My Brother

1

Amid the pine tree windbreaks and foamy Pacific shore, Sea Ranch, California, is a wonderful place to be dumped. The wild lilac and ill-tempered sea lions—they'll distract your attention for at least a few minutes after the woman of your dreams leaves you at the altar. That, and a hell of a lot of booze.

My younger brother, Kurt, and I arrived early at the only dive bar in town, a place where the bartender would wince if he heard the words *mojito* or *caipirinha*. We gave the bearded keep twenty dollars in advance to keep the drinks flowing. He put a few more beers in the cooler and promised to take special care of the group that would soon gather for the evening. It was going to be a long and interesting night.

The century-old Gualala Hotel greets visitors with white pillars and an Old West porch. Close your eyes and imagine the thirsty cowboy tying his horse to the front rail. Open them and see tourists sitting around picnic tables in the dining room, devouring family-size bowls of minestrone soup. The hotel's bar, with its knotty pine and boar-head decor, sits off the main entrance. It had one of those electric beer signs on the wall that morphed scenery from mountain to beach.

Kurt bought me a Budweiser and asked how I was doing. I didn't open up. I looked at his newly gray hair and thin face and realized I *couldn't* talk to him.

Growing up, the teenager's code of conduct prohibited me from associating with a brother two grade levels my junior. To impress my friends, I did everything I could to avoid him. He was happy to do the same. Since then, we saw each other only a handful of days a year. Usually around Christmas. Details of our lives were relayed through our mom. Neither of us took the initiative to do more.

I wanted to talk to Kurt. I needed to talk to Kurt, but I didn't know how. I felt an awkward paralysis, like a child who can't relate to his parents. I couldn't pull out the words. I remembered the days in the backseat of the light blue Ford station wagon. We could talk about anything back then—secret hiding places (always behind the built-in shelves in my room), optimal ways to torture our younger sister, Lisa (pin her down and pretend to spit), or that baseball card game I always seemed to lose; lay Tito Fuentes against the wall and try to knock him over from ten feet away with a Wilbur Wood or a Dusty Baker. Despite the distance between us, Kurt was still the first person I called after I learned, five days prior, my wedding was off.

I'd reached him on my cell phone as I sped up the 405 Freeway from my house in Newport Beach to my fiancée Annie's small, rent-controlled apartment in Santa Monica with the industrial-strength carpet and refrigerator in need of a cleaning. I couldn't remember the last time I phoned him. Probably to relay some bad news, like the death of our grandfather. We'd grown apart during the last decade. Kurt sold real estate in Seattle while I pursued a political career in Washington, D.C., and California. He sounded surprised to hear my voice. I sensed he knew something must be wrong. I needed him like I'd never needed a brother before.

"What's up?" he said.

"Not much. Weather's nice. Played golf the other day. My wedding's off. Did I mention the weather?"

Silence.

"Serious?"

"Serious. I'm on my way up to Annie's to get dumped right now. Her brother Gerald just called me to tell me she's not going to be able to go through with it."

"Man, I'm sorry," he said in a hushed tone. "What the hell happened?"

"Long story. I'll tell you later."

"What are you going to do?"

"I have no idea. Everything's paid for. People have rented cabins for the weekend. Some folks from overseas are already en route. Nightmare."

"Hmm."

"I haven't even been dumped yet and the only thing I can think about are those hundred phone calls I'll need to make tomorrow."

"That, um, sucks."

"I hate to ask you this, but is there any way you could fly down here to give me a hand? I'll pay for your ticket."

"No problem," he said without hesitation. "And you don't need to pay for anything. I'll leave you a message on your answering machine with my flight info."

I talked to my mom briefly after that, telling her the wedding was about to crash. I'd spared her from the rapidly rising list of problems in the previous weeks, though I knew she sensed them. Delays on invitations and unworn wedding rings are red flags to moms.

"You have no choice," she tried to console me. "She's doing you a huge favor by telling you now as opposed to after the wedding. Franz, it's a blessing. You'll see that. It might be a while, but eventually you'll see that."

I knew my parents would be hugely supportive. They always were. At times, maddeningly so. That didn't stop me from feeling I'd failed. I knew I couldn't talk to my father yet without breaking down. I just kept thinking about the photo display shelves in their living room, the ones packed with shots of their wedding in Yuba City four decades before, sister Lisa and Doug's the previous year, dogs present and past, favorite babysitters, the photo of my great-grandfather during his years in China. There'd be no Sea Ranch shots. And I wondered how long it would take until my mom removed the ones with Annie.

Speeding up the 405 Freeway, I rewound the ten-year relationship in my mind like a cheap VCR whirring around for a scene.

Don't fold on me, Annie. Don't fold.

What about the children's names? We had them all picked out. Or the split-pea-soup dinners when we couldn't afford anything else? Don't you remember the bad puns lobbed back and forth for hours during car rides?

What happened to the night we made love so fervently we both had to hold on to the bedpost at that remote guesthouse in the Hudson Valley? The one with the old lady who paused before renting us the room. Don't you remember me staring at you, stroking your hair when you opened your eyes the next morning?

What about life, our life, our entire adult life spent with each other? Doesn't that count for anything?

Annie waited in Gerald's apartment, down the hall from her own. Sitting on his white leather sofa in faded blue jeans and an old gray cashmere sweater, she didn't look at me when I walked through the door. I sat across from her, bending my head like a turtle to read her face. I could see her eyes were beet red and I felt awful. For both of us. She played with a rumpled Kleenex in her thin hands, squeezing it, touching it to her colorless face. Gerald began with some awkward comments about nobody being wrong and nobody being a bad person. I just stared at Annie, still wondering what direction to take.

Why couldn't you say something a few months ago? No, forget it. Mom's right. You're doing me a favor.

I was angry, embarrassed, overwhelmed, numbed, despondent, and . . . relieved. I then knew the best tactic to take was no tactic at all. For the first time, I could see the relationship was over. Like a balloon slipping through a child's hand. Up, up, then it's gone. Nothing to do but watch it vanish. Still, I loved that balloon.

Slowly, Annie lifted her head, let out a deep breath, and said, between sobs, "I'm sorry. I just can't do it. I've tried, but I just can't do it."

She looked like a little girl, years younger than the elegant woman I knew.

"It's okay," I said, taking her hand.

As I drove home, arms extended and locked on the steering wheel, glassy eyes focused trancelike on the car lights ahead, I felt a weighted object fall into my lap.

The band on the expensive, granite-face Tag Heuer watch Annie had given me as a birthday gift a few years back had suddenly worn out.

It wasn't my idea to go ahead and have the "wedding" anyway. I wasn't that strong. It was Ben's plan, my friend and longtime roommate. He blew off his public relations clients to help me make phone calls the next day. Kurt flew in from Seattle late morning. To speed the process, we established a call system involving two cell phones and my home line. One of us would break the news to a friend, and then pass the phone around.

My first call was the hardest. I hung up several times before reaching my ninety-eight-year-old step-grandmother at her retirement home in Sacramento. LaRue loved weddings. And Annie. Last time I visited her she had talked for hours about Sea Ranch, a coastal resort community a few hours north of San Francisco. She wanted to know all the details—the color schemes and the procession order and such. At one point she stopped me midsentence.

"I'll make you a beautiful wedding cake," she said.

I noticed a cake-decorating newsletter on a glass table nearby, dog-eared to a few different ideas.

"Um, okay," I said, not really sure if it was right to have a ninety-eight-year-old woman spread icing for hours.

I don't remember her words when I called her, but I remember her tone— warm and soothing and calm. Especially in comparison with mine. She sounded far from surprised, and that surprised me. I thought about all the afternoons she must have spent savoring an event that would never happen. I started the conversation feeling I'd let her down, and ended it feeling all was fine. Five minutes later and my mind raced anew. For those moments of pause, I was in debt to LaRue.

After LaRue, the calls became easier. Still embarrassing and awkward, but easier. The consolations were tender and reassuring. After a couple of conversations, I realized most of my friends had heard the gist of the story through others. My job was to fill in the gaps and to muster my bravest "I'm fine" after they asked how I was doing. Some friends were angry with Annie ("That *bitch!* Oops. Can I call her that?"), though most felt bad for her. The men talked about logistics like gift registries and down payments, the women probed deeper into my state of mind and Annie's. I encouraged them to reach out. "Phone her, hug her. It's nobody's fault." They offered to help with calls and told me they loved me. A few of the men threatened me with bodily harm if I ever got back together with her: "I'm not kidding, Wiz."

The term support network had always sounded like some corny phrase from a Tony Robbins pep talk. For the first time in my life, I discovered its depth, power, and meaning. Sure, I knew friends had long surrounded me. I found out that day that crises have a way of rallying everyone in from the hinterlands, placing them on a line, and forcing a roll call vote of warmth and support. I felt like a drill sergeant listening to people report for duty.

Annie and I had picked a hundred-year-old barn at Sea Ranch as the ideal site for our vows. A Russian fortress, Pomo Indian community, sea otter trading center, sheep ranch, and outpost for whiskey and rum smugglers—the area had a rich history. In the early 1960s, developers purchased the property to build an environmentally sensitive community featuring single-story homes made from wood that would gray and fade into the hillsides. Yards and sidewalks were discarded in favor of natural landscaping, open spaces, and walking trails to beaches.

The wildflower-wrapped structure on the edge of a bluff had seemed so naturally simple when we chose the location. That Friday it morphed into an out-of-the-way pain in the ass. Kurt, Ben, and I called dozens of caterers, musicians, florists, gift registries, and hotel staff to cancel reservations and beg for refunds. I watched the bulk of my savings whither away. The band from Los Angeles kept their five-thousand-dollar deposit. The bagpiper from Mendocino said he was sorry, then let me off the hook for payment. You can still buy my CD if you're interested, he said before hanging up. I told him I'd get back to him, then never did.

The honeymoon splurge to Costa Rica was the only issue I couldn't resolve. *Oh, the honeymoon. I was really looking forward to that. The champagne breakfasts and bird-of-paradise bouquets. Bed nettings and teak writing tables, verandas and Pacific Ocean views.* I'd call the travel agent on Monday to see if the rooms were refundable. And I gave up trying to reach the airlines after a half hour of pushing 0-0-0 in the hope an operator would magically see the urgency of my call and take me off hold. That could wait, too.

Early in the afternoon, someone asked Ben about the rented Sea Ranch cabins. Another friend from the East Coast said he had nonrefundable plane tickets and planned to come anyway. Inspired, Ben started telling people the wedding party was still on . . . there just wasn't going to be a bride.

"I don't know, Benny," I said, still numb and spinning from the fast-changing circumstances.

"Think about it," he answered forcefully. "You should be around friends. Your friends want to see you. Your friends will be at Sea Ranch. *You* should be at Sea Ranch."

I agreed, halfheartedly, then by late afternoon became more enthusiastic about the idea with each conversation. *Why not? No. Okay.* We settled on the large cabin with the oceanfront Jacuzzi as ground zero. Golf times were secured, carpools from the San Francisco and Oakland airports arranged, and assignments given for food and booze supplies. Kurt compiled a list of names on a napkin. Seventy people said they'd attend.

"No moping or tears," Ben prescribed in his faded Boston accent. "Especially you, Wiz."

Now, this is ironic, Annie. For both of us. One of your biggest criticisms of me was spending too much time with friends.

"C'mon," Ben ordered. "Let's take a break from the calls and go grab a flick."

"What do you want to see?"

"*Fight Club*. It'll toughen you up a bit."

I laughed. "All right."

The phone message machine blinked "23" when we arrived home after the movie. Kurt began to return the calls. Well practiced, we had the spiel down to five minutes. In a strange sense, I now looked forward to them. The words of condolence and encouragement continued to energize me and give me hope for a quick recovery.

"The outpouring of love and support is amazing," I told a friend. "I'm almost tempted to do this every year. Almost. I said almost."

Ben turned on a college football game and promoted his vision for the weekend. "We'll do up a big ole tri-tip one night. Pick up a couple cases of wine. Organize some hikes for the golf haters." Grabbing his cell phone, he called a friend who worked as a chef to see if he could make it. "Peter, we'll supply all the grub, you just have to cook it," he explained. The enthusiasm gave me a lift. And the self-sell job grew.

This is going to be easier than I thought. Maybe it's a blessing. Maybe I'll escape without too much damage. Yeah. Yeah.

Late that night in bed, I shoved aside the covers, crept into Kurt's room, and began to cry.

Five days later, I didn't know what to feel sitting in the Gualala Hotel bar with Kurt. I'd never been to a brideless wedding before, much less my own. I'd never read a how-to article in *Modern Bride* or *Men's Health* about spending a weekend with your closest friends and family after the woman you'd pursued for nearly a decade decided she didn't want you anymore.

Is this a celebration? A tear-fest or a drunken bender? All of the above?

My friend and mentor Larry Thomas was the first to walk through the door. He wore a pink button-down shirt and looked much younger than his fifty-four years. I wasn't surprised he led the onslaught. Ever thoughtful and protective of his protégés, Larry was always quick to give me a hand, to grab me by the nape, and to guide me higher and higher through jobs and life. I knew I'd never be able to repay him despite my constant vows to do so. I trusted his judgment and valued his friendship. He had recently left The Irvine Company for what he labeled a pause to pursue an "ever growing personal to-do list." Like Kurt, he didn't talk about Annie.

"Wizard," he beamed, "lemme buy you a beer."

I held up my full Budweiser.

"Better yet," he continued. "You buy me one."

"How's The Irvine Company treating you?" he inquired.

"Don't ask." I said. "The place keeps getting weirder."

I pointed to the scene-changing Coors sign and asked him if he knew how it worked. Pausing, so I'd focus on his words, he said he was proud I'd chosen to go through with the "wedding." His words gave me an immediate confidence boost and raised my expectations for the weekend. *Maybe I'll get through this after all.*

I'd seen only snippets of the old *This Is Your Life* show, but that night I sensed exactly how the contestants felt. I planted myself at the end of the bar and watched with anticipation as the swinging doors opened and, one by one, my closest friends walked in.

There was John Dawkins, a prankster from grade school currently mining telecommunications riches in Moscow. He banged through the doors like a Wild West sheriff, yelled my name, and gave me a big hug.

"Dawkins, you smell like Red Square."

Jonathan Terra, a PhD candidate working to finish his dissertation while living in Prague, hit me right off.

"Where's Annie?" he joked.

My sister, Lisa, and her husband, Doug, drove from their home in Sacramento.

"I love you, big bro," she said midsqueeze. That hug crushed me.

Lisa, I'm so sorry. You're supposed to see me as perfect. Not like this.

The rest of the group straggled in throughout the evening, an eclectic bunch that included a music producer, writers, a Deadhead/reporter for the *San Francisco Chronicle,* a wine wholesaler, documentary filmmakers, teachers, a banker, a Santa Cruz surfer, frustrated lawyers, political hacks, a private pilot, and the founder of an Internet site for Jewish products. Within minutes, I was awash in drink offers, tasteless jokes, promises to fix me up, encouragement, ribbings, and, above all, love.

My college roommate Jeff Clyburn strolled in with his girlfriend, Alix. They'd flown from Washington, D.C., that afternoon.

"I really appreciate you guys making it," I said after Alix confessed to feeling queasy during the drive up from San Francisco on the exaggerated S-turns of Highway 1.

"Of course," Jeff bellowed with a look that said he'd never considered otherwise. "We got your back."

For the first time in my life, I understood how many people "had my back." They were all there, in a beat-up old saloon we'd completely taken over, except for the town drunk at the end of the bar. Attending were people who called daily and others with whom I'd lost touch. Some members of the friend pods from Davis,

Washington, D.C., Sacramento, and Southern California overlapped. Most did not. At one point in the evening, I looked around the room, laughed to myself, and decided it was the most meaningful event in my life. Not in a mushy, hyper-sentimental fashion. Instead, I felt more like a biographer who'd carefully examined his subject's history and pinpointed the key moment.

This is really screwed up. The only time in my life I'm going to get all these people in one room is if I get married or die. I probably won't be able to enjoy the first and definitely won't be able to enjoy the latter.

Right then, I fantasized about hijacking an IPO so that I could buy an island with no insects and plenty of snowy white sand and fly everyone there for a blowout Friends' Day party once a year.

By 2 A.M., we'd succumbed to the last-call pleas of the bartender to retire the evening. Ben ordered everyone to "Wizziepalooza headquarters," the cabin with the hot tub. We piled into vans and cars, handing keys over to the few sober ones: pregnant women, recent moms, and God-fearers, mostly.

I don't need shrinks to get over the breakup. These people are better than shrinks. They're not aloof, two-hundred-dollar-an-hour psychologists with no idea who I am. Like that squishy counselor Annie dragged me to see. I know she must have done a number on me in previous visits. No wonder he stared when I first shook his hand. Must have thought I was somewhere between a wife-beater and a psychopath. These people know me. My strengths and flaws. This is my team, the people I picked. If anyone can get me through the next couple months, it's this bunch.

I envisioned a group of sedate, reflective, wine-swilling friends sitting on the floor by a fire, dissecting my relationship and preparing a sensitive plan of recovery. I'd sit on a big chair to the side, nod my head at their suggestions, and tell each one how much I appreciated his or her support: *Thank you. No, thank you.*

Instead, I was greeted by a group of twenty drunk, naked men and women piled into a Jacuzzi with a capacity for ten. Jeff Kubiak, a childhood friend and former American record–holding swimmer, demonstrated proper technique for the spa breaststroke. Others encouraged me to jump in.

Maybe a seasoned psychologist isn't such a bad idea.

Finding an open space, I peeled off my clothes, plunged in, and listened to Jonathan and his Czech girlfriend, Ivetka, talk about Prague. "Anything goes, Wiz. It's like America without the Christian Coalition." John Dawkins pontificated on life and love in Moscow. Another friend had just returned from Cuba. He'd showed me his pictures earlier in the day. The conversation turned into a debate over which country had the best women.

Wait. Maybe this is a psychology session? These guys are talking about thrills and happiness found in different corners of the globe. Maybe I can be happy living abroad now. Just like John and Jonathan.

I stumbled out of the hot tub and into my bed, fell asleep immediately, and plowed into a disturbing dream about a babushka in Russia who lectured me on how to achieve a Soviet-style twelve-step recovery plan while she administered a painful massage.

Saturday morning I woke feeling groggy and depressed despite the previous night's laughs—a hangover more from emotion than booze. It didn't surprise me. This was to have been my wedding day. A thick, cloudy, gray sky reflected my brain. I was heartbroken, sure. The worst was knowing my scars would take longer than a weekend with friends to heal.

You're at the beginning of a long, downward slide.

Annie! Why did you have to do this to me? I had this thing all teed up. All you had to do was say "I do." I'd have taken care of everything else. You screwed everything up.

I turned over and saw John Dawkins lying at the foot of my bed.

"How you doing, man?" he asked between yawns.

"Well, this isn't exactly how I envisioned waking up on my wedding day. But other than that, I'm fine."

Throwing on a T-shirt and pair of jeans, I walked out to inspect the damage. An impromptu couple slept on the floor under a mound of blankets and pillows. Someone had broken a redwood railing on the deck. Wine stains (Heitz Cellars Cabernet, 1983, a gift from Annie, a bottle we promised to savor at a "big event") spotted the white kitchen chairs, and empty beer bottles were strewn everywhere. I actually felt good about the mess. It gave me something to do for a couple hours, a temporary respite from the onslaught of depression. I grabbed a rag and started to clean.

Soon, the houseguests rallied, and others appeared from neighboring cabins. A group of a dozen decided to walk down from the cliffs to a beach a half mile away. John Dawkins led the trek down, then attempted to convince us a nude swim in the cold November waters was the ideal cure for the previous night's poisons. Without hesitation, we passed. The preferred backup plan was to steal John's clothes as he jumped into the waves alone. Before he noticed, we were halfway up the cliff, laughing hard at the thought of him, naked, walking past tourists out for a Saturday stroll.

John had other ideas. He grabbed a long, rope-shaped piece of smelly brown seaweed and tied a belt. He then found a bigger flap of sea debris and fashioned a fig leaf cover. He looked ridiculous. The rest of the group scurried back to the cabin, grabbing cameras and positioning themselves on the deck to witness his arrival.

Rarely embarrassed, John strode up the open path along the cliff at a leisurely pace and with a look of purpose.

"Franz," he yelled loudly over our cheers. "Get your ass down here. We're going to have a wedding. Now's the time."

I glanced down at my new watch (Timex Triathlon, thirty-five dollars). He was right. It was five minutes before two, the scheduled hour. The wedding party whooped for the spur-of-the-moment ceremony.

"Do you, Franz, take this freak of nature to abuse and peruse for as long as you live, so help us all?" my brother asked.

"I guess I have to say yes, since I woke up next to him," I said, laughing hard.

"You're free to kiss the bride," Kurt ordered to chants of encouragement from the wedding party.

A former wrestler, John grabbed the sides of my head, pressed his lips against mine, then tried to dart his tongue into my mouth, gecko lizard–style. The entourage howled and snapped photos as John and I walked arm in arm back to the cabin.

"You know we love you, Wiz," he said. "Look at all these people. Lotta love here for you."

"Dawkins, you know I love you guys as well. I can't tell you how much it means to me to have you clowns here.

"But can I ask you a serious question?" I continued.

"Sure."

"How did you ever get laid with a kissing technique like that?"

My plane back to Orange County was delayed. Heavy rains, the desk agent said. The weather reports predicted it would last for days.

2

"Franz," said my secretary, Lisa, from her cubicle. "It's the assemblyman on the line."

"Tell him I'll be with him shortly."

Instead of taking the call, I reclined on my black leather couch and stared out the window over the elite Big Canyon golf course (shoes shined between rounds) and the Newport Beach skyline. He was an assemblyman, so I'd make him wait for a minute. Those were the rules of the game. If the call was from a congressman or a senator, I would have picked right up. For city council members from towns where we didn't do business, I'd tell Lisa to take a number.

"Franz!" the assemblyman said with the enthusiasm of a fraternity brother. "Great to hear your voice. How's The Irvine Company these days?"

"Fine, just fine. As long as you keep the enviros off our backs, we'll be fine."

"Hey, I have this event coming up in a few weeks. You should have received an invitation by now."

"But, Assemblyman, you don't even have a race."

"Yeah, I know, but I need to show a large amount in the bank before the next reporting period to keep others out."

"Well . . ."

"Listen, this is going to be a great fund-raiser, Franz."

After a few minutes of courtship, I gave in. I always did. Politicians across the country knew I had a million-dollar bank account from which to dole out hefty donations. On the political fund-raising circuit, I was known as an ATM. All they had to do was call, say a few nice words, and the money would flow.

I hung up the phone and started to laugh. I got a kick from groveling politicians. I loved the different techniques they used—the apologies ("Hey, I hate to ask you this, but . . . "); the guilt trips ("C'mon. If you guys don't show up at my event, everyone will ask what I did to piss you off."); the whiny begs ("Franz, pleeeeeaaasse, this is my only event of the year."); the not-so-subtle threats that I'd have problems if I didn't give the money ("By the way, I see where your legislation is up in committee next week."). The best fund-raisers knew Lisa's name, the status of bills I followed, and my penchant for events that included rounds of golf, expensive wines, and dinners in fancy homes.

Overseeing government relations for The Irvine Company was like playing shortstop for the New York Yankees or taking wildlife photographs for *National Geographic*—it was the job coveted by most in the field. The Irvine Company is a corporation unlike any other in the United States. It owns and develops approximately fifty thousand acres in southern Orange County along with business properties in San Diego, Los Angeles, and Silicon Valley. There are many other American developers with large land holdings, but what makes The Irvine Company different is that its land is in the middle of a large and wealthy urban area. Other developers build homes. The Irvine Company builds cities.

Roots of the company date back to the California Gold Rush, when James Irvine, having made a fortune selling pickaxes and blankets to the miners, purchased Mexican land grants totaling 125,000 acres, approximately one-fifth of present-day Orange County. While neighboring communities cropped up like prairie grass to accommodate waves of "Go West" adherents during the following hundred years, the Irvine family continued to work the land as a profitable ranch and farming operation, opting for cattle, beans, asparagus, and oranges over people.

Ownership having passed through several generations and many divisive family feuds, the Irvines ultimately decided to incorporate and pursue the housing market. They took a unique tack. Instead of building tract houses and bedroom communities, they decided their first step would be to give land away. The recipient was the State of California, which received one thousand acres in 1960 for the construction of a new university, the University of California, Irvine. A quirk in state law prohibited gifts, so contracts were quickly rewritten to sell the prime land for a dollar. It was the smartest profit they would ever net.

The university gave the planners at The Irvine Company the nucleus around which to craft communities, business parks, open-space reserves, schools, shopping malls, apartments, and tens of thousands of homes. The company went so far as to commission the architect of the university to map out the new City of Irvine, the country's largest master-planned community. Since then, the mission of the company has been to implement the vision. They've made billions of dollars doing it.

A big reason for the company's success has been its willingness to engage in vigorous government relations. Large campaign contributions helped elect pro-housing politicians, who would fight environmentalists or anyone else trying to halt development on private property. To do this job effectively required an enormous political bank account. That's what made my position so powerful and enviable.

When I traveled to Sacramento to lobby for a piece of legislation, senators left floor debates or committee hearings to find out what I needed. Lobbyists called to see which candidates I planned to back in upcoming elections. The Irvine Company was one of the biggest political players in the state. For five years, I had been the one holding the checkbook.

"Franz," said Lisa from her cubicle. "It's Gary on the line. He wants to see you right away."

Lisa had this way of placing every call in a no-big-deal frame. Maybe it was from her military training. I loved her for that. Especially that week.

Gary Hunt was my boss. Pulling on my suit coat, a mandatory procedure for visits to the ninth floor, I sensed the news wouldn't be good.

The top floor of The Irvine Company headquarters is far more formal than the stories below. There's an awkward stillness along with the polished marble and flawless orchids. Secretaries sit behind tall wooden cubicles, unable to see passersby. The executive offices are filled with glossy stone tables; tinted window walls overlooking the Newport Beach harbor; and large abstract oil paintings, part of the company's museum-quality collection of contemporary California art. *Jerry Maguire* was filmed in the twin building next door, the one-time office of real-life sports agent Leigh Steinberg.

Gary's tall body hunched over his desk. A wall-size abstract painting of a city scene hung above to his left. I wondered how many of the company's top execs actually liked the art. Gary didn't look at the painting. He stared at an organizational chart. I noticed it right away. It wasn't as big as the artwork, but, in my mind, it was close. Large boxes in reds and blues, dotted lines and straight ones. I tried to steal a glance at the names on the paper before he folded it up and set it aside. Instead, I stared at his perfectly parted gray hair and, for some odd reason, tried to guess the type of superstrength gel he used to keep it in place. Joico ICE? Brylcreem? He leaned back in his ergonomic chair, smiled at me through his thick glasses, and asked if I wanted coffee.

Offering me coffee. This really is going to be bad. Maybe I don't want to see the chart.

I declined. Casually sliding his hand underneath his desk, he pushed a secret button underneath his desk that closed the door I'd just entered.

I'm locked in.

13

Gary began by telling me I was doing a "fantastic job." He recounted a couple of my recent "atta-boys," then launched into a spiel about the company's focus on local issues and local government.

"You are so valuable to this company that we want to shift you off Sacramento and Washington, D.C., and focus you exclusively on Orange County," he explained.

I felt the air leave my body as if the wind had been knocked out of me after a bad fall. It was the first stumble in my twelve-year career, and it was a big one. I struggled to look calm and continued to stare at his slicked-down hair. Now I hated the hair.

"Have you already made this decision or are you soliciting my opinion?" I asked.

Startled, he paused. "Well, we've already rearranged the group, and I've told the others, but you know you're always welcome to voice your opinion."

Why bother? It's too late. He's already made up his mind. I'm screwed.

Part of me actually felt sorry for Gary. I knew he hated to give bad news. I asked him about the details of my new assignment and reporting structure. My background and my passion were firmly planted in state and federal government. I'd worked for five years as a press secretary in the U.S. Senate and for California Governor Pete Wilson in Sacramento. I'd run campaigns and opened a successful public affairs firm that focused on state political issues. Shifting me to local government was like hiring a pilot to drive a truck. It didn't make sense, and Gary had a hard time explaining the logic.

He smiled and asked if I was okay with everything. We had a good relationship. He was one of the first people to call me with comforting words after Annie canceled the wedding. Apparently, our friendship wasn't strong enough to stop the demotion.

"I know you're a team player," he said.

Team player. Team player. Screw team player. Team player always means giving something up. Why can't someone tell me I'm a team player and give me a better deal?

I didn't even try to sleep that night. The two pillars of my life, the two passions I'd pursued for a decade, had now crumbled on top of me.

More than anything, I was stunned. After Annie called off the wedding, I planned to shift all my energies to The Irvine Company. Now they told me they didn't want me either, or at least not in my former role.

What the hell is happening to me? Do I have some horrible body odor or a giant "Kick Me" sign stenciled on my forehead? Dumped and demoted, dumped and demoted. Not bad for a month's work. What else can possibly go wrong?

I woke with a sore throat, itchy eyes, and a pinpoint sinus headache. The symptoms stayed for weeks. After several cartons of Claritin and Sudafed, and several more of Advil and Tylenol to cope with the antihistamine headaches, I discovered my condition was caused by mildew, rust, and holes in my home's forty-year-old heating system. It would cost me several thousand dollars to fix.

3

I walked back to The Irvine Company after a late lunch and found the company's petite and polite facilities manager in my office staring at my black leather couch. She carried a tape measure that she casually shifted to her side, out of my view. I had never thought of her as sneaky. Now I did.

"What do you want to do with it?" she asked.

"With what?"

"The couch."

"Uh . . . keep it where it is?"

"It's not going to fit in your new office," she said with a forced smile.

"My new office . . . right. Let me get back to you."

A few days later, Gary again summoned me to his office. He wanted to talk about taxes and elections. The week of my nonwedding, the City of Irvine had held an election to raise property taxes to help the local schools. Good schools sold homes. The Irvine Company pushed hard for the measure's approval. It was my top priority. It was also one of the farthest things from my mind. Measure B gained 62 percent of the vote, yet failed because California law required a two-thirds majority for such measures to pass.

During the election, I'd bled the company's vendors and subcontractors to raise $250,000, an astronomical sum for a local election. Hundreds of volunteers walked precincts and manned phone banks at night and on weekends. Everything that could have gone our way, did. Except for the outcome. Gary called me in to tell me they planned to try again with another election in a few months.

"You're a miracle worker, buddy," Gary said, smiling from across his desk. "If anyone can make it happen, you can. Just know that your bonus in July depends on this one passing."

I groaned. "Any way I can run this election in another city? Somewhere more liberal, say Berkeley or San Francisco?"

"You can do it, Franz. Just think bonus, bonus, bonus."

The privately owned Irvine Company closed its fiscal year on July 1, then paid employees generous bonuses two weeks later. The payments were calculated on the basis of overall company profits, seniority, and personal accomplishments. I knew the City of Irvine would never vote for more taxes and cringed at the thought of explaining a second lost election a few weeks before bonus checks were issued.

"We really need you to focus on local politics," Gary said as he walked me to the keyed elevator after our meeting about the second parcel tax election. "It's the bread and butter of this company."

More like a butter knife in my side.

"I understand," I said. "Say, Gary, I heard through the grapevine I might be getting a new office. Know anything?"

"I was meaning to talk to you about that. It's on the seventh floor. Talk to Human Resources. We're going to give you an ocean view. You deserve it."

On the way back to my office (*Pfffew, the couch is still there*), I stopped at Lisa's desk and asked if she wanted to see our new space. She sprang up and followed me downstairs. Walking past glass-wall offices, I imagined one hundred stares, like a prison ward watching an inmate walk to his new cell. Lisa tried and failed to hold her laughter when we arrived.

"Well, it's got a nice view," she giggled.

"Lisa, it's a third the size of my current office."

"It's fine."

"Wow. I can't believe this. But they're right about the couch. No way it'd fit in here. I'm not so sure we can even get a desk in here."

She started to scour the hall for her new cubicle.

"I'm going to take off," I said. "Cover for me, will ya?"

"What'll I say if anyone calls?"

"Just tell them I'm at Toys 'R' Us buying furniture."

"Furniture?"

"Yeah. Little, bitty furniture."

I ducked out of the building, jumped into my car, and sped home.

And on the way, I had an epiphany. Not a radical, fall-on-your-knees revelation. Just a moment of clarity that made me smile.

Of course. Why didn't I think of it until now? Why not? Why the hell not?

The couch, the Mini-Me office, the meeting with Gary, his perfect hair, the whole crummy week—it all triggered an idea. I sat in the car and turned down the stereo to think it through. Then I made a few calls to my travel agent and raced home to tell Kurt, who'd decided to take some time off work and stay with me for a couple weeks.

"Kurt, KURT! Where are you?"

"Out here. On the patio."

He sits in the sun too much.

"How'd you like to go on a honeymoon?"

"Who's the gal?"

"Me."

"Dude. Think about it. You have close-cropped hair and an art collection. I own a shih tzu. People will talk."

"Let me rephrase that. How would you like to go on an all-expenses-paid trip to Costa Rica? I've got a couple first-class plane tickets and a bunch of hotel reservations."

"For real?"

"The tickets say Wisner. You should be cool. Just bring an ID and say your nickname is Andy if anyone asks. Say Annie's a typo."

"All right. I'm in."

"Great, perfect. We leave tomorrow."

I walked to the back of the house, threw my coat on the bed, and stared at Annie's belongings pushed into the spare bedroom. A nine-year collection of relationship reminders spread out across the floor and spewed from closets. "Clutter" for all those years, now an endless supply of remember-whens. From the piles, I lifted a small painting of a Sacramento street scene painted on a cigar box.

Miles Hermann. Remember his show? You said you adored the cigar boxes. I came home late that evening. You chalked it up to the governor's office, but the truth is I snuck out and bought the painting. I'm sorry for not giving it to you that night. You would have known.

Sifting through her books, I hesitated. Then stopped.

This is it. The end. The last connection I have to her. Gerald comes to pick up this stuff, and that's it. All those years, pfffffttttt. Gone. The breakup in the apartment was surreal. This is final.

I love you so much, Annie. How come that's not enough? Scrape away everything else, and you know my heart lives to attach itself to you.

Grabbing her thin, red sweater, the one she brought to the air-conditioned movie theaters, I slumped down on the floor and felt my eyes well up. I pounded my brain for missteps, a round-the-clock effort that had consumed every synapse and storage unit in my foggy brain. A stack of baskets in the corner forced a respite.

Who keeps all these baskets? And what do you ever use them for? One basket, that's all you need. There should be a one-basket limit. Otherwise they grow and multiply and pretty soon you have a collection. Like this. Baskets being stored in baskets. I'm going to have to buy more boxes just to store stuff used for storage.

I started to pack away a few books, the easiest place to begin. Art history texts from Brown University, several graphic design manuals, Raymond Carver paperbacks. *You loved Raymond Carver.* And her projects. Box after box of logos she'd designed, newsletters for politicians, family announcements. And the silly stuff. Like the *Puppets for Pete* bumper sticker with Pinocchio endorsing the Wilson for Governor campaign.

That was funny. But they didn't laugh, did they? Just us.

After I finished the books, I moved to the CDs. *Get rid of all that Lilith Fair music Don Young told me to lose.* "Wiz, you really want to sit around listening to Sarah McLachlan these days? If you want to kill yourself, how about I lend you my Smiths collection?" A small binder grabbed my attention. It looked like a school notebook. I froze.

Just forget it. Put it in the box and seal it up.

I grabbed a roll of packing tape and started another box.

Just a glance. C'mon. Quit beating yourself up over this. Let her tell you in her own words. . . . Maybe she left it on purpose.

Slowly, I lifted the schoolgirl spiral with the date 1992 written on the inside fold, staring in disbelief as if Annie herself had leapt into the room.

A page or two, that's all. I don't have to read the whole thing. Of course she's going to trash you. That's what all women do in their diaries, isn't it? Lord knows I deserve it.

I couldn't do it.

I can. She owes me an explanation.

I shot a quick glance down the hall to see if Kurt was looking before opening the seven-year-old journal. She summarized most days with just a sentence or two.

This is crazy. What the hell are you doing? What good can come of this? You're just giving yourself more ammunition for self-inflicted wounds.

"Tried to talk to F today," it read. "He doesn't seem to listen anymore. Work occupies all his time."

Oh, I heard you. I didn't always show it, but I heard you. I knew you were hurting. Didn't you see my pain, too?

Her words pulled me deeper.

"I took F to a seminar last night, but I still don't think he gets it. And that's a problem. I don't have a lot of support or answers these days. I'm scared."

It was killing both of us. I just didn't want to say it. Upbeat, stay upbeat. If we had any chance, we'd have to fight it that way. You looked so scared. And that made me scared. But, c'mon, be honest. My work wasn't the problem. It wasn't the reason you were frightened.

I continued to leaf through pages, past days and diatribes about my work demands or her family in Utah, scavenging for clues why she left me at the altar.

"Packing up her junk?" Kurt asked from the doorway.

He startled me. I turned my back so he couldn't see the notebook.

"Yup. Figure it's better to get it over with. Gerald promised to come down and pick it up."

"You okay?"

"Yeah, fine."

"Hey, what time's our flight tomorrow?"

"Red-eye out of LAX. Leaves at eleven."

4

Politicians love charts. Any kind. The more colors and bars, the better. Bonus points for using animated symbols, like green dollar signs to show expenses, or overflowing garbage cans to show waste. If they're big enough to require an easel, better still: "Of course I'm right. Says so right here on this HUGE CHART."

Ten years prior, on my first day on Capitol Hill as an assistant press secretary for Senator Pete Wilson, I learned the U.S. Senate was no exception to the chart rule. I saw them all day on C-SPAN. Day two: I learned making charts was my responsibility. Day three: I learned of an upcoming agriculture committee meeting to discuss legislation for the wine industry. I spent the afternoon gathering information about grape production in California and fantasizing about burgundy-colored pie charts. Day four: I walked down to the graphics department, where the Republican senators produced their fancy, taxpayer-financed newsletters, "franking privileges" to them, junk mail to everyone else. A striking, dark-haired, young graphic artist with cream skin and arched cheekbones toyed with her computer. On day four, I had a different outlook on the chart business.

Karen, the cheery manager of the graphics studio, saw me hesitate and asked if I needed help. I mumbled something about wine barrels while trying to steal glances at the pretty designer. Karen scanned my information and said they could have something done in a couple days, smiling mischievously before announcing she'd have Annie work on it. *Annie, got it. Annie.*

I debated what I'd say before picking up the charts a few days later. Asking her on a date seemed a bit unprofessional. Premature, too, since my only introduction was a stare from across the room. A Senate office reception was a better option, though I didn't know of any good ones in the coming week. I still hadn't made up my mind when I entered the studio. Annie saw me and walked to a stack of charts piled against a wall. She made some comments about "the wino stuff" and asked me if everything looked fine.

Rather than examine them, I stared at her lustrous cobalt eyes. She wore an oversize shirtdress with a black and white pattern like the back of a Holstein cow. On anyone else, it would have looked like a Halloween costume. On Annie, it looked playful and chic. Her confidence made her seem much older, though I guessed we were about the same age. Her jesting, self-effacing demeanor was rare for an attractive woman, making her even more attractive. I ignored the charts, told her they looked perfect, and then walked back to my office. Dateless.

You wussy. What happened to the follow-up? The shame.

A crate full of watermelons arrived at our office the next day courtesy of a farmer we'd helped with an amendment to a bill. I grabbed one on the way to my desk and stared at the dark green bands.

Perfect. I'll give it to Annie as a thank-you.

"It's lovely," she joked, rocking the watermelon in her arms like a baby. "I just don't know if I have a big enough vase."

Along with the fruit, I planned to invite her to a small party at a colleague's house the following week. By now I'd ascertained that:

a. Annie's boss was a good friend of my boss;
b. Annie was single though coy;
c. her apartment was two blocks away from the party;
d. she'd talked to Karen about me.

Never mind that her comment was something along the lines of, "Who's the intern?" I saw it as solid progress. And I was armed and ready to convince her to come to the party. Only thing was, she strutted off for lunch before I could work up the nerve. So I shifted tactics like any decent press secretary. I walked over to Karen's desk and invited the entire office to go. Karen understood.

The night of the get-together I arrived with a group of friends who cared little about politics, much about parties. They exchanged verbal jabs while I waited with anticipation, like a child in the darkness before Christmas morning. None of them knew about my pathetic attempts to woo Annie. Late in the evening, I gave up hope she would show.

As I babbled with my roommate Jesse, he shifted his eyes to the entryway and made a comment about a gorgeous woman coming in. I didn't even finish the sentence, let alone the story I was telling him. I immediately swiveled on pointe and walked straight to Annie. She looked elegant even in faded jeans and a simple white cotton sweater. Her smile made me stumble for words. Finally, I blurted a question about a drink. She inquired if Karen had been at the party, then muttered something about a "setup" when I told her nobody from her office had shown.

It didn't matter to Annie. She leaned back on the couch, sipped her wine, and proceeded in her witty fashion to joust with me about white trash cooking ("split-pea soup with hot dogs are far better than pigs in a blanket"), presidential trivia, and movie lines from *This Is Spinal Tap*. And not the line about the amps going to 11. Rookies threw that one out. No, she lobbed Howard Hessman's dialogue about needing "to wait in the lobby for the limo." I was in love.

I learned we both grew up in the West, attended private universities in New England, and moved to the nation's capital to launch our careers. Our families were large, close, conservative, and Americana-corny (black-and-white photographs of family members in prairie costumes, and such). We loved our jobs, and neither of us had cynical, jaded, or self-important attitudes that often accompanied political martyrs or people who'd been in Washington too long.

As the crowd dwindled and the hostess began to clean up, I asked Annie if she wanted to continue the conversation at the Hawk and Dove bar around the corner. I told her my friends planned to go, though I had no idea what they wanted to do. She saw through my ploy and said she'd call a "safety friend" to meet us as well. We drank Guinness (Guinness!) and joked about our families, our work, and ourselves until last call. She gave me her number and said she was free Sunday for dinner.

And that was it. Deal done. I knew from the moment she walked into the party that she was the woman with whom I'd grow old. Just knew.

Before our first date, I polled the two friends I knew who did date and, based on their advice, decided on a high-end Italian restaurant packed with rich lobbyists and Washington, D.C., political celebrities. I stopped at an ATM two times before picking her up. Annie looked genuinely happy when she opened her town-house door. I gave her a warm hug and offered to carry her sweater. She said good-bye to her cat, Oedipus (*Cat, okay, I can live with that*), and we started to walk through the Capitol Hill neighborhood.

"Where's your car?" she asked after we'd walked five blocks.

"Uhh, I don't have a car. I thought we were walking to your car."

Annie shot me a mock glare, shook her head, smiled, then grabbed my arm to walk back to her house.

"If you want me to drive, you need to ask me to drive. Preferably before we leave the house."

We talked all through dinner with an ease I'd never experienced. I looked over at Annie, poised, dark, beautiful, and knew for the first time in my adult life what it was like to crave another human. Here, after half a date, I realized I had an insatiable appetite for her. I wanted to see her on Monday and Tuesday, and again and again and forever. I wanted to fast-forward to the parts when we'd wake up next to each other. Trying not to look too anxious, I invited her to my apartment "to watch the eleven o'clock news." She said okay.

The eleven o'clock news?

I flicked on the apartment lights, turned to Annie to take her sweater, then quickly spun back around to make sure I saw what I thought I saw in the living room. I did. And I panicked. Dozens of industrial-size boxes of condoms were stacked in the corners, others opened and in plain view. Hundreds of condom samples were strewn on end tables and across the floor. Pink, purple, green, and white packets covered my entire living room, making my apartment look like a free clinic after an earthquake.

"I know this seems a little odd," I babbled. "My roommate works for the State Department. Something to do with population control in Third World countries. These must be samples from his work."

She shook her head, made a crack about my roommate being a "real stud," and cleared off a batch of purple condoms from the couch. She sat down and smiled in a way that let me off the hook for the whole evening. I loved her at that moment. Annie was fine with me. And us.

"Call me tomorrow," she said as I walked her out to her red Honda coupe an hour later. After the news. "I'm free all week."

She gave me a kiss on my cheek. I rubbed it like a genie bottle as I bounded up the stairs to my fifth-floor flat. George, my other roommate, was awake when I returned. Trancelike, he stared at the television. I was so thrilled with the way the date had ended, I forgot to give him grief about bringing his condom cornucopia home from work. Annie was "free all week." Annie was "free all week."

For some reason, she wouldn't open her menu. Maybe it was because we decided to order wine. Or maybe she preferred to soak in the candlelight and distressed-pine antiques. I think it was because that's how Annie moved through life—peaceful, relaxed, graceful ("slow" when we were late for somewhere). Our relationship was in its tenth month.

Before the meal, I arranged with the waiter to place a United Airlines ticket to California in Annie's menu. When she ordered, it would fall in her lap. Theoretically. But she didn't touch the menu. The temptress. Instead, she just smiled at me and asked about my trip to San Diego to be with Senator Wilson on election night.

Shortly after I started working for him, Pete Wilson announced his campaign for governor of California. With conflicting emotions, Annie and I assisted the effort from Washington, D.C., calling California radio stations from Republican party headquarters on Capitol Hill with sound bites for their news programs, producing fliers and fact sheets during our off hours for the campaign staff. We were eager for him to win, though we knew a victory would end our comfortable situation and send us into the great unknown of Sacramento. "Field Poll has him up five points. That's good, right?"

I had this grand plan to fly her to San Diego for election night festivities. In the case of the Wilson group, this usually meant a large ballroom at the Grant Hotel, a video message from Charlton Heston, and a show tune sung by Gayle Wilson. One of those ditties where she'd change the lyrics to say something nice about her husband: *The votes will come out tomorrow. You can bet your bottom dollar that tomorrow, Pete'll be guv.*

If Mrs. Wilson's prophesy failed, Annie and I would fly back to Washington, D.C., and resume our routine of tuna sandwiches in the Hart Building cafeteria and my flimsy excuses for the senator to use charts. "He'll have to have a visual if he meets with the Saint Helena Little League team. Those kids need some sort of attention-getter."

I also wanted her to come to California so that she could meet my parents in Davis.

"Make sure you tell her we live on the same block as the Mormon church," my mom kept repeating.

"She's a Jack Mormon, Mom. I don't think that's going to score you any points."

"Can't hurt."

"I'll let her know."

On the sly, I arranged for Annie to have the time off. But her boss warned me not to spring it on her the day of the flight. "And don't even think about packing her bag," she said. "Trust me. You'll really mess that one up. A woman has to pack her own stuff."

Tickets and time off, a favorite restaurant, a bottle of Cabernet—it was a perfect plan . . . except she wouldn't open her menu. I nudged it to her. She stared away. I asked what she wanted to eat. She shrugged.

C'mon. You're killing me.

"Are you ready?" the waiter inquired.

Annie snapped out of her daze and unfolded the oversize menu. The tickets dropped to her lap. With a look of confusion, she opened it and saw her name in black ink on the top of the itinerary. Now beaming, she leaned across the table to kiss me. Half of me thought I should be on one knee. We both knew "till death do us part." And I was more than ready to love and, yes, obey. My heart said, "Will you?" My head listened to conventional wisdom extolling the virtues of "waiting before you get married." We were both twenty-three.

We spent nearly every day together that first year. After the rare day apart, we'd jokingly chastise the other "never to do that again." Weeks were filled with long walks and road trips to New England, meanders through art galleries and bookstores, celebrations at horse races and warehouse parties. The best times were spent nowhere at all—the long stares over coffee, that extra hour in bed.

I loved everything about her—the way she finished my half-done crossword puzzles, how she threw her hair in a ponytail and looked better than a runway model, or railed against media efforts to embarrass my boss. I loved her poised stance, bad jokes, and her preference for macaroni and cheese. I loved her because she loved me. Friends called us "Frannie"; we were inseparable.

Being with a confident woman gave me confidence. Gone were the fumbled pickups and watermelon props. I could strut a little those days because I had Annie on my arm. The boost carried beyond my love life. "You're a good writer," she'd say, encouraging me to submit speeches I would have never attempted. Soon the senator read them during floor debates. She led me deeper into the fine arts and literature, travel and foreign film, helping me feel enriched and whole. "You can do it," she'd say.

Final result: Wilson 52 percent, Feinstein 48 percent.

Again, I had it arranged. Well, almost. A one-bedroom flat with pink 1950s bathroom tile and a rose garden. Annie loved rose gardens. That's why I picked the unit. The flowers and the Murphy bed that unfolded from the wall in the living room. Perfect for visitors or those late-night Letterman shows when we'd doze off before he'd get to his first guest. In the best part of Sacramento, too. East Sac. I prayed she'd like the city. She was a Westerner, I told myself during daily rituals of wishful thinking. Of course, she'll love it here.

My mother came over that afternoon to help get the place ready. We splashed Murphy's Oil Soap on the hardwoods and cleaned the windows. We stocked the cupboards with Golden Grahams and Diet Cokes, her favorites. I wanted it to be perfect the next morning, when Annie would see it in the light for the first time. She'd quit her job in the Senate, cleaned out her apartment, and given away her cat, Oedipus, the one that swooned like Pepé Le Pew and, for his amorous adventures, preferred a stuffed bear to female members of his own species. Annie thought Oedipus would prefer a farm in northern Virginia, so he stayed. She'd given up her East Coast life to take a chance on us. I wanted her to feel good about the decision from the start.

As I shifted furniture, my mom reached into a bag and pulled out a light blue bundle of felt cloth that muffled the sound of rattling metal. With focus, she unwrapped it. The silver knives and forks, with the W crest my grandfather designed, spilled onto the table. They shined like a mini row of mirrors. I knew she'd spent the afternoon polishing them. I struggled for something to say.

"I . . . well . . . are you sure you want us to have these?"

"Oh yes. I talked to your father about it last night. We decided they don't get any use at our house. And, well, you need some silverware. And you and Annie are starting out. Together . . ."

"Give me a hug," I said, sparing her, deciding that only sitcom moms do those speeches well.

Annie was to fly in that night. Dulles to Sacramento International Airport. The "International" always prompted a chuckle from the locals. Either the airport went out of its way to schedule one flight a year to Vancouver or some overanxious sign maker just assumed Fresno was abroad, they joked. I looked at my watch and knew I had to leave to make it to the airport on time. Forget the shower. Just a few more minutes of cleaning, decided my mom. She'd finish the house and lock up. I gave her a kiss, grabbed a couple garden roses from a vase, and sped up Highway 5.

Annie hated our realtor. Hated her orange and lavender lipsticks that matched the colors of her belts and shoes. Hated her insistence that every house in Sacramento was "perfect for you two." Hated her feng shui comments about where the couches and chairs should go in the house on Santa Ynez Way, though we both fell in love with it immediately.

"You're never going to believe this," Annie said. "I just hung up with Peg. She says our offer is causing marital stress on the people who own the house. She suggests we up our offer another ten thousand dollars."

"How about we counter with the same bid but throw in counseling sessions?"

Annie insisted we stick with our price and dump our agent. She got half her wish. We stuck with Peg but with the understanding that only I would talk to her. After a few more battles, we got the house and moved from the Murphy bed apartment to a California bungalow with gray walls and white pillars on a Dutch Elm–canopied street in a one hundred-year-old part of the city. With her eye for color and design, Annie started to reshape the place, scraping children's wallpaper from the bedrooms, installing an old pharmacist's display case in the bathroom, and removing every remnant of the previous owner. The home became our home. Peg didn't make the list for the housewarming party.

Our house. Just say it. Over and over. Our house.

Those nights, before the kitchen was redone, we'd eat McDonald's cheeseburgers on the front porch and talk about the future of each room. How we'd need to add a second bathroom someday. Had to have a second bathroom if we were ever going to have kids. That's the plan, we'd say to each other while sharing fries. Someday.

I felt grounded in the new house. Empowered. I felt I was on a mission. I had even greater clarity in my life. In the new house, lovemaking took on an added depth. I devoured those Saturday mornings, her nudge on my shoulder, the stream-line curve of her side, the taste of her sweat. The intensity during. The levity after.

"You know, making love to you is nothing to write home about," I said.

"What? What did you say?"

"Like I'm going to get out a pen and paper and write my folks on what it's like to make love to you? 'Dear Mom and Dad . . .'"

I got up to go to the bathroom.

"You know," she said, "that's not a good look for you."

"Huh?"

"Naked. It's not your style."

"You'll pay for that," I said, and then headed out the front door. In the early morning hour, I started to streak around the house.

"No, no, no," she yelled, laughing, out the bedroom window as I jogged around the lawn. "I didn't mean it. It's a good look for you."

I kept streaking.

"Okay, okay, it's a great look for you. Get that white ass back inside."

I dreaded very few days in Sacramento. When I did, I'd know it the night before as I struggled to sleep. The fears were usually amplified by a dream starring a mania-cal newspaper editor, bedecked in green visor, chasing me around with a knife and yelling, "You said it! You said it." In real life, I'd hop out of bed as soon as the news-paper hit the front porch, tear to the story about Pete Wilson, and groan. "Yuck. I said it. I said it."

The bad quotes could be broken down into categories. There was the revenge quote, for which a reporter from a recently scooped newspaper would clip and paste my words to fit the "gotcha" theme of his story. This was similar to the way movie studios take reviews like "a mind-blowing waste of good film" and just use "MIND-BLOWING" on their ads. Then there was the setup quote. I'd espouse the company line at the top of the story, then the reporter would spend the rest of the article explaining to a half million readers that an imbecile served as press secretary. My friends chose those days to call. "Hey, read your quotes in the *L.A. Times* today."

There were the misquotes, the misinformed quotes, the missed-the-deadline quotes. And then there were the just plain dumb quotes, like the time I justified spending cuts for nursing homes to *The New York Times* by saying something about not needing to put expensive artwork in every room. My logic went some-thing like: "What if the patient is comatose?"

"Congratulations," the communications director told me the next morning. "You just lost us the coma vote."

Fortunately, those days didn't come too often. They decreased in frequency as I discovered how reporters bait, bitch, and beg for anything that will help them please their editors. The blunders diminshed after I learned to say, "Sorry, can't help you there," as if we were both reaching to obtain the same goal. The good news was that when the bloopers did happen I'd forget them by 9 A.M., thanks to the fifty pink call slips on my desk and a phone that blinked as if I worked at the Jerry Lewis Telethon.

The bad quotes did little to kill the buzz of the job. I loved most everything else about it. Like the editorial board meetings at the *San Francisco Chronicle* or *Los Angeles Times* (good discussions, bad food), the top-floor lunches with ARCO or Bank of America execs (boring discussions, better food). I loved that the cuff-link and loafer lobbyists knew my name, or that I could stop a press conference that had strayed into taboo subjects with a simple, "Thanks, everyone." I enjoyed the way friends and relatives asked for the inside scoop, hearing the governor espouse words I wrote, and wearing the "don't-fuck-with-me" security pins on the lapels of my cheap Macy's suits.

I loved the perks with equal fervor. Planeside boarding, for instance. The official aircraft was a 1970s prop plane that doubled as Department of Fish and Game transport to stock the lakes. I could tell by the smell in the craft if the state's waterways were low on trout or bass that week. In deference to the fish, we scheduled most of the governor's press trips on commercial flights. We'd avoid the two-dollar-a-bag skycaps and block-long ticket lines and drive the black Suburbans straight onto the tarmac and beside the plane minutes before takeoff. Flight attendants swooned, passengers wondered if they should get an autograph. I was a reptie rock star.

In Annie's eyes, my celebrity status was beginning to dim. The work hours in the Senate were long, but the hours in Sacramento were all-consuming. Starting my days with a dozen newspapers at dawn and ending them with a press release rewrite during the 10 P.M. news didn't leave a lot of time for relationship-building. She'd found nine-to-five employment with an arts funding agency. I assumed our love was strong enough to bind us for the time being and tried to chalk up the canceled dinners and scrapped weekends as "working for our future." Annie talked about our now.

After a series of late nights, I promised to make it up to her with a romantic weekend in Carmel. Her birthday weekend. On the drive down we talked about restaurant recommendations and a long walk on the beach. We checked into the bed-and-breakfast and embraced before our bags hit the floor. Then my pager went off. We turned to stare at it in unison. It was as if a fire alarm had gone off for the umpteenth time. Do you ignore it or flee the building?

It was one of those tipping-point moments, the kind trial lawyers point to and say, "Aha!" Annie or Pete, Annie or Pete. I called the office; she slumped on the bed with her hands over her face. The Oakland Hills are burning, they said. We had a state-of-emergency declaration and a helicopter tour planned in the coming hours. If Annie and I left that moment, I could make it back to Sacramento in time to fly down with the governor.

Usually a shaggy dog story would do the trick, one that ended in a play on words. Annie couldn't resist those. Cornier the better. I used to craft them with punch lines that sounded similar to people's names, like "Fawn's Wiz Near." Ha, ha, ha. Five minutes, tops, and I'd get a smile. Every time. She'd laugh, then get angry about not being able to stay angry.

A bad pun wouldn't have worked that day. I didn't even try on the silent ride home.

I looked in the rearview mirror to see if she was still behind me. The rain and darkness obscured the headlights that followed on the highway. Annie had promised Joanne, her boss at the arts agency, a ride from the Sacramento airport. Sacramento International Airport. She drove Joanne's car with plans to give it to her at the terminal. I drove Annie's red Honda, which took on so much water during a rain we were forced to keep a Tupperware bowl inside for bailing. We were forty-five minutes late.

Her headlights seemed to sway to the side of the road. They became smaller and smaller. I pulled into the emergency lane, hit my blinkers, backed up, and trudged out in the rain to see what happened.

"Is there something wrong with the car? You out of gas?"

I saw a hint of panic in her eye and perspiration on her forehead. She told me she was having heart palpitations and a hard time breathing. Staring ahead, trying to inhale, she said she was fine, but needed a few minutes before she could continue. The way she forced her words made me more worried than assured.

"You need an ambulance? Forget the car. We can leave it here."

"No, no, I'll be okay. Joanne's probably wondering where I am."

Rain bulleting, cars flying by, we sat in Joanne's car for several minutes saying nothing. Like a ten-meter platform diver on her final attempt, Annie gathered herself, rehearsing in her mind what she needed to do. Fighting distractions. Focused. Scared. I knew it, because I was, too.

After she gave me an unconvincing, "I'm good now," I hopped back into the Honda, and we drove at forty miles an hour until we reached the airport, a few minutes away. Joanne idled on the curb. Her plane had been delayed, so she hadn't waited long. Annie apologized and mentioned she'd felt "a little dizzy" on the way over. "No big deal." Joanne sensed otherwise and urged her to take a day off.

With long pauses and short answers, Annie and I talked about her attack on the way home. She struggled for an explanation, saying over and over, "It felt a little like a heart attack." She had been working late hours at the arts agency, on that we both agreed. A night person, she often pulled into the office midmorning only to stay until 9 or 10 P.M. With my frequent trips and fourteen-hour days in the governor's office, we saw each other less and less. She'd been sleeping poorly and hinted at stresses from work. With increasing frequency but always with clever humor, she complained about the communication gap with her Mormon parents in Utah and the time requirements of my job. I chalked up the airport drive incident to a lack of sleep. Or maybe her diet. All that macaroni and cheese. And Diet Cokes. I vowed to talk to her about it the next day.

Annie had another attack. A small one at home. She had a third at work. Then a big one on a Monday night. On the most important Monday night of the year for me—the State of the State address from the capitol. I'd worked for weeks on the event, preparing supporting documents (including charts, of course), briefing reporters, coordinating the satellite feed to television stations. Minutes before the address, an intern told me Annie was trying to call me from a doctor's office. I gave him a couple instructions on what needed to be done post-speech and fled the capitol. "You'll do fine, Ron. This is your call-up to the bigs. Go for it."

My dad was there with her. A skin pathologist, he'd come over from his hospital after she'd failed to reach me a few times. Usually I'd get frustrated with the noncommittal way he'd describe anything medical. Bug bites, headaches, Trivial Pursuit anatomy questions, anything. "You should see a doctor," he'd say. I told him we should pass a law requiring physicians to have an opinion. Annie and I had been searching for answers for several weeks ourselves and had come up blank.

"She's in the next office talking with the doctor. She's better now. Had some sort of an attack while driving. I thought we could take her over to Mercy for tests. Make sure she's fine."

"Yeah, yeah. Good idea. Did she tell you? She had an attack like this before. Couple weeks ago on the way to the airport. Bizarre."

The doctor emerged, told us not to worry, and led us back to see Annie. Struggling to look composed, breathing like a child after a hard cry, she explained the attack as before. Pounding heart, lack of air, and an overwhelming sense of claustrophobia. Annie's world was becoming a circus fun house—rooms spinning, lights flashing, the ground keeling.

Only this one wasn't enjoyable. She couldn't find an exit. She smiled and grabbed my hand. "Let me rest," she repeated. "Just a minute."

We drove to Mercy Hospital and checked Annie into the emergency room for a series of late-night tests. My father and I sat in the waiting room trying to pinpoint her illness. After an hour, the attending physician walked up and explained the examination showed no abnormalities. She was perfectly fine, according to his measurements.

"You mean she's making this stuff up? In her mind?" I asked. "I've been there when she had an attack. I swear the symptoms are real."

"Look, I don't know exactly what she has. But sometimes, the mind can convince the body it's having attacks like this. You should get her to a specialist."

My dad nodded his head in agreement.

She said it felt like something, someone, wanting to burst out of her skin. A demon inside that would speed her pulse, take away her breath, spin the walls. Her usual first reaction was to flee, but the spirit would trap her and steal away any escapes. Highways became hallways without doors on high-speed conveyer-belt floors. Her office seemed like the NYSE floor with everyone clamoring for her attention. Couldn't they see she needed more space?

How could she feel like this? She scrambled for answers, but had a hard time even knowing where to look. So she knocked on many doors—doctors, blood testers, library research, book searches, talks with friends she trusted. All the while the attacks continued, triggered by everything from loud music to a crowded elevator.

After months of dead ends, we found a name, if little else. Anxiety disorder, the doctor at the UC-Davis Medical Center called it. We learned that attacks can come at any time, last from a few seconds to more than ten minutes, and often include dizziness, trembling, heartburn, numbness, nausea, choking, sweating, and fear of dying, among other symptoms. We hoped for a quick fix but soon learned that recovery efforts focused more on long-term coping. There was no instant cure. That didn't stop Annie from plowing through books and alternative treatments, attempting to tackle this new monster.

Anything with crowds or noise was out. Forget about concerts, sporting events, dancing, political rallies, even large dinners. No more highway driving. Streets would have to suffice, even if the trip was across town. My Pearl Jam and Smashing Pumpkins CDs were moved out in favor of Joan Armatrading and Shawn Colvin. These were the little changes. She slept less, many times preferring the couch to our bed. She pushed aside my embraces and overtures for intimacy.

My hours in the governor's office increased after a personnel shake-up in the press office. A mother with an infant and a father with a grade school girl replaced my former workmates, two single guys happy to take trips with Governor Wilson. The new flacks decided that travel wasn't in their job description, so I assumed the bulk of the trips throughout the state. Hello, Ukiah and Borrego Springs.

I know, I know. I could have set my foot down here and insisted we split the travel. But you know me. I loved those trips. Fueled off them. I didn't realize how much you hurt.

After five years together and a year of panic attacks, Annie told me she needed a change of environment. She said she wanted to move into her brother's apartment building in Santa Monica. No discussion or tears. Just a simple decision. She said she thought it best to put the relationship on hold until she was better. Sacramento had begun to depress her. A change of scenery and a new job would do her good, she argued. I was suddenly the one having an anxiety attack.

After Annie told me she planned to move out, I did what every bright, rational young American man would do. I panicked.

It wasn't just the decision to propose to her. Even then I had an inkling marriage wasn't the guaranteed panacea for all relationship ailments. I just thought that it might help, concluding that the proposal would prove to her that I was not wed to my life in the governor's office. We both knew we'd get married someday. Why not now? Plus, it would be much harder for my two married colleagues in the press department to slough off all the press trips on me.

Maybe work that last bit in after we've called her parents to tell them the good news. They should be happy. Their rationale will be something along the lines of: Well, she's not marrying a Mormon, but he's close.

The proposal, though a stretch, was somewhat rational. Where I really panicked was in the execution. Start with the diamond ring. I didn't shop around. I bought it at the closest place to our house, Nordstrom. I paid twice its value just so I could have a hyper-polite salesman with close-cropped hair explain the "four c" process in painful detail. I flirted with the idea of flying her somewhere exotic for the "Will you?" (Maui, maybe, or at least Santa Barbara), but decided I didn't have enough time. Not with Annie fleeing to Los Angeles soon. No, I needed to act.

I told her I wanted to take her to dinner at a fancy Italian restaurant, then ignored her when she told me she was tired, cranky, and preferred to eat leftovers. Already made the reservations, I announced, as if it would be impossible to cancel them. She griped about the arts agency, and Sacramento in general, through salads, antipasta, and gnocchi. Something about a new boss who dressed in overalls and muumuus. Over dessert, I tried to steer her into a preparation phase by talking about how we'd managed to overcome so much. The words stumbled as they came out, sounding desperate and confused. The confidence I'd accumulated over the years, stockpiled thanks in large part to her boosts and love, was now falling away.

No, no, no, no, no.

She said she had a headache when we got back to the house and started for bed. No, no, no. Wait a sec, I said as I scrambled to put a CD in the stereo.

Where's Al Green when you need him?

I grabbed the only one I could find in its case. Enya. *Oooooofffff.*

Play through. No big deal. Enya, headaches, muumuus—you can still pull this one out.

I asked her to sit on our couch before turning out the lights. Then I flipped the switch back on, because I couldn't find the matches to light the Presto log fire I'd prepared before. She'd changed into a T-shirt. Enya's whining from the stereo drew her attention and a look of confused disgust. The Presto log did zippo, and we were back in the dark for a few more minutes as I fanned the flames.

Nervous, no. I felt derailed. The thought of her leaving kicked my press secretary spin into gear. I started a spiel with some lines that I'd "considered all the hokey options out there for such an event"—the boat rides in stagnant ponds, or sporting-event scoreboards that would flash our names. I'd discarded them all in order to ask for her hand "in the place where we can build our lives together."

Let's review. Lead-in—horrible. Logic about not wanting to do anything special for this event—reeks of desperation. Closing line—translation: PLEEEEESE Don't Go! And did you even ask her to marry you? Transcript says no.

Annie smiled and rubbed the side of my head.

"Give me some time, then we can get married."

"So is that a yes or a no?"

"You know I'm in no condition to get married now."

Now that's a no.

She gave me a hug and said we should go to bed. To sleep. I told her I'd be there in a minute. Just needed to put the sputtering Presto log out of its misery and turn off the CD.

Enya. What were you thinking? Of course she's going to say no.

As I walked around, the house seemed enormous all of a sudden. As if it were a large hall after a dance, with dulled wood floors and discarded plastic cups and streamers. I thought about the antiques and artwork she'd probably take with her to Los Angeles.

She dumped you, and you're thinking about armoires and oils.

It was true. I wasn't as devastated or sad as I thought I might be. Maybe because I'm an optimist. When her panic attacks stop, we'll recover, I thought. I tried to rationalize our problems and started to convince myself that Santa Monica would be good for her. In a couple months, we'd be back to our old, comfortable relationship.

In fact, she kind of said yes back there, didn't she? That part about getting married as soon as she's better.

Oddly, we never talked about a split or pause, about dating other people or ground rules to continue our relationship. A few days later, she just left.

5

"Holy shit," Kurt blurted as he slammed on the brakes of our four-wheel-drive Isuzu mini-jeep. "That's a body." He paused. "Go check it out."

"Me, why me?"

"Because . . . because I'm driving."

"Kurt, that makes no sense. Try honking your horn."

The body remained motionless on the dirt road. I got out of the car.

"Amigo, amigo," I yelled. Nothing.

"Amigo, amigo," I continued, shaking his shoulder. Still nothing.

"Is he dead?" Kurt yelled from the driver's window.

"I don't know."

"Check for a pulse."

I placed my finger on the man's wrinkled neck, against the creases of outdoor labor.

"There's a pulse," I yelled back to Kurt.

Cresting like small waves, his chest expanded and collapsed. I smelled the booze on his breath and through his pores. He moaned and moved his head. Using a tug-of-war, heave-ho motion, I dragged the man out of the isolated country road and onto a grass field. Our guidebook promoted a posada up the hill. Convinced he would be fine for a few minutes, we decided to get help for our friend at the guesthouse.

Twenty minutes and no posada later, we shined the Isuzu headlights on the drunken man, who was now sitting up, head buried in hands, mumbling incoherent Spanish about *borracho* and "mama."

"His hangover's going to be worse than the one I had at Sea Ranch," I said.

We decided to drag him farther off the road to a grass bed where he could sleep off the celebration. Just another Saturday night in rural Costa Rica.

"You looked like you were going to faint when you touched that guy," Kurt said.

"Listen to you, Mr. I-refuse-to-get-out-of-the-car."

"I should have honked the horn when you felt for the pulse."

"Then there really would have been a dead body," I said. "Yours."

I looked at Kurt on the ride down the remote hill and it struck me how few hours we had shared since childhood. My mind tried to assemble his story, patching together bits of information. Sitting there, I realized how little I knew about him. I felt like someone who'd watched a soap opera for years, tuned out for a decade, then tuned back in. The characters were the same, but I knew I'd missed many plot lines. All those episodes dealing with boarding schools, amnesia, and evil twins.

He ate snails as a kid. I remembered that. Garden snails. The large tortoise-shell ones with bubbling slime coming off their faces. My parents told him it was wrong, then joked about it with their friends. That encouraged him to continue scouring the garden.

At a very early age, he proved his street savvy during a family trip to the King Tut exhibit in San Francisco. Standing at the end of a long line to see the gold masks and bejeweled mummy caskets, Kurt suddenly limped forward and motioned me along. I followed as he hobbled like a child with a broken leg. The masses in front of us began to part and step aside, allowing us to walk to the cases. I could see my father waver between condemnation and grudging approval. The lines were long.

I remembered he always gave our grandparents a long hug and usually volunteered to walk our mutt, Terra. His room had a ceiling fan, scores of BMX trophies, an OMD poster, and dozens of cologne bottles arranged like a church pipe organ with taller ones on the sides. I didn't ask, but I'm convinced he kept his high school girlfriend because she worked at Pioneer Chicken. Kurt loved free fast food.

Our parents cut him a lot more slack when it came to bedtimes and grades. But, man, did my father seethe when the policeman knocked on the door one night and told him Kurt had blown a drug sting by pulling over an undercover cop car with a police light he bought in Mexico. I could almost see Dad working the punishment out in his mind as he thanked the officer multiple times and promised to deal with the incident "immediately."

I also saw the panic in his face the night the hospital called to say Kurt had been a passenger in a car wreck. The convertible had slid off the gravel road at eighty miles per hour and hit a tree, the Napa Valley paramedic said. Kurt survived because he wasn't wearing a seat belt. That says enough about him right there. The impact shattered his femur and launched him twenty feet from the accident. He came home from the hospital the day before I flew to Boston for college. I didn't want to leave him.

Kurt attended the University of Oregon in Eugene, then chased his college girl-friend to her hometown, Seattle. Her sister sold real estate, so Kurt gave it a try. A natural salesman with a knack for connecting with strangers, he had many of the attributes needed for success—"selling the dream," as he described it. He also had an aversion to long hours and a low threshold for pleasure. To Kurt, work was the vehicle to pay for trips to Las Vegas, courtside Sonics tickets, and tee times at his favorite golf courses.

A coworker of his told me Kurt had the "highest kill ratio" in the office, the most home sales per attempt. "He makes more than most, but only works half-time," the broker explained. "He could easily be the number-one salesman if he put in a few more hours."

The same breezy approach didn't help with his marriage. His wife seized the golf weekends like a hammer and a shield for her own shortcomings. She was twenty-three when they married, never having lived alone, never knowing the joys of dorm life and IKEA furniture. His divorce took place a year before my split, two and a half years after he and his wife exchanged their vows. Kurt's friends chalked it up to a lack of birthdays: hers. I knew there must be other reasons, but talked to him about it on only a few occasions and in even less detail. "She feels like she skipped a stage," I think I remember him saying. I'll wait until I can ask him more in person, I rationalized at the time. But the silent days stretched to weeks and months and soon I was too embarrassed to inquire. Like a wedding gift you fail to send: after a year, you hope the couple forgets. I convinced myself Kurt was fine.

I had no idea how we'd travel together, but got a glimpse before we left LAX on the overnight flight to San Jose.

"Come on, Fritz, let's go scam our way into the United Airlines lounge," he ordered as we waited for the flight.

"Nice to see you again," he told the United representative with excessive mascara at the reception desk. I knew he'd never been there.

"Yeah, you, too," she replied.

"Brought my crazy brother with me this time. He needs a little TLC. Just got left at the altar."

"Oh, I'm so sorry," she said with real concern. "Go on in and get him a drink."

Minutes later, we saddled up to the Red Carpet Club bar, drinking free beers, and leafing through the United in-flight magazine.

"Hey, man, you're going to love this," Kurt said. "Guess what movie they're showing?"

"What?"

"*Runaway Bride.*"

"I think I'll skip it. I've already seen that story."

After an all-night flight in a plane ripe for a makeover ("I thought you said this honeymoon was first-class?"), we headed to a car rental lot a couple blocks from the airport. Dusty, dingy four-wheel-drives huddled tightly around a dirt lot with a makeshift office that resembled a portable classroom. Kurt began to sniff around for the car of his choice. A sign on the door read *Back in Ten Minutes.* We waited for an hour.

"You guys flying in or out?" asked the fiftyish gringo with faded blue surfer shorts, Hussongs T-shirt, and a face weathered from years of waves and waves of years.

He shook his head and looked sheepishly at the ground when I told him we'd just arrived. Mike was a homebuilder from San Diego who worked half the year, then worked down his savings the rest. Cheap, sunny surfer paradises like Indonesia and Costa Rica were his preference. Living on credit, he'd run out of money a couple days earlier and was heading back to Southern California to "bang some more nails." He talked about upcoming trips and his "surf and saw" lifestyle as we gave him a ride to his hotel, the Del Rey. "Come on by tonight if you're not doing anything." An attractive woman in a leather skirt walking out of the lobby strengthened our resolve to do so.

"Meester and Meesses Weezner," said the man at our hotel, a few blocks away. "Welcome. I have you staying in the honeymoon suite, no?"

"It's actually Mr. and Mr. Wisner, and a plain old room would be fine."

"Your bride, she will join you later?"

"She's been . . . delayed."

"Ah, I see. For long?"

"Long story."

"I will put you in room five."

"Two beds?"

"*Sí.*"

"Thanks."

"But please let us know if you need any champagne or food to celebrate."

"I'll let you know. Thanks."

Declining the bellhop's offer to help with our bags, we made our way to the distinctly unromantic confines of room five.

"No," I said, barely containing my laughter.

"C'mon," Kurt prodded.

"No. I'm not going to carry you over the threshold."

"It's your honeymoon."

"I'd drop you on purpose."

The deal we cut before the trip was this: I'd pay for everything—flights, hotels, car rentals, and meals. In exchange, we'd cancel all honeymoon suites, flowers in the rooms, chilled champagne, his-and-her bathrobes, massages and manicures, and any attempts to carry each other over thresholds. Beer and hammocks, I told him. Now Kurt was reneging on the deal, and, deep down, I was happy he tried. The whole thing was so surreal—a honeymoon with my brother—I needed ample mockery to help pull me through.

Kurt and I walked around town for a few hours, then headed over to the Del Rey hotel for the evening. We settled into the Blue Marlin Bar, drank our first Imperial beers, and wolfed down tortillas with rice and strip steak. A gorgeous, latte-skinned cigar girl asked if we wanted a smoke. Several large-screen televisions aired a football game between the Green Bay Packers and the San Francisco 49ers. Blackjack tables beckoned from an adjoining room.

"I like our man Mike," Kurt said. "I like his lifestyle. He's got everything he needs."

"Yeah, I guess."

"He's got no obligations, no other mouths to feed. He can pick up and go whenever he feels the itch."

"Yeah, sure," I said, paying more attention to the football game.

Kurt scanned the room full of polished women in clothes more characteristic of San Jose, California, than San Jose, Costa Rica.

"Pros," he said. "Mike's chillin' at a combo Vegas casino and whorehouse."

An attractive young woman with a light brown business suit and bobbed hair leaned over from a stool next to us and started to chat. She had a "May I help you" smile and a reserved, professional manner like a law-firm receptionist.

"Are you here on business?" she asked.

"We're here on my . . . honeymoon," I said.

"Qué?"

"My honeymoon. It's a weird story. Short version is I got dumped at the altar and decided to come on the honeymoon anyhow with my brother, Kurt, here."

She giggled, more out of confusion than sympathy, a laugh to fill space. I didn't blame her. I wondered what I was doing myself.

"You guys ready to go upstairs?" she said nonchalantly after a few more minutes of innocuous conversation about rain and California women.

"No. Thanks anyway."

She smiled and started to move from her chair. I reached for her arm.

Please. Don't go. Can't you see I'm lonely?

"Um, wait. You mind if I buy you a drink and ask you a few questions about your country?"

With a shrug she sat back down and ordered a whiskey and soda. Kurt pushed off, saying he wanted to play a few hands of blackjack and to pay a visit to Mike. Still looking a bit befuddled, the woman introduced herself as Maria.

"Nice to meet you, Maria. My name's Franz."

"So what do you want to know?"

I want to know what I'm doing here on my honeymoon with a Costa Rican prostitute. And a brother I barely know. Are we going to drive each other crazy this week?

I want to know why the love of my life deserted me in the final seconds of our lift-off. And why my work spit me out.

I want to know if Mike is truly happy or maybe, just maybe, he has those days where he longs for a big family and a house in Fontana that looks just like all the others on the block.

Instead, we started with tourist sights. She mapped a few of her favorite beaches and national parks on the back of a napkin. Next to each she scribbled names and phone numbers of friends.

No, don't ask her why she does this for a living.

"You say you are on a honeymoon?"

And that triggered it. It was all I needed. A crack, an opening to tell this stranger about my dented heart and the mass confusion swirling around in my head. During the wedding weekend, I'd largely passed on opportunities to talk in depth. Now I wanted to vent, to tell someone, anyone who'd listen, how I'd lost my two loves—my fiancée and my career. So I started in and gradually worked up my confessional to include things I hadn't told Kurt. Like finding Annie's diary. Or the time we went to dinner with her brother and I learned she'd kept our wedding plans secret from him. Not once did it occur to me that I was having a heart-to-heart with a woman who faked orgasms for a living. Maria dove into the conversation, prompting me deeper and deeper with a series of questions. Her drink sat untouched, her work for the evening set aside. And I continued on for a half hour until Kurt walked up.

"The blackjack dealer wins on a push here," he said. "How the hell can that happen? Even in the crappiest casino in Nevada, a push is a push."

"So you didn't do so well?"

"Yeah, they took all my money."

"You see Mike?"

"No, I went up to his room, but nobody answered. You about ready to go?"

I looked at Maria.

"I need to go," she said.

"Go," I said. "But, hey, thanks."

The guidebook advised us to take cabs at night. Having blown all our money, we decided to walk the eight blocks back to our hotel.

"What's the worst thing that could happen?" Kurt asked.

Cue, stage right. A group of five lively transvestites approached from the opposite side of the street and began to fumble with our pockets and backsides. Decked out in high heels and tightly fitted dresses, the group moved in unison, arms grasping like an octopus reaching for prey.

"Whoa," I said. "At least take us out to dinner first."

We quickened our pace for a half block before breaking into a jog for the rest of the way to the hotel. The room number and the napkin were gone when I emptied my pockets.

"Mike's gonna have a hot time *tonight*," Kurt sang.

The roads in and out of San Jose are like a giant snarl in a young girl's hair: the more you try to force your way, the worse the problem. Without warning, highways wind their way through residential neighborhoods. Traffic signs are occasional and occasionally followed. Breakdowns litter the sides of the road and clog arteries.

Kurt smiled behind the wheel in the middle of the morning mess. He rested one arm out the window and adjusted his sunglasses. Some people see chaos as chaos. Others view it as an opportunity. At that moment, I realized Kurt saw it as a jackpot. Everyone trying to go east just meant the roads west would be free and clear.

Kurt dubbed our four-wheel-drive "Burrotico" for its size, stubbornness, and stability, inspired by Costa Ricans who tack on the word *tico* (or "little") the same way Americans plaster *mega, super,* or *ultra* on supermarket items. He'd eyed it at the lot, and then convinced the agent to rent it to us at a reduced rate. Four-wheel-drives were essential in Costa Rica. Potholes that morning punctuated the point.

"Paint it Black" by the Rolling Stones blared through the radio, followed by "La Bamba" by someone other than Ritchie Valens.

"Love the randomness of the radio down here," he said. "I'm so sick of that programmed and packaged crap in the States."

"Agreed. It's all geared to some hyper-defined demographic. Just that word. *Demographic*. Yuck. I think we've over-demographiced."

After a couple hours avoiding bumps in the road and countless Costa Ricans, who loved to walk on the sides of the highways, Kurt turned the wheel over to me.

"Oh, tie a yellow ribbon round the old oak tree," sang the radio.

"They still need some help with the tunes," he said.

"Yeah, they need a little help, or, shall I say, help-tico."

We flew past a little bald man waving his arms. He kicked dirt as we drove by.

"Was that a cop?" I asked, pulling over.

The *policia* and his young sidekick rambled up in their dilapidated jeep. The dirt-kicker sprinted toward us. My two semesters of college Spanish helped me translate about two of his words, though I knew he was berating me for speeding. His breath smelled like the stale cart food from San Jose.

"*No hablo español,*" I chanted, half realizing I was speaking Spanish to tell him I didn't speak Spanish.

Exasperated, he grabbed a pen, scribbled the number forty on the top of his palm, then smiled and said, "Lee-mit." He wrote an eighty below the forty, shifted his grin into a scowl, and said, "You," tapping the eighty with his pen.

My *no hablo* mantra immediately changed to a chorus of *por favors,* with Kurt adding harmony from the passenger seat. Worn down by our begging, our friend waved us on with a disgusted flick of the wrist and a confused look on his face.

"We need to work on our ticket rap," Kurt noted in the same fashion a singer would talk about fine-tuning a song.

By the third day, we fell into a comfortable travel pattern. Rich coffee and tropical fruits in the morning. Swim and a little sun. Hiking or exploring in the afternoons. Siestas. Big dinners of grilled fish and rice. Close the day with a beer and a Cohiba cigar on a restaurant patio. No thresholds. Kurt did most of the driving and all of the negotiating. I scoured the guidebooks and fumbled through translations. Driving slowly on dirt roads, we worked our way up the coast to the Nicaraguan border, then drove back down the center to stomp through the country's legendary rain forests. And there were actually times, minutes, mind you, when I didn't think about Annie.

Kurt and I deciphered surfer conversations in Tamarindo, learned to mimic and agitate howler monkeys on jungle treks, forced our chain-smoking guide into a jog up the mountain to the Barra Honda caves, stared in amusement as anal birdwatchers fought over credit for sightings, and listened to several Americans brag about plans to build retirement homes and lure Costa Rican brides with bribes. One man showed us his newspaper advertisement for a wife. He said he received five offers of interest within a week.

Note to self.

"Have you guys seen anything living?" asked the harried New York woman in the middle of the verdant Monteverde Cloud Forest. I winced. Kurt pounced.

"Yeah, we just saw a black panther about fifty yards back," he deadpanned.

"Really? I thought they were nocturnal?"

"Well, the rain forest is so dense, they have a hard time distinguishing night and day."

"Honey," she yelled as she turned toward her husband. "They just saw a *pan*-ther."

Our guide Pedro shook his head. "You guys are going to get me fired," he said "Come on. I'll show you a couple things and teach you a couple tricks.

"Don't look at specific areas, scan for movement and listen," he explained. "Look for dark clumps on trees, falling leaves or rustling branches. There's usually something there."

Though he'd given the tour hundreds of times, Pedro talked with the excitement of a high school freshman on a first date. He defined life in the rain forest as a "battle for light," using strangler fig trees and wide-leaf ferns as examples. The flora-and-fauna lessons were spliced with narratives about Costa Rican life. He talked about the country's pride in education programs and national parks, about the importance of family, about Oscar Arias's Nobel Peace Prize, and the ancillary benefits of not having a national army.

The rain increased like the blast from a steering wheel–size showerhead at a high-end hotel. It continued for the next several days as we moved on to the Arenal Volcano.

"No, no. I don't want any cream in my coffee," Kurt said as I tried to pour him some the next morning.

Our Arenal hotel offered a proper English breakfast with scones and boiled tomatoes. A friendly boxer sat next to Kurt in hopes of a scrap. A snooker table beckoned on the open-air patio nearby. A slice of Britain in the heart of Costa Rica.

"I thought you liked cream?"

"Nonfat milk."

"It's got no taste."

"I like it."

He cut away the gristle from a piece of ham.

"When did you turn into such a healthy eater?"

"I've always been."

"No, you haven't. I've seen you load piles of bacon between two slices of Wonder Bread and go back for more. And whatever happened to your motto of eat it now or regret it later?"

"That was a while ago."

"Not that long."

He paused.

"Actually," he started, "I decided after my divorce that I never wanted to be overweight again. It seemed like the one thing in my life I could control."

I paused.

I don't know you, do I? Don't have a clue about your feelings after the divorce or even how you like your coffee.

"Hmmph. Well, you look good. Healthy. Maybe I'll start running, too. We can go together."

"Yeah, okay."

Gary, a former British Navy sailor and current owner of the hotel, joined us at the table. He lit a cigarette and started talking about Premier League soccer. And honeymoons.

"I must confess I had a bit of a scare when I saw you two lads. You know, with the honeymoon reservations and such. Assumed you were a couple poofters from California. Blokes can get married there, can't they?"

"Thanks for not spreading rose petals on the beds," I said.

"Don't mention it."

"We'll take some champagne, though, if you have it," Kurt interjected.

"I'll see what I can do. It's still a honeymoon, after all."

A woman's voice yelled from an adjacent building.

"Lads, don't ever get married," he counseled. "My wife was thirty pounds lighter and a hundred times nicer before we tied the knot." He excused himself from the table.

"Is it just me, or are you noticing all these signs?" I asked Kurt. "Everything from the watch Annie gave me dropping from my wrist the night we split to *Runaway Bride* being the movie on the plane to Gary talking about his crappy marriage. Maybe I just didn't pay attention before, but it seems like I'm being bombarded by a lot of messages big and small."

"Sure."

"I'm serious. Someone's trying to tell us something."

"Here's a message—the rain. It's telling us to get out of here. Remember, I live in Seattle. If I wanted to hang out in the rain, I could do that at home."

We agreed that prepaid hotel reservations and prearranged tours limited our flexibility. Vacations, like life, needed room for improvisation. No more, we swore. Kurt pulled out a map, pointed Burrotico to the Pacific Coast, and we were off.

"Everybody was kung fu fighting," blasted the radio.

We made it to the coastal town of Quepos just in time to enjoy a tangerine sunset over the Pacific from an empty restaurant with a cracked concrete patio and palm frond umbrellas. A bushy-haired man bolted from a parked car across the street and scampered over to take our order. The entire drive down I struggled, trying to place everything together in some semicoherent shape. My life before seemed so orderly.

Maybe too much so. Strip away the perks and what do you have? Reward? Satisfaction? Love?

Now it was a jumbled mess.

My biggest fear. The bane of the firstborn. Why am I being pushed into territory I've spent my whole life trying to avoid?

Like an archaeologist on the brink of a find, I dug and dug, trying to decipher the tidbits and see the greater form. Trying to make sense out of overnight failure. *God, I've never done this. And I know I'm not good at it.* Trying to grab the fallen pieces and arrange them in a shape to convince everyone—especially me—that all was not lost. *I'm nervous, and scared to let go. And now pissed. At her and the company. Fuck 'em. That's healthy to say that, right?* Trying to find the pony in the room full of manure. Trying to . . .

"You know, we should take a big trip," I said, surprising myself.

"You mean to Russia or somewhere?"

"No, no. I mean take six months or a year and go everywhere. Russia, China, Africa. Wherever you want."

"Well, I guess we . . . "

"Think about it, Kurt. Neither of us is married. We don't have kids. We hate our jobs. We have a little cash to do it. Why not?"

"Maybe. Buy me dinner and a margarita, and let's talk about it."

"Look at it this way," I urged, becoming increasingly convinced as I talked through the idea. "If we don't do it now, we'll never do it. One of us will be married or locked into a job. You'll be sixty before you go out on the road for an extended period of time."

"What about Fritz and Riley?"

"We'll find a dog-sitter."

"Maybe Mom and Dad."

"No way Mom and Dad."

"What about my house in Seattle?"

"Sell it. Move in with me for the time being."

"Fritz and Riley, too?"

"Bring 'em."

He chewed on the idea for a few minutes, then bit, something I could never have done in the past.

"When would you want to go?"

"Irvine Company gives their bonuses in late July. Cash my check, give my two-week notice, and we're gone."

"That would give me enough time to sell my house and wrap up my listings. You really want to do this?"

"I don't think I have a choice. Feels like I'm on autopilot these days."

We talked through dinner and on the way to the hotel, hashing out logistics like ways to pay bills online and friends abroad off whom we could sponge. "John's begged me for years to go to Moscow, and Terra has that new apartment in Prague." Kurt became more and more intrigued. I was sold from the beginning, a refreshing role reversal. I went to bed convinced the trip was going to happen. A year on the road. Just me, Kurt . . .

Wait a minute. You just strapped into a year, a year with Kurt. You'll want to kill each other after a month. Not knowing him is a hell of a lot better than wanting to murder him. He's a morning person, you're night. He likes sun, you prefer shade. He'll always push for the dives, you'll want the nicer hotels. And that's just the stuff you found out this week. Think of all the little things that will drive you—and him—crazy.

"Hey, quit grinding your teeth," Kurt said from the other bed.

"Huh?"

"You're grinding your teeth. I can't sleep."

"Sorry. I'm all stressed out these days. I need to get one of those mouth guards, so I don't wear my teeth flat."

"If I'm not here when you get up in the morning, I'll be on a run. Back before breakfast."

Somehow I knew then that I could deal with Kurt for the year. Sure, we might have our rough patches, but as he did with the teeth gnashing, he'd tell me when I was doing something that bugged him. We're brothers. We at least do that part well. He wouldn't hesitate to do his own thing whenever it suited him. He's a Libra. He does that well.

I fell asleep thinking about DEAs. That's what our father called them: Dad's Exciting Adventures. We'd rarely know the destination, only when to be ready to go. "Pack a bag or a swimsuit," he'd say. "The DEA begins at noon, sharp."

The trips started small—train rides to the Sierra Nevadas or treks to the fish hatchery, where Kurt fell into the water trying to grab a salmon. When I was twelve and Kurt ten, our father announced a special DEA, a sabbatical to New Zealand for six months. Without finishing our food, we rushed to the big globe in the living room to find our new home. Then the horror set in.

"What about Little League? Or my paper route? I can't go, Dad. I just can't."

He reassured us we would be back in time for baseball, paper routes could be given to friends, and, yes, we could even bring our skateboards. "One each." Hours spent plowing through the New Zealand entries of our encyclopedia set sparked curiosity about glaciers, beaches, and "Look at all those sheep, Kurt."

We landed in Dunedin the Friday before classes began. On the plane ride over, my mother explained New Zealand schoolkids wore uniforms. She took me to the local department store the following day to purchase an outfit of gray wool shorts, matching gray socks, white polo shirts, and a navy V-neck sweater with red trim. I sported the schoolboy attire around the house to the amusement of Kurt and Lisa, who escaped a similar fate on account of their ages.

Sack lunch in hand, I walked to Dunedin North Intermediate and into my homeroom. I looked with anticipation around the room, hoping to find an instant friend. Instead, the kids talked among themselves in a brand of English I found difficult to understand. I'll just wait for recess and then approach someone, I reasoned. With luck, I'd meet a kid whose accent wasn't too thick.

Break time, still no contacts or conversations. Lunch was the same. I ate by myself on a bench and watched the boys play cricket, trying to decipher the rules while attempting eye contact with someone. Anyone. For the rest of the afternoon, I sat depressed at my desk, wondering how the granddaddy of DEAs had morphed into a nightmare. When the final bell rang, I couldn't leave fast enough. I grabbed my books, slumped my head, and began the agonizing march home. A bus full of classmates passed me a few blocks later, slowing for a stoplight.

"Poofter . . . poofter. The Yankee's a poofter," the kids on the bus yelled in chorus. "Poofter . . . poofter. The Yankee's a poofter."

Crushed and confused, I ran the rest of the way.

"Hey, Franz!" my mom said in her patent enthusiastic voice. "How was your first day?"

"I hate New Zealand. They called me a poofter."

"What's a poofter?"

"I don't know. But I don't like being called one."

"Maybe it's a compliment?"

"Why did you and Dad bring us here?"

Later that afternoon, an older boy from next door explained *poofter* was slang for homosexual. Kids were sometimes called poofters, he said, if they wore their wool socks up to their knees, as was the style in California at the time, 1970s skateboard chic.

"Try pulling your socks down tomorrow," he said. "You should have better luck."

Fresh start. Day two, socks around my ankles, way down, two Maori boys approached me before I could get to my desk. Problem solved. That day and in the many enjoyable ones that followed, my classmates asked me dozens of questions about America, while detailing essential subjects for a New Zealand boy in 1976, including lollies, meat pies and chips, cricket and rugby, ABBA and Tintin comic books, and why their relatives with tattoos on their faces did that funny dance while sticking out their tongues.

After the sock controversy, California became cool. Classmates crowded around me to ask about movie stars, surfing, and a land seen in magical terms. I didn't bother to explain Davis was one hundred miles from the beach. Or that the town often smelled like cows from the surrounding fields and tomatoes from the local Hunt-Wesson processing plant.

Hey, I can do this. I can live outside California and still have fun.

During long weekends and vacations, we'd pile into a small white Ford sedan with lipstick red seats. The trips introduced us to sheep-shearing contests and sheepdog trials, kiwis and keas, and a world supply of wilderness packed on a couple of islands in the far South Pacific.

Four years later, we took another sabbatical, this one to Fremantle, Australia.

Kurt and I enrolled at a local high school and immediately embraced the local beach scene with its idolized lifeguards and zinc-covered noses, Mad Max movies, INXS and Australian new wave music, Aussie Rules football, and local teenage girls.

"Keep your socks pushed down around your ankles," I warned Kurt on our way to school on day one. "Just in case."

Kurt and I didn't want to leave when the sabbaticals ended. And Davis became a springboard to journeys elsewhere. Our appetites were whetted at a young age. Whetted, then set aside.

"All we are is dust in the wind," boomed Burrotico's radio the next day on the way to Dominical, in southern Costa Rica.

"See?" I said. "Dust in the wind? All we are is dust in the wind."

"Don't get carried away."

We were somewhere between discussing the best way to break the honeymoon extension to our parents ("together, that's a must") and carnival plans in South America when Kurt pounded the brakes at the beginning of a one hundred-yard single-lane bridge made with wood slats and railroad ties. Passengers from other cars sat on hoods, smoking cigarettes.

"De-vas-ta-ción," someone proclaimed as we walked to the other side of the bridge to investigate the holdup.

A semi truck had somehow flipped a dozen railroad ties into the river fifty feet below. Several river crocodiles made us scratch retrieval off the list of repair options. The driver of the rig argued with an old man missing several teeth. Others stood and stared.

"Amigos," Kurt boomed to my surprise and theirs. *"Vamos."*

He grabbed a teenage local by the arm and asked me to follow. After walking back across the bridge, Kurt pried a nailed tie out of its position. He and the local boy carried the tie to the accident site, and then pushed it in place. I worked on another tie with an older motorist who grasped the plan. Soon, twenty men worked in unison under the command of a gringo who knew maybe twenty words in Spanish.

"Let her rip," Kurt signaled to the truck driver, who stopped his argument, hopped into the cabin, and eagerly revved his engine.

A whistle-filled roar went up as the truck safely passed. Men patted Kurt on the back and honked their horns as they passed. Kurt stood proud, like Alec Guinness in *The Bridge on the River Kwai,* soaking it all in.

"Forget the world trip," he said. "I'm running for mayor of this place."

6

Annie's departure from Sacramento sent me to the nightmare of every bachelor—limbo, a place where egos are crushed and conspiracies hatched by the minute. Just hearing the word triggered cringes and sympathetic responses of "duuuuuu-uude" from my male friends. Were we dating? My answer depended on the day. Sometimes—Fridays and Tuesdays, I think—I'd tell my friends I was on the market and ready to be hooked up. Tall brunettes preferred. Other times I'd sing Annie's praises and nod to all that we were doing okay. "Don't worry. We're still on track."

Growing up, I had a stuffed dog, Rover, with glue-stained fur, several stitch jobs, and only one eye, courtesy of Kurt's early experiments in ophthalmology. Though Rover was a tad disheveled, I loved him. To justify my spot in limbo, I convinced myself Annie was Rover. A little dinged up, sure, but still I loved her. Forget about my issues, our situation was nothing a little TLC wouldn't cure. Fortunately, I never got around to telling Annie I equated her with a one-eyed stuffed dog.

A few months after Annie left in 1994, I ran into Larry Thomas in the lobby of the Sacramento Hyatt across the street from the state capitol. Tuxedoed, with a beautiful blonde in tow, my mentor from political circles was now working as an executive at The Irvine Company, a position that allowed him to move in and out of state politics and escort gorgeous women to black-tie events.

"Wizard! Where the hell you been? I've been trying to get a hold of you. I want you to come work for me," he said as he and his date made their way to a banquet at the other end of the hotel.

I joked that I was turning into a Sacramento lifer but promised to call the next week. The truth was I loved Sacramento. But "forty-five minutes" crept into my mind. Annie's apartment was just forty-five minutes from The Irvine Company headquarters in Newport Beach. Maybe I could take the job with the company, buy a house, and convince her to move down? Sacramento was the problem, right?

Maybe anxiety disorders dissolved in the bright Southern California sun. Maybe. Yeah, yeah. That was it. Maybe she'd fully recover, and we could live happily ever after? Maybe, yes. I discarded the dream and Sacramento and started a new one along the Orange County coast.

It was the most remarkable gift I'd ever received. I just stared at it, unfolded on my lap. Annie grinned with pride, nudging me to "open it, open it." I gave her a big hug and then turned back the large black binder. We sat side by side on the blue and white ticking cloth couch in my Newport Beach apartment.

Slowly, graphically, on Kodak four-by-sixes and scripted verse, my life unfolded. Here were crayon drawings by young cousins; a Happy Birthday card from my nursery school teacher; embarrassing photos with friends (*ouch, that haircut; I didn't even like Flock of Seagulls*); notes from my old high school football coach ("Hey #44") and the friendly Davis mailman; poems, stories, haikus, press releases, collages, and letters composed by family and friends who shaped my first three decades. Here was my life.

"Well, do you like it?" Annie asked. "Do you like it?"

"Ann, I don't know what to say. I'm . . . I'm blown away. This is remarkable. Thank you, thank you so much. I love you so much. How did you do this?"

She explained she mailed a letter to a couple hundred friends, cousins, old teachers, governor's office colleagues, college roommates, travel agents, the dry cleaner and the owner of our favorite antique store, reporters, and countless others. She asked them to mail a story, card, photo, or any creative item to commemorate my thirtieth birthday. My mother helped track down addresses and round up responses. The replies were as creative and eclectic as my circle of friends.

I knew she'd spent months compiling the entries, months more arranging them in the book. I looked at her and felt a tidal wave of warmth. Here was a labor of love. Here was love. Anyone that would gather and glue photos of me for months had all the attributes necessary for marriage—creativity, industriousness, competency with school art projects (thinking of the kids here), contentment to stare at my bad hair.

Let's go. Hop in the car and go to Vegas. Enough dicking around. Let's get married. Now. Please.

The job with The Irvine Company had brought me closer to Annie. Still in limbo, though nearer its exit. It wasn't the same as living together in Sacramento, but the weekends with her gave me hope for a renewed union ahead. I'd wait. Wait for Annie to declare she was ready to return. Wait for her to upgrade her answer to my proposal.

The best gauge of her well-being was her car. Since the Sacramento incidents, Annie refused to drive on highways. She explained they made her feel trapped and claustrophobic, and frequently triggered attacks. The fear turned her twenty-minute commute to work at a Los Angeles museum into a forty-five-minute trek through urban streets. Visits to Orange County meant trips on the train. Highway driving would signal she was less anxious.

Time and distance ate steadily away at our relationship, like ocean waves attacking a shore. The status quo was a killer. I saw the erosion, which was easier to grasp than in Sacramento. The days apart afforded a better view of the whole. I griped about the limbo, yet still waited. Months, years. Limbo.

In 1997, eight years after I met Annie, I gave up. As she continued to insist she was improving, the stack of self-help books in her apartment continued to grow. They had titles like *A More Perfect You* or *The Essential Phobia and Fear Cope Book*. Despite the cover promises, I didn't see the signs of progress. We were stuck. I wanted to get married despite her condition, reasoning that we could fight it better together. She insisted on overcoming her situation alone before we went forward.

"I'm sorry, Annie, but I just can't wait any longer," I told her at a Santa Monica coffee shop.

We sat outside despite the cold and the fog. On that, I insisted. I didn't want either of us to have a false comfort of home. I fought hard not to look back to the table as I walked away. It had been three years since I'd proposed to her in Sacramento.

Sitting alone in my car, I was more frustrated and numb than sad. Maybe it was because I still believed we'd eventually work things out. Part of me thought love was enough, that it would eventually bridge the gaps in our relationship. Maybe she'd call tonight and say, "Okay, Vegas is fine."

Work was the obvious distraction, and I poured my energies into the job. The long hours were rewarded with promotions and more money. Golf outings, trips to Europe, political campaigns, Anaheim Angels games, and time with friends filled my calendar. I started dating others, fighting to convince myself Annie and I were through. One year, no contact. It was the only way I could plow ahead.

After a weekend in San Francisco with a new girlfriend, I flew back to Orange County late on a Sunday night. The phone ring surprised me. It was Annie.

She stammered, sounding more nervous than I'd ever remembered. Following a couple minutes of "How you doing?" talk, she got to the point, saying she wanted to see me in person. Was I free for dinner the following night?

My mind flooded with suddenly open passageways, dark memories, and muted frustrations of waiting. A sharp ray of love pierced through. I could feel it deep inside, a spotlight on a suppressed passion.

"Just be cool and find out what she has to say," my roommate Ben counseled. "We all know you still love her. You haven't fooled any of us. Just don't jump back in without thinking. Remember, there's a reason you aren't together right now."

Early by an hour to our rendezvous, I walked along Redondo Beach, a depository that afternoon for two-star tourists and sand volleyballers trying to complete a final set before the sun disappeared. Emotions, packed away, flooded anew like a desert river after a storm. What to say? What to say? And there she was.

I hugged her as I would a friend's bride at a wedding—loving yet tepid, not wanting to wrinkle the wedding dress. She breathed a deep sigh after unwrapping her arms. So, how's your family? she asked. Fine. So, how's your job? she asked. Same ole. I wondered how long she would continue with the chitchat. It was her evening, so it was her move. *Right, Benny?* She looked thin and sounded more confident than she did on the phone. *Did you drive over on the 405 or through city streets?*

"Just so you know, I'm one hundred percent fine," she announced. "I've worked hard for the past year to heal myself with the goal of restarting our relationship.

"I've learned a lot," Annie said with quiet force and a touch of nervousness now. "One thing is that I can't live without you. Another is that I don't want to live without you."

Boom. Crash. The shell that had encased her for years, the shell that prevented me from getting too close, had been cracked. The daughter of a family that preferred secrets, Annie usually kept her feelings to herself. Some judged it as a cool aloofness. I knew she was deathly uncomfortable with emotion. Her words floored me.

"Are you saying you want to get married?" I asked. "Now?"

"Yes," she said.

"You mean drive-to-Vegas-tonight married?"

"If you want."

Whoa. Remember. Slow down.

"You know, emotions are weird things," I offered. "You don't just turn them off and on. I've spent a lot of time working out of this relationship, shutting down feelings and dreams. Now you're talking about starting them up again."

She looked down at the floor, and I knew she wanted to hear more.

"This dinner means a lot to me, Annie. I know those words don't come easy or without thought. Most of all, I'm thrilled you're better. You look beautiful."

She smiled a bit, but her eyes stayed down.

"You know I love you, Annie. I'll always love you. But I need some time. Just give me some time. I'd like to see you again."

I didn't tell her I was dating someone else.

"Well, I've waited a year," she said. "What's a little more time?"

"Annie, I've waited many years."

We agreed to start anew. With no timetable or preconceptions. It was an Annie I hadn't experienced in years—loving, energized, reaching, embracing. Never before had I seen her so preoccupied with my happiness. That didn't make me happy. Out were her sass and that frustratingly seductive indifference. In were comments along the lines of: "I'd love to spend New Year's Day at the Rose Bowl with you and your buddies, drinking beer and cheering two colleges neither of us attended." The over-solicitousness threw me . . . for a couple weeks. Then I just sat back and enjoyed it, figuring her old attitude would reappear soon.

We started the relationship again to the approval of family and friends. My dad, especially, gushed about having her back in the fold, telling Annie's parents several times that he and my mom were getting a better deal in the exchange. We went on dates, old-fashioned dates. To Cirque du Soleil and black-tie openings at the Los Angeles museum where she worked in the public-relations department. We filled in the spaces from the year apart and eased back into the shared history that bound us. I told my girlfriend in San Francisco that I could no longer see her.

Washington, D.C., I thought. This is just like the time in Washington, D.C. Here was the one person in my life whom I'd loved. Wholehearted, unconditional love. Here was the woman who made me fantasize about Huggies and Diaper Genies. In addition, there was logic. Even if I wasn't sure things would work out, I knew I'd regret it for the rest of my life if I didn't try. So I did.

We practiced driving to conquer her fear, the one issue, she admitted, that still lingered. The crowning moment came when she drove from Santa Monica to Newport Beach on the crowded 405 Freeway. "You're doing great," I yelled as she steered her BMW from the granny lane to the middle lane.

The pace of the relationship continued to accelerate as well. Our love was solid, comfortable. On a drive to pick up my sister at the Ontario airport, we decided to become husband and wife the way two longtime business partners finalize a deal. There was no "Will you?" or bended knee, no fancy dinners or rings in cakes (or Enya and Presto logs, thank God). She already had a ring, and I'd already proposed. We just started talking about locations. I threw out the idea of eloping somewhere. Annie thought her mom would be devastated with a spur-of-the-moment service, so we forged ahead with plans for a wedding that fall.

"So we'll pick a spot and get married, right?" I said at the end of the conversation.

"Mmm-hmm."

After visiting several venues in Southern California with coordinators who struggled to sound excited about "your big day," we decided on Sea Ranch as the site of our vows. We flew to San Francisco in May, then drove the two hours up Highway 1 to finalize dates and details with the Birkenstocked wedding planner. Annie giddy-up'ed as we walked through the wildflower fields surrounding the old barn, talking about a bagpiper to lead the procession and a simple ceremony overlooking the rocky Pacific shore. Maybe peonies in buckets, she said. And no wedding attendants. Just her sister and Kurt by our sides. Keep it informal and fun.

When we hopped back in the car, I could see something had made her pause. *You should be happier.* I tuned in the San Francisco Giants baseball game on the radio. They were tied. An hour into the drive, she turned and asked me not to get mad if she told me something. *God, I hate that lead-in. I don't think I've ever not been mad after that preface.*

"Sure," I reassured her, but not me.

Picking the words carefully, she said she had started to experience the anxiety attacks again. "Little ones."

True to form, I was mad. Both at her and this monster that kept coming back to attack each of us. I wanted to scream, but instead asked if there was anything I could do. "No, no. I'll be okay." The Giants lost in extra innings.

Though she struggled, my mind was made up. We were to be wed. Friends and family knew. That alone sealed it. Like political campaigns, once a decision has been made, you did everything possible to see it through. I ignored the signs and insisted, *I can make her happy. I can solve her issues.* Maybe deep down I sensed the marriage plans aggravated her anxiety. Maybe the feelings weren't even that deep down. Still, I wouldn't admit it. Summer and the red flags continued.

"Why isn't she wearing her engagement ring?" friends asked at the Schaible wedding in Colorado.

"Just shy," I reassured them.

"Why aren't the wedding invitations out?" my mother queried.

"That's just her typical, last-minute style," I replied. "They'll be late, but they'll be beautiful." (They were, actually. A mixture of fibrous green stock and mini wheat stalks crafted to match the rural feel of the barn.)

To everybody: "That's just Annie. No big deal. Everything is fine. Everything is fine. Quit asking me, because everything is fine."

It was a broken-record conversation that stretched into the fall.

"Let me know, Annie, if you can't do this. It's all right if you can't go through with it," I said, though we both knew this was the last attempt.

She gave conflicting replies, saying she loved me and didn't want to lose me, but confiding more and more that she wasn't comfortable.

"All I know is that it's not supposed to feel like this. It's supposed to be easier."

Two weeks before the wedding, we went to a marriage counselor to talk about her growing anxiety. "Oh, I wish you had come to me sooner," he kept repeating. Annie moped and shrugged on the way out, dodging my questions about whether the wedding was still on.

Invitations out, flowers selected, music picked, flight and room reservations made. One hundred fifty people would attend. Saturday, November 6, 1999. Part of me hoped the resistance would soon be chalked up to a bad case of cold feet. We'd joke about it with our kids. Inside, I knew the problems were unresolved and deepening.

"It's a knot, Franz, a knot that I can't get rid of," she said one night in bed after a perfunctory and quick lovemaking session. "The wedding just tightens the knot."

"What do you want to do?"

"I don't want to lose you," she said, not really answering my question. "I don't want to lose you."

My mind darted between rage and the desire to hold her in my arms and tell her everything would be okay.

"All I know is that it's not supposed to feel like this," she said.

She started to cry. I panicked for a moment, then decided humor was a better approach.

"Ann, honey, c'mon. It's me, Franz, your dream man."

I didn't get a laugh. The tears continued.

I froze, then, inspired, jumped out of bed.

"Hey, I almost forgot. I got you a present."

I'd been at the mall that afternoon and decided, while walking past the windows with the bored-looking mannequins swathed in flapper pearls, that a gift would give her a boost. She unwrapped the box from TSE with the claret pashmina shawl, smiled for a second, set it aside, and continued to sob.

Her brother called me a few days later.

7

In the ten miles between Newport Beach and Laguna Beach rests Orange County's best-kept secret—Crystal Cove. During warm summer days, most tourists flock to the Newport Peninsula to watch boogie boarders challenge the legendary Wedge or to wedge themselves onto a crowded piece of sand in Corona del Mar or Huntington. They leave Crystal Cove State Park and its miles of banana-shaped shores and sage scrub hills to naturalists and locals in the know.

The run from my house to one end of Crystal Cove and back took fifty-five minutes to complete. Exactly. I know, because I made the trek every day despite my vehement opposition to running and a surgically repaired knee with two screws and a plastic gizmo that looked like an IUD.

I ran daily to escape growing problems at work. Assignments continued to fly from my desk to the in-boxes of others. The ones that remained had little appeal, like "constituent building" with the local homeowners association dominated by attorneys with too much time on their hands. They turned perfunctory meetings into four-hour debates about palm trees. I wanted a superior to tell me I had done something wrong to warrant the decline. Anything would have been better than the silence of "You're doing a great job."

I ran to escape the emptiness of my house. Kurt had gone back to Seattle to sell his house and unplug his life up there. I begged him to move down as soon as possible. Silence was something I long avoided, preferring boisterous groups over solitude. Now it was killing me. *Hell of a time to learn to be alone.* So I ran.

I'm running for you too, Kurt. I'm thinking about sunset jogs through cobblestone squares and along desert roads. Us, on the trip. Talking most of the time, though cut me some slack at the end of the runs if I'm a little quiet. With your willowy body, you can run much farther. I'm trying.

Friends who experienced misfortune told me the low point comes weeks later, after the visits and encouragement to cheer up have slowed to a trickle. Those months, I knew what they meant. The Sea Ranch "wedding" had lifted me, and the honeymoon to Costa Rica had given me an idea. But that was over now. People stopped calling to see how I was coping, assuming my optimism had regained control. The hugs ended, but the pain remained.

I knew the support was out there, but I didn't want to pick up the phone. Guys don't call "just to talk," I believed. I was scared they'd see through the flimsy excuses ("the Niners have to do something at cornerback") or, worse, that I'd start to cry.

So I cried on my own. On Friday nights in front of the television. Standing in the shower, not wanting to go to work. *Just another minute. As soon as the mirror completely fogs, I'll get out.*

Needing diversions, I bought a satellite system and a programming package that allowed me to watch every NBA basketball game. Though I'd ignored the sport in the past, I convinced myself it was now all-important. The Sacramento Kings became my cause. The Kings are me, I rationalized. Cellar-dwellers now but with the potential to become winners.

And I ran. And walked. And thought along the shores of Crystal Cove.

I thought about the trip and the days until Kurt moved down. About the exit strategy for my job. About Annie, telling myself I was lucky not to be with her, though I didn't believe it for more than a few minutes.

"You look thin, Franz," said a kind secretary at work one day. "What's your secret?"

"I'm on this great new program. You just get dumped before your wedding and demoted at work, then lose fifteen pounds within days."

For the first time in my life, my strategy was to exist. Not to live, just exist. Hang on until Kurt joined me. Survive until summer, when I could quit and start anew. This was the bottom. I knew it. And I couldn't dig myself out. At the same time, the submarine ride down inspired a newfound appreciation for the range of human emotion.

So this is how far down I can go? I didn't know I had this feeling on my play list. I still feel like hell, but for those split seconds it's an out-of-body experience watching someone else feel like hell.

It heightened senses and opened my eyes to an entirely new landscape. An islander being shown snow for the first time. In a sense, I felt I was becoming more human. Emotional depths I never knew existed surged through my limbs like a shot of tequila. I felt alive. Miserable, but alive. Plowing through valleys I never knew existed, I felt as if I were taking the anti-Prozac.

I sat, alone, in coffee shops and along the shore. But now . . . my heart pulled for the kid with smudged, thick glasses or the overweight girl. I'd seen them before. Many times. Now I really *saw* them and thought about the teasing they likely faced at school. I was warmed by the spirit of a new mom as she leaned over to cinch the hooded sweatshirt of her newborn and grieved for the elderly neighbor being loaded into the ambulance with an oxygen mask clipped to his ashen face. The tanned, wrinkled homeless woman in the neighborhood became a person, not just someone I avoided when refilling my latte. I stopped to talk, actually listening to what she had to say, and thought about her words afterward.

I noticed little things in better detail, like the smell of the white star jasmine on the neighbor's fence or the feel of my bare feet on a sisal rug or the taste of fresh strawberry milk shakes at the Shake Shack near Crystal Cove. In a strange sense, the spiral down was the ultimate ego trip. Everything related to me.

Climbing into my car one day, I sat on my wire-rimmed glasses, breaking a lens and snapping a metal arm. I swore to myself and called Lisa to tell her I'd be late to work so I could drop the glasses off for repair.

And it happened. Or, better, it didn't happen. I didn't get a headache during the next couple days despite not having a backup pair of glasses to wear. It was the only reason I wore them in the first place.

"Can your eyesight just improve suddenly?" I asked the optometrist.

"Sure," he said after administering an eye test. "You're still slightly nearsighted, but if you don't get headaches anymore, don't wear the glasses. Your eyes will adjust and your vision might continue to improve."

Someone had just given me my vision back. I could see. Clearly now. And up. The eyes gave me something about which to feel positive, upon which to build.

I'm not deteriorating. I'm on the mend.

It was a small turn of events, but it *was* a turn of events.

8

"Watch this," Kurt ordered as we pulled off Walnut Avenue and into the Eskaton retirement complex in Carmichael, California. "Just keep the window up and wave to the guard. He'll open the gates without making us sign in."

I hadn't been there for several months. Not since before Sea Ranch. I knew I needed to go. Not for her so much as for me. LaRue gave me strength. I needed strength. During the Easter holiday, Kurt and I drove to see her at Eskaton, a half hour from our parents' house in Davis.

The Hindu guard smiled and waved us through, past the pink stucco buildings and lifeless entryway pond. Past the Cadillac El Dorados with whitewall tires and little-used RVs. Past the overweight nurse pushing a slumped-over man in a wheelchair. Kurt pulled to the right of the complex and parked directly in front of LaRue's building, the one with the apartments. The care facilities were on the other side of the complex.

It's never hard to find a parking space at a retirement home.

We walked down the hall, pausing to look at the cubbyhole in front of her neighbor's apartment. Most of the units at Eskaton have a display cove next to the door. Grandmothers decorate them with holiday pictures and greeting cards, with miniature Christmas trees and partial nativity scenes. Grandfathers opt for war medals and golf memorabilia. In hers, LaRue always had a picture of Ray. He was her first husband. She loved Ray.

"Oh, thank my stars," she sang from behind the front door after Kurt pushed the bell. "I'm the luckiest woman on the planet."

She adjusted the wire glasses that left deep pits on the sides of her nose before giving Kurt a big kiss on the lips. Despite her frail body, LaRue demanded bear hugs and warm kisses like that. Pecks on the cheek just wouldn't do.

"Hey, you look great, LaRue," I said.

"Oh, I need a haircut," she said, playing with her frizzy and thinning gray hair. "I look like a lion with this mane."

She did look great. Sure, her eyesight was poor. And the cancer had stolen parts of her insides. It didn't take her drive. Or her ability to garden or do needlepoint under that magnified lamp that looked like a dentist light.

"Here, I made something for you," she said, handing me a ceramic dish with a painted robin in the middle.

"Thanks, LaRue."

"Do you use them?"

"Yes." *They sit on my mantel. I wouldn't dream of eating on them. They're far too precious.*

"What time is it?" she asked.

"Eleven-thirty."

"Ohhh, we're late for lunch."

She led us down the hall, past the rows of apartments, pausing at every other one for a comment.

"Clarence, now he's a military man. He likes to come early for breakfast. And Vivian, well, she needs a hip replacement."

Residents standing in the hall paused when she walked by. They all knew her name, the unofficial mayor of Eskaton. An octogenarian using a walker smiled, expecting the same in return. "Oh, I don't like to see that," LaRue said, pointing to the metal legs. "We need to get rid of that thing soon."

With LaRue in the lead, we piled plates of salad, meat loaf, and string beans on our cafeteria trays. "I can manage fine, honey." Then we stood with the food in hand for what seemed like a half hour as LaRue introduced us to her friends, half of whom we'd met many times before.

"These boys are my grandsons."

We weren't, though. Our grandfather, at the age of sixty-three, decided to divorce our grandmother and marry another woman. That one ended in divorce as well after a few years and Howard then introduced the family to LaRue, a woman ten years his senior. To say I greeted her with reservation would be an understatement. Complete avoidance would be more like it.

I changed my mind at a family reunion. In a corner away from the festivities, LaRue asked me to sit next to her and tell her about my life. She had a sincerity in her smile and a warmth in her words. "Everyone in the family says you're our expert on politics. Do you mind if I ask you a couple questions about the election?" At that moment, I knew why my grandfather fell in love with her, and before finishing my brisket and corn bread, I'd promised to come see her during a free weekend. Those visits became more frequent after Howard passed away and LaRue moved to Eskaton.

"LaRue, there's something we have to tell you," I said after settling down at a table and into our meals. "We're here with some news. Kurt and I are planning a trip, a big trip. We're going to quit our jobs, sell our houses, and travel around the world for a year."

"Wonderful!" she said without pause.

"You know, you're more than welcome to join us for a stop or two," I said.

"Well, I just might," she said. "I love travel. It's one of the few things in life you never regret. So, now, tell me where you plan to go."

"Probably start in Eastern Europe," Kurt said. "We have some friends over there who—"

"I'll buy pins and chart your trip on my world map," she said.

"Maybe Asia after that."

"Doris, Bob, come over here for a minute. I want you to meet my grandsons. They're off soon on a world trip."

"Great. Where you going?"

We detailed the trip several times for a handful of people that afternoon. To a person, they endorsed the voyage with enthusiasm and a hint of envy. Our parents' generation would stumble over specifics. "Can you go back to your job after the trip? How will you pay for it?" The seniors grasped it immediately, telling us again and again, "I wish we had done that when we could." Those at the end of their journeys embraced ours.

"Promise me something," LaRue interjected.

"Sure."

"Promise you'll send me a card from every country you visit."

"Of course."

I had broken the news of the trip to our father a few nights before.

"Wait. Stop," he said. "Just so you know, we're not going to look after the dogs."

"I'm not asking you to take care of Kurt's dogs. Deal with him on that."

"Just wanted you to know."

"Understood."

"No dogs."

"No dogs."

"Where was I?" I continued. "What I'm trying to say is my job sucks. My love life stinks. Kurt and I have the time and a little money to do it. We don't have kids. Why not? Why not take a year off and see the world?"

"Have you talked to your superiors at The Irvine Company? Told them of your displeasure?"

"It's pointless. They've already made up their minds to shift me down a few levels."

"You shouldn't burn any bridges there."

Dad, I know a walkabout is foreign to your generation. And I know this is your job and your comfort to play devil's advocate and question my decisions. But I need a bon voyage this time. I'm questioning it enough on my own.

"I don't care too much about bridges these days, Dad. I just lost the two pillars of my life. Everything I've worked for over the last decade. That's all gone now."

He paused.

"Let me ask you, what do you plan to do about insurance? What if you need a blood transfusion in one of those countries?"

Insurance? Blood transfusions? You're such a doctor. Your questions about insurance are as good as your saying, "Go forth." Thanks.

Mom was next.

"I don't think your father is too keen on watching the dogs," she said.

"I know, I know. He told me."

"I wouldn't mind. I could run them around the cul-de-sac on my bike and—"

"Mom, I honestly feel this is all happening for a reason. Everything is pointing me in a different direction—the marriage, the job, everything. It's as if someone is telling me, 'No, you aren't going to spend your life with someone who doesn't love you. You're going to bond with your brother and learn a little about the rest of the world.'"

"You two wouldn't separate, would you?"

"No, we'll do the whole thing together."

"I'd worry if you were apart."

Funny. If it was just one of us, this would be considered flaky. Two and it's brotherly love.

Throughout my life, I'd made plans, set goals, and saw them through. Just like the chore lists my dad would leave on the kitchen table each day before school. Now I was discarding plans, going on feel, listening to signs. The experience felt strange, yet oddly promising. I wanted to dig deeper, yet I struggled to let go.

You're a Republican. You just don't do this. It's got all the ingredients for a disaster—a brother you barely know, big expenses and zero income, limited planning, and few objectives other than to see what's out there, plus no job at the end of the trip.

My life turned upside down, I'd seen my American dreams crash, and yet still I wavered. I struggled to make order of the chaos, and I looked for excuses that would justify a continuation of my Newport Beach life—like a new assignment at work or a new girlfriend in the neighborhood. I feared if I didn't continue to take steps toward the trip, I'd find an excuse to back out. So I continued planning, hoping to do enough preparation so that it would be impossible to cancel the honeymoon with my brother.

"Kurt, Kurt," I yelled one day after work. "C'mon. We're going to get shots."

The county offered low-cost immunizations for world travel. We took a number and a seat among the rows of Hispanic and Asian kids and their mothers. The registration form had a line for planned destinations. We drew arrows pointing to the back of the sheet, then scribbled the names of about thirty nations in margins and across the bottom. We stopped when we couldn't think of any more.

"Hmm," said the no-nonsense nurse in tennis shoes, blue jeans, and open white lab coat. "You guys might as well get comfortable. You're going to be here for a while."

With a look of purpose, she gave us seven shots in each arm. Kurt was sick for the following week.

Back at work at The Irvine Company, Gary gave me more unsavory tasks.

"I need you to raise another two hundred thousand dollars for the parcel tax election in Irvine."

"You want me to raise two hundred thousand dollars from the same people I hit up a few months ago? For the same initiative we lost?"

"You can do it. You're a miracle worker."

Arrrrrrggggggggg!!!!!! If I could work a miracle, I'd keep it for myself.

"Kurt, Kurt," I yelled during my lunch break home. "C'mon. We're going to get some visas."

A few weeks earlier, I'd sat, late and bored, at a fund-raising luncheon for Chapman University. Pledge of Allegiance, student-produced slide show, and the like. An olive-skinned man in an expensive business suit to my left looked equally apathetic. Safe ground, I assumed, before leaning over and making a crack about being "suckered in." He laughed and looked around to see if anyone else heard. Detecting a slight accent, I asked his nationality.

"Syrian," he replied.

"Whoa, Syria," I said.

"You sound surprised."

I guess I did.

"I guess I am. I've never met anyone from Syria. Please tell me about it, because I'm contemplating a long trip this summer with my brother."

We talked in hushed tones and at a rapid clip for the next hour, oblivious to the string of podium speakers extolling the virtues of Chapman. Hazem turned out to be a full-time Newport Beach physician and part-time Syrian consul. He had attended school in the U.S., raised a family in Southern California, and built a successful radiology practice near my office (the couchless one). A few years earlier, the Syrian government asked him to open a consulate in California.

While an energetic man ranted about fund-raising goals, Hazem talked of ancient souks and khans with vendors hawking carpets and silver from cramped kiosks on labyrinthian streets. He gushed about castles from the Crusades and mile-long Roman colonnades devoid of tourists. Of T. E. Lawrence treks and Saladin victories, of baba ghanouush and spiced hummus, mother-of-pearl inlay and olive oil soaps. Most of all, he talked about a curious Syrian population eager to embrace Western emissaries. "They'll be very intrigued to see you."

I'm supposed to go to Syria.

"Kurt, Kurt," I said that night. "Guess where we're going?"

"Sushi?"

"No, on the trip."

"Canada."

"Syria. I sat next to the Syrian consul today at a lunch. What are the odds of that? In Orange County?"

"Ninety to one?"

"Can't you see? You and I are meant to go to Syria."

"Whoa, whoa. Dude, I'm game to go to Syria. And I hear you on this omen stuff, too. Just don't go nuts on me. You're beginning to sound like a Deadhead or something."

Keep walking toward walking away.

Plane flights seemed the logical next step. Who canceled trips if they already had the tickets? Round-the-world tickets were our first thought. A couple of friends had used them in the past. Similar to train passes, they theoretically allowed passengers to make multiple stops for one fare.

"Oh, yeah, one of those tickets," the operator said in his Midwestern, 1-800 accent. "I better get my supervisor to do this. Just a moment."

"May I help you?"

"Yes, please. I'd like to buy a couple of your round-the-world tickets."

"Do you know your dates?"

"As soon as I can cash my bonus check and before I blow it on something stupid like a new, black leather couch."

"Excuse me?"

"Sorry. August fifteenth."

"Going to?"

"Everywhere you fly."

"Sorry, sir, but that's not how these tickets work. You need to give us exact dates and locations. We calculate the fare based on the overall miles."

70

"You don't have something that'll just let me go to the airport and jump on any ride? Like those VIP passes they hand out at Disneyland."

"No, sir."

"All right. Lemme go get the atlas. This may take a while."

I grabbed Kurt, plopped the oversize map book on the dining room table, and put the phone on speaker mode.

Kurt and me: "Iceland." "No, Turkey. Then Iceland." "Forget Western Europe. We can do that when we're seventy. Remember what our friend Tedd said: 'Go deep.' "

The speaker phone: "No, we don't go there." "Those dates aren't available." "Okay, but that will cost you an extra couple hundred dollars." "You've exceeded your mileage limit." "No, no, no."

Us: "This sounds a lot like the conversations we have with you guys when we're trying to use frequent flyer miles."

After numerous frustrating phone calls to all the major U.S. airlines, we concluded round-the-world tickets weren't the way to go. Back to the Internet for more research. Yahoo! popped up several Web sites that specialized in relatively inexpensive, multiple-stop tickets. Some offered the ability to punch in desired destinations with world maps, model planes, and dotted-line routes like those used in black-and-white road movies. I tinkered with them for hours at night while Kurt slept, the firstborn still trying to plan while the second-born assumed details would fall into place.

"How about this?" I'd spring on him the next morning over coffee. "Russia–Prague–Romania–Bulgaria, hang with the weight lifters–Turkey–Syria, hook with Hazem's family–Lebanon–Jordan–Israel–Egypt–Uganda, gotta see the gorillas–Tanzania–Zanzibar–Zambia–Zimbabwe–I just want to be able to say that, 'ZanzibarZambiaZimbabwe'–South Africa–Brazil–Peru and Machu Picchu–Ecuador and the Darwin freaks–Thailand–Indonesia–Vietnam–Nepal–India–then some cushy resort in the South Pacific to recover and *bam,* we're home."

"What happened to flexibility? You're doing more planning for this than you did for your wedding."

He was right. In Costa Rica, we preached whims and ever-changing desires. If we stumbled upon a great village or beach, we wanted to stick around for a couple days. If the place was overrated, we wanted the ability to bail right away.

So I let it go. And the trip framework took on a life of its own. A friend from Davis asked Kurt to serve in his November 2000 wedding. He could skip it, but preferred not to. My college roommate, Jeff, planned to marry Alix in May 2001, and I didn't want to miss that either. Our parents suggested a family reunion in Kona, Hawaii, mid-January 2001.

Instead of one long trek, the journey evolved into several multimonth trips. We'd pick a continent, explore for three or four months, typically the longest stay allowed by the airlines before they charge an extra fee. We'd then fly back to California to go to the weddings, check on the house and dogs, and rejuvenate quickly for the next land mass. The first leg would be August through November, the second November through January, the third February through May, ending with May through whenever.

Eastern Europe became a natural starting point. Jonathan Terra and John Dawkins offered free rooms in Prague and Moscow, respectively. I'd been to Russia and the Czech Republic before, but wanted to see more of each. Kurt had yet to set foot in either. Better still, Eastern European countries wouldn't drain our limited budgets as quickly as a few months in, say, France or England.

I want to see Havel chain-smoking during some ribbon-cutting ceremony. Or Yeltsin, just smashed at a street parade. Putin's not going to be as fun.

"Let's start north, then chase sun," Kurt said.

Indonesia, Vietnam, and Thailand were also high on our to-visit lists. We gravitated toward cheap prices and warm winter. Southeast Asia logically became the second phase of the walkabout. We'd leave a couple days after Kurt's friend's wedding and return in time to join the family in Kona Village, Hawaii.

We'll be like Mel Gibson in The Year of Living Dangerously. *"This is Guy Hamilton in Jakarta." Drinks at the old-school hotel, the "yes, boss" driver, black fez-type hats.*

Latin America during our winter, its summer, was the obvious next segment. But that was too far in advance. What if one of us fell in love with a tour guide from Thailand? What if we wanted to make some money teaching English in Indonesia?

What if Kurt and I want to strangle each other?

We decided to wait on purchasing airline tickets. I forgot about the planes and fretted instead about Kurt's dogs and my house. The three-thousand-dollar monthly mortgage would drain my savings, I knew. I thought about selling, but preferred to have a place to crash between trips. So I clung to the one remnant of my Orange County lifestyle—DeAnza Drive, access to the private beach, no trees higher than rooflines.

Having sold his house in Seattle for a six-figure profit, Kurt was set financially for a while. He worried mostly about the dogs.

"Problems solved," Kurt told me one day. "Natasha is going to take care of the house . . . and the dogs."

Natasha was a longtime friend and Kurt's favorite running partner. She was the type of person who'd say, "I love you, guys," each time we saw her and sound like she meant it. During a jog with Kurt and his Jack Russell, Fritz (good for five miles, not including side jaunts to chase rabbits), she complained about finding affordable housing in Newport Beach. She told Kurt she wanted to share a place with two friends near the beach.

"How do you feel about Fritz?" Kurt asked. "Because I might have a deal for you."

In exchange for reduced rent, Natasha and two girlfriends agreed to live at my house, watch Kurt's dogs, keep our furniture in place, and allow us to stay there between trips.

Trip logistics continued to fall into place as if the whole process was preordained. My car lease expired the week before we planned to leave, as did Kurt's. Bill and mortgage payments were adjusted to be paid automatically and online. A local insurance agent located a health plan that would cover us around the world. Except for the airline tickets, we were set. I pushed to pull the trigger on a few flights to and around Eastern Europe when Kurt came up with a better idea.

"How'd you like to cruise through Poland and Turkey in a brand-new Saab, music pumping, Eastern Euro hotties begging for a lift?" he asked.

He explained the carmaker offered a plan through which motorists could purchase a Saab in the U.S. and pick the car up at the factory in Sweden. Saab paid for two round-trip airline tickets from anywhere in the U.S. along with a night's stay at a posh hotel. New owners could drive around Europe, Turkey, and the Middle East for up to six months with insurance and roadside assistance provided by Saab. After touring, motorists needed simply to drop the car at any of their selected ports throughout Europe. Saab would ship it back to the U.S. at no additional cost.

"We'd probably spend several thousand dollars in flight and car rentals anyway," Kurt explained. "Why not buy it, then sell it back in the States? We'll lose a little on the resale, but not as much as we'd pay to rent a car for four months. Plus, Saab will buy our tickets over to Europe. And we'll be able to go anywhere we want in a nice new ride."

"Sold." The final piece was in place. In style.

My love life, meanwhile, was still a jumbled mess. No matter how many times friends attempted to pair me with someone, the dates unfolded the same way. They'd make the connection ("you'll love her"), I'd find an overpriced restaurant for dinner, and she'd look great. Then, without fail, between drink orders and entrée selections, I'd launch into a line-item recap of my wedding wreck. Most of the time with little to no prompting.

"So I hear you went to Costa Rica recently?"

"God, I loved her. Nearly ten years. I thought we were perfect. And then, *bam*, she dumped me."

They'd listen, some with interest. They'd try to steer me on to other topics, none with success. I knew I was killing my chances, but couldn't help myself. I was obsessed with taking this journey to its bottom. A sap at a low-end casino watching his chip pile quickly erode.

Just one more bet. I know I'm going to lose. I almost want to.

"Why don't you call me in a couple months or so? After you've worked these things out," they'd say after the waiter brought the check.

We both know I won't.

Still I pressed on, propelled by clichéd, animal-laden advice about "getting back on the horse" or the existence of "other fish in the sea."

And then I met Laura. Mutual friends Ed and Jennie introduced us at a Newport Beach restaurant. A tan brunette with an aerobic instructor bounce, she wore low-cut jeans and clutched an expensive purse that night. A few incoherent words spilled out of my mouth after Jennie mentioned Laura had just moved down to Southern California from San Francisco. Probably to escape a relationship, I suspected, though she and Jennie skirted the issue with cryptic references and rolled eyes the rest of the evening.

Four filets and two bottles of Cabernet later, Ed announced plans to take the group to the horse races at Hollywood Park the coming Sunday. He had box seats and offered to drive. The chance encounter now seemed more like a planned setup. It worked.

"I'm in," I blurted, not too subtly.

Should have been out, I told myself on the drive home. A couple of big assignments at work loomed, along with the large bonus check that would follow should I finish them. The house needed packing, reorganizing, and cleaning before Natasha and her friends could move in. But there was a bigger reason.

"What are you thinking?" I asked the mirror before going to bed. "You want to chase a woman a couple weeks before you go on the road for a year?"

The next morning I went to battle with the mirror again. Heart trumps head, I concluded. Here was someone who'd given a jump-start to mine. *Feel, not rational thought—that's what the trip's all about. Lose the planning and go with the flow.* A phone call from Ed the day after the races confirmed there was mutual interest. Still, I knew if Laura and I saw each other we'd soon have an "I've got to tell you something" conversation.

"I've got to tell you something," I said over dinner a few weeks later, after a few runs along Crystal Cove beach, a day in San Diego, and a couple double dates with Jenny and Ed. "I'm, ahh, going to quit my job next week, rent my house, and travel around the world with Kurt."

"Nice," she answered, a frozen smile plastered on her face. "Good for you."

I couldn't tell if she was shocked, or excited, or pissed, or a combination of all three. I stared at her hand, fidgeting with the wineglass, and half expected her to douse me any minute. The politician's smile didn't leave her lips the rest of the meal. The conversation zigzagged between flirtation and a halfhearted agreement that pursuing the relationship would be irrational. She said she needed time alone in the coming months regardless, time to learn her new job and mend from her former romance. I encouraged her to join us in the country of her choice whenever she could. Southeast Asia later in the year was a possibility. We'd stay in touch through e-mails.

9

In the reassembled Irvine Company pyramid structure, Dan Young became my new supervisor. A former mayor of Santa Ana, Dan had a skilled politician's touch for making others feel good about their situation. He struggled to put a happy face on mine.

He knocked on my door in July and asked if I had a minute, motioning me down the hall. We talked about the second parcel tax election, which received the same 62 percent approval as the first, again a few percentage points shy of the two-thirds needed for passage. I felt awful. I couldn't understand why people balked at a couple extra dollars a month to improve public schools. And the value of their homes. I also felt awful for me, assuming another losing campaign would whack my year-end bonus. The two-star hotels became hostels.

Dan looked at his watch and then apologized, saying he was late for a lunch. He handed me a brown envelope and told me I'd done a good job during the year under difficult circumstances. We'd talk later, he promised.

Only if it's at Angkor Wat.

I thanked him, tucked the envelope into my jacket pocket, and walked back to my new, shrunken, couchless office next door. "Please, please do me right, Uncle Irvine," I prayed, tearing the envelope with care to avoid ripping the bonus check inside. I worried daily that the company had learned of my travel plans and would slash it accordingly.

Seventy-seven thousand dollars. Seventy-seven thousand! There it was, staring at me. Seventy-seven thousand dollars. I glanced at the attachment to make sure taxes were already withheld. They were. Seventy-seven thousand dollars! I estimated a few more paychecks and money due for unused vacation time, and quickly calculated I'd leave The Irvine Company with close to one hundred thousand dollars. It was more than enough to keep my house and pay for a year abroad with Kurt. Or longer. I felt like a high school senior whose parents had taken off for the summer, leaving him alone with keys to the house and sports car.

Seventy-seven thousand dollars. Seventy-seven thousand get-your-ass-on-the-first-plane-out-of-here dollars.

Love The Irvine Company.

Telling my secretary, Lisa, I was going to lunch, I sprinted to Wells Fargo. The lines were long, but I didn't want to use the ATM outside. Too much money. I settled in behind a young mother scolding her boy for playing with the rope and stanchion.

It's okay, little guy. I'm about ready to do something similar.

"May I help you?" asked the Vietnamese teller.

"Yes, I'd like to deposit this check, please," I said, trying to look casual.

"I need to get my manager because this is a large check," she said.

Actually, it's a backstage pass to the planet.

Her manager sauntered to the window. She wore a set of keys on a coiled, pink plastic chain around her wrist, toying with them as she looked at my identification.

C'mon. You're killing me here.

"Guess it must be Bonus Friday," she said. "We're getting a lot of big checks today."

I flew out of the building, smiling at the leather-skinned woman coming from the realtor's office next door and the paint-speckled contractor stuffing a stack of checks into a deposit envelope. The ring of the cell phone grounded my orbit.

"Bubba!" yelled the voice of my friend Mike Lutton, a type-A, French-cuff-and-white-collar dealmaker extraordinaire who'd left The Irvine Company a few years prior to start a successful commercial development firm. He could always make me laugh.

"Hey, man!" I replied.

"You sound like you're in a good mood. What's going on?"

"Nada. You know me. Always in a good mood."

"Say, Cedillos and I are over in your neck of the woods. Gonna grab some lunch at the Ritz. Care to join us?"

"Well, I was going to go have some leftovers at the house with Kurt. He's in Newport now. But what the hell? It's Friday. Let's celebrate."

The maître'd pointed me to the end of the bar, past the yachtsmen and highball lunch crowd. Mike already had a bottle of expensive French white wine opened. Ron Cedillos's voice boomed from behind. "Franzie!" I knew Ron from my days in the Wilson administration, when he raised millions of campaign dollars for the governor Wilson. He and Lutton were partners in crime.

Mike grabbed the bottle and escorted us to a corner table on the trellised patio. A long-legged waitress followed behind. In her Ritz uniform of tuxedo jacket, black leotard, and sheer dark hose, she looked like a David Copperfield assistant. She beamed at Mike, the smile to a regular.

"Good to see you, Bubba!" Mike said after ordering gravlax, lump crab cakes, and filet mignon tartar for the table, veal Oskar for his main course, and another bottle of the white. Ron chimed in with osso buco.

"So tell us what's going on," said Ron.

"I'm going to quit on Monday and travel around the world with Kurt for the next year."

"No, serious?" said Ron.

"I'm serious. Look at the grin on my face."

"Bubba, a toast," said Mike, raising his glass. "To you getting the hell out of Dodge."

"Hear, hear."

"And," he continued, "to The Irvine Company bonuses."

I stared at the gold label on the bottle of wine, then over at the plates of expensive food being delivered to the other tables. And my smile vanished. For a second.

"You fuckers!" I said. "No wonder you chose the Ritz."

They exploded.

"That's the first tradition you need to learn after you leave The Irvine Company," Mike said. "Always know the bonus day."

I started to laugh with them. A hard, tension-relieving, lottery-winning laugh. The bill was five hundred dollars. I didn't care. I was already on a plane . . . to everywhere.

Within the next two weeks, I'd quit my job, turned in my leased car, canceled the cell phone, and happily dumped my pager on Lisa's desk. Kurt used a nine-iron on his. We shuttled off to Goodwill Industries two carloads of sweaters and khakis, paperbacks, kitchen utensils, linens, bad gifts planned for recycling, and anything that reminded me of Annie.

Make sure you include that faux granite clock. I always hated that thing. Especially when she told me she gave the same one to that goofy friend of hers.

I stashed the computer, shifted artwork and music collections to friends, gave my suits and ties to job-seekers, and stuffed jeans, T-shirts, shorts, running shoes, and a handful of short-sleeved collared shirts in a ratty black backpack I borrowed from Ben. Pushing my arms through the straps, I felt the happiest I'd been in many years.

Each shedding amplified an intensely satisfying liberation. It became addictive; I wanted to do more. I'd pack a box for Goodwill and immediately look to pack another. I'd worked most of my life accumulating, an endless quest often with diminishing returns. Nobody ever told me it would feel better to leave everything behind and walk away.

Strip. Strip it off. If I want to remodel my life, I need to gut it first. I know that now.

My sister, Lisa, and her husband, Doug, had their baby in Sacramento a few days later. Elizabeth Grace. Our father called us with the news as we moved the last of our belongings out of the house and helped Natasha and her friends Mirka and Erin settle in. We gave Fritz and Riley a bath, penned a list of instructions, and jumped in Kurt's car on our way to Northern California. We'd stop there for a few days to meet Elizabeth before driving up to Seattle, our debarkation city.

"Honey, I just want you to know that the pressure is off," said Mom as we entered the hospital room.

I looked at Lisa, pale from the delivery yet still animated, and saw a montage of scenes. The swim meets and sun-bleached hair, the sticker collections and sleepovers, the countless letters during college saying she was proud of me. I looked in Lisa's arms and saw a pink, tabula rasa face with the beginnings of a smile. And I saw strength. Suddenly my problems seemed a little less severe.

"Good-bye, LaRue."

"I bought those red pins for the map. And told everyone here at Eskaton. We're ready. So remember to write."

"I won't forget."

"The good stuff."

"Of course."

She handed me a small bundle of handkerchiefs, paper thin and ironed. They had the initials of her first husband, Ray. I stuffed a few in my backpack and gave her a kiss good-bye.

The Seattle Mariners were getting crushed. The packed Safeco Field stadium groaned in unison with each opposing run. With our minds on the trip, we hoisted a couple Red Hook beers and congratulated ourselves on the getaway, clean even though we'd shut down years of work in two weeks.

A friend gave Kurt a couple Diamond Club tickets to the game, which entailed plush seats behind home plate and all the food and beverages a fan could conceivably consume. We were midway through the world record for hot dogs, when I asked Kurt, bun in mouth, about the passports.

"Oh, yeah. Must have left them at Mitch's office. I need to go there tomorrow anyway. We'll just swing by in the morning and pick 'em up."

Mitch was Kurt's former colleague at Windermere Real Estate in the working-class, though increasingly yuppiefied, neighborhood of West Seattle. We'd dropped off the passports at the Lebanese embassy in San Francisco a few days earlier in order to purchase visas. They FedExed them to Windermere, attention Mitch. No worries, we assured each other as we sat back and enjoyed the game.

"What do you mean they're not there, Mitch?" Kurt asked over the phone early the next morning. "They were sitting on your desk yesterday afternoon. How many people are in the building at night? A cleaning lady or two? We're coming over."

Three hours of searching, urgent pages to the staff, overturning furniture, detectivelike questioning of the cleaning service, several garbage dump dives, and we still couldn't find the passports. Only an empty FedEx envelope remained on Mitch's desk.

"Well, there's nothing else we can do," Kurt said. "I'm going golfing."

"You're what? You think countries are going to let you in based on your golf scorecard?"

"Relax. There's a passport office downtown. They can issue us new ones in twenty-four hours. Friend of mine had it done recently. No big deal. And who knows about the power of my scorecard? If it's low enough, they just might open their doors."

"Okay, but to have the process completed in twenty-four hours means you have to start the process. And we leave in less than forty-eight hours."

"I'll just play a quick round, then swing by the office midafternoon. You can go now and start the process for both of us. We have photos and copies of the lost passports in the backpack."

Kurt continued. "Think of it this way. This is just a test to see how we handle adversity on the trip. Someone's testing us. We'll be fine."

We passed the test, securing a couple new passports hours before our flight to Europe. They cost us 250 dollars and some serious begging to the INS agent to issue them without birth certificates. "If I told you I got dumped at the altar, would that speed anything?"

Passports in hand, we were on our way.

"It makes no sense," Kurt said on the flight to Eastern Europe. "Where on earth could they have gone?"

The Case of the Missing Passports.

EUROPE

Atlantic Ocean

NORWAY

SWEDEN

North Sea

DENMARK

NETHERLANDS

Baltic Sea

Oland

St. Petersburg

RUSSIA

Moscow

Oslo

Stockholm

Göteborg

Copenhagen

Gdańsk

POLAND

Amsterdam

Köln

GERMANY

Prague

CZECH REP.

Kraków

Baden-Baden

FRANCE

SWITZ.

Lake Como

Milan

SLOVENIA

Venice

CROATIA

Split

Brač

Hvar

AUSTRIA

SLOVAKIA

Budapest

HUNGARY

Zagreb

BOSNIA

Sarajevo

SERBIA AND
MONTENEGRO

Cluj-Napoca

ROMANIA

Bucharest

Dryanovo

BULGARIA

Black Sea

Istanbul

Goreme

ITALY

GREECE

Chios

Izmir

TURKEY

Athens

Bodrum

Ovacik

Aleppo

Homs

SYRIA

Mediterranean Sea

0 Miles   250   500

0 Kilometers   500

© 2004 Jeffrey L. Ward

10

The first several weeks of our honeymoon felt like a ride on a new bike with training wheels. That's because we chose to spend it with friends who lived in Eastern Europe, Jonathan Terra and John Dawkins. Despite my comments to family and friends in the United States that the trip "was no big deal," I had multiple worries about life on the road with Kurt. Would we get bored after a few months and decide to sprint back to our former lives? Would we come to blows during an argument over a woman? Could I take him if we did? On top of that, I stressed about the planning details—accommodations and transportation, money and visas. The whole thing, I concluded, had the prerequisites of a bonfire.

When Jonathan and John suggested we all meet in Croatia for a summer vacation to start the honeymoon, I convinced Kurt we should join them. The car was ready to be picked up in Sweden, but it could wait, I argued. We should spend a few weeks in Dubrovnik, and on the islands of Brač and Hvar, bonding with friends, easing into our vagabond status. I didn't tell him it was a toe-in-the-water approach. If he had any doubts about the honeymoon, I didn't see them.

We spent most of the days with the group, skinny-dipping in the Adriatic, eating pomegranates and olives on the balcony of our three-room villa, wandering along cobblestone streets and dulled marble plazas in towns that clung to their fishing village identity, though losing their grip to moneyed pleasure-seekers from neighboring countries. The church-to-disco ratio was still well below that found in Italian or Greek coastal resorts. On some mornings, before the others were awake, Kurt would roust me out of bed for an early morning run or a quest for a large-drip coffee.

We talked about reconnecting with old friends and decided there's a special bond with them that outlasts changes of scenery and mind, but that such friendships are best when fed and nurtured. I realized that in Croatia. Despite the ease with which they resumed, the friendships, I knew, had been taken for granted. I thought about the other people I'd like to see during the year, the ones I'd taken for granted. I tracked down a small Internet café on the island of Hvar and sent out an e-mail urging them to join us in a country of their choice. It didn't occur to me that my best friend was already there.

At the end of the vacation, John pushed for us to fly to Moscow to experience his Russian life. I could tell Kurt preferred to go to Sweden to pick up the Saab, but I hesitated about breaking off on our own. My corporate mind still preferred the order of an arranged stay. We decided to go to Russia only after Kurt read the fine print in the materials from Saab stating they'd insure his car in every country in Eastern Europe, "except Russia."

"Franz, let me introduce you to Franz," said Kurt from his midrow seat on the crowded flight to Moscow.

His firm grip and short haircut gave the instant impression of prior military service.

"Always good to meet a namesake," I said. "There aren't too many in the States."

"Yes, of course," he said. "Are you German?"

"We're mutts, a mixture of a bunch of nationalities. We're also fourth-generation Californians."

"Why the German names?"

"My father says he wanted traditional and unique names to go with our German surname. I think he and my mom watched *The Sound of Music* too many times."

Franz didn't see the humor.

"I've been talking to your brother about Moscow. He says you've been there before. Long ago?"

"Yeah, about fourteen years ago. I'm curious to see the changes."

"You'll be amazed. Many, many changes. Moscow is like any other major Western city now. More corrupt, of course. But similar."

Franz explained he traveled often to the Russian capital on business, splitting time among his native Austria, home in Australia, and Moscow apartment. I gazed out the window at the green and brown quilt of farms spread across the Russian countryside and tried to imagine what kind of business had ties to the three locations.

Mob. Definitely mob. Only he doesn't have the heavy jewelry. So maybe weapon sales. Nah. What kind of munitions would the Aussies make? Only other common denominator is meat. Bad meat. Like frozen beef pies or something. Yeah, he's a pork salesman.

"You guys need to know something very important," Franz said as our plane began its descent. We leaned toward him.

"The immigration line at the airport is usually horrendous. They often have just two or three officials stamping passports. After we land, run—don't walk, run—to the immigration counter and make sure you are in the front of the line. Otherwise, you may be stuck for hours. I do not joke. It's happened to me several times."

Stuck in the back of the plane behind a mass from many nations, Kurt and I looked at each other, shrugged, and grabbed our bags from the overhead bin to make the Olympic sprint through Sheremetyevo Two Airport. We thanked Franz for the tip and told him we'd save him a place in line. "We're fast. See, running shoes."

Franz was wrong about the number of immigration officers. I would have taken two or three. They had only one. One painfully slow immigration officer. Winded from running, Kurt and I still found ourselves behind about two hundred people.

"A couple hours?" I said. "This could take a couple days. And Dawkins is supposed to be outside waiting for us in ten minutes. We're hosed."

Franz sauntered by as we debated our plan of action.

"Come with me," he ordered.

He must know someone in the government or have access to a special immigration desk for VIPs, we imagined. Anything was better than the enormous line that snaked its way across a hall, up two flights of stairs, and into the upper terminal. We followed him with confidence, but Franz didn't have a connection or special access. His plan was simply to cut in front of everyone else.

"He's just bogarting the line," Kurt said in amazement.

We wanted no part of his scheme. But as we looked back, the line continued to grow and our spaces were gone. Morphing from opportunists to ugly Americans, we lowered our heads and prepared for the abuse.

"What the hell are you doing?" a man yelled. Others grumbled loudly in Russian and German.

Franz turned around and explained to the line that we had another plane to catch. "You would do the same thing." His lie did nothing to appease the increasingly hostile crowd. "We all have planes to catch. Get back in line."

"*Bardak*. Means 'whorehouse'. Typical Russian chaos," Franz said. "Trust me, they're used to it."

"*Bezsovestnaya svoloch,*" barked a Russian man.

"Franz, what did he say?" I asked.

"Don't worry. Just something about you being a bastard without conscience."

"Oh, okay."

"You Americans think you don't have to wait in lines?" a Frenchman yelled to Kurt.

"Actually, I'm Canadian," said Kurt.

"Fuuuuuck youuuuuu," yelled an elderly woman.

Hey, old ladies can't say that.

"This is *bad* karma," I whispered to Kurt. "But what can we do? No way I'm going back to the end of that line."

The next fifteen minutes dragged slower than the final bell for summer recess in grade school. Franz translated the verbal abuse, which shifted from personal insults to angry diatribes about the United States and how our country was responsible for Russia's problems of crime, poverty, and alcoholism.

Great. I'm going to rekindle the Cold War by cutting a line with an Austrian meat pie salesman.

Finally, a young Russian couple let us go before them. We handed the oblivious immigration officer our passports and hurried to baggage claim. After clearing customs, we jogged through the ratty airport lobby, past a group of babushka cleaners arguing around a mop and bucket. Exiting the terminal, we prayed we'd see John idling in his car. No John. So we dropped our gear and waited. Waited at a pickup curb directly in front of passport control. Waited at a spot passed by every single person on our flight. One by one, the people we angered in line walked by and said something repulsive in their native language. Death by a thousand cut-downs. I tried changing shirts. Kurt pulled down a baseball hat and adjusted his sunglasses. Still, we couldn't flee the abuse. I told him I needed to go to the bathroom. He grabbed my arm and said I wasn't going anywhere.

"*Eto te kozli kotorye vlezli bez ocheredi*," shouted a Russian man.

"I have no idea what that meant, but I don't think it was 'Welcome to Russia,'" I said.

An hour later, John pulled up to the corner, honking his horn like a madman. "Hit it!" we yelled, jumping into his old Saab before it came to a complete stop. He apologized for being late, saying he was bickering over the size of a bribe with a government technician he'd convinced to install a small satellite on the roof of his apartment. "You wouldn't believe the bribe inflation in Russia these days." The Summer Olympics were to begin in a couple days, and John had never been one to wade through bureaucracy.

John Dawkins had landed in Eastern Russia ten years earlier after a post-college trip around the world. He perfected his Russian, jumped from fish hatcheries to oil refineries to communications technology, moved to Moscow, and married a girl-next-dacha sweetheart from Kazakhstan. Lena laughed at his pranks and tolerated his wild schemes. Hyper-creative, adventurous, sentimental at times, John had been a close friend since grade school. His room back then was usually decorated with snakeskins, skulls and jaws, Eastern tapestries, pictures of old circus freaks, live ferrets, dead birds, and lots of incense. The surroundings were tame compared to his wanderlust mind. Prone to preaching, he'd espouse the virtues of things like wrestling, Bob Dylan, or lychee nuts. Travel with John and you were immediately cast in the Marlow role to his Kurtz. He's the type who, given the choice between two paths, would choose a machete.

John and Lena married three months earlier at the Dawkins family ranch, nestled in the foothills near Davis, California. Professing tradition, John had asked me to wear an embroidered Cossack shirt and Russian fur hat. He had donned a magician's cape and Renaissance frock, and had insisted on performing the ceremony atop a white horse. I led him down a hill on horseback to take Lena's hand in marriage. John swore it was an authentic Kazakhstan custom. Seemed more Barnum and Bailey to me.

Lena still had a newlywed grin when Kurt and I walked through the doors of their modest, fifth-floor apartment with worn parquet flooring, a cramped kitchen, large balconies, and a bronze statue of Ganesh greeting visitors in the entryway. "Pure power, Wiz." Their slightly bohemian, Chistye Prudy ("Clean Ponds") neighborhood sat in the center of town, a fifteen-minute walk from Red Square and two blocks from a filthy man-made pond lined with empty vodka bottles and potato chip wrappers. Lena's mother scurried in the kitchen, preparing food for John's birthday party that night. An aroma of spicy Indian food wafted from large pots. Without sampling or asking, John threw a handful of small red chilies into the biggest one.

"My brothers!" Lena screamed, giving Kurt and me bear hugs.

John handed us a couple Baltica pilsners and led us into the living room. Thai tapestries, West African drums and spears, Siberian artwork, and Uzbekistani carpets hung from the walls and shelves. *Same ole Dawkins.* Nusrat, his hyper-curious white ferret, bounced from behind couches and chairs, prowling for stuffed animal conquests and smelly shoes. John told us, in an earnest tone, we were his first American friends to visit.

John was one of my best friends in the world. A foreign world. And his life had become foreign to me. Sure, we saw each other on holidays, exchanged e-mails, or sent ribald gag gifts on occasion. But had I really listened to him over the last decade or asked him about the challenges he faced and successes he savored? Why did he change careers so often? Or not marry Svetlana, the high-jumper with the daughter who liked to dance? I tried to explain it away as the normal demands of my career and my relationship with Annie. I could have carved out more time. Should have. But life sets in and years fly by until you wake up one day and see how wide the divide has grown.

Nusrat knocked over a bottle I'd placed on a windowsill, prompting a warning from John not to leave sunglasses or wallets within the creature's reach. Shooing the ferret to the bedroom, John talked in fast-forward about his life in Russia, like a child spitting out a long story to a parent. Soon, friends began to arrive for the birthday dinner and we were awash in curry and vodka toasts in two tongues. "To you, my friend."

The night ended in the morning at a cavernous disco with Broadway lighting, a stadium sound system, and hoards of svelte, bored-looking young women in miniskirts. They were much prettier than I remembered. They'd lost the cheap, light blue eye makeup and brightly colored rouges, but had gained an arrogance and a cupidity. Kurt danced with one for half the night. He woke with glitter on his neck and face.

"New Russians," John explained. "Hopefully a species on the decline. It's all about money and showing everyone you have it. The more expensive, the more *krutoy*, cool. No taste, just flash. So you get a lot of beautiful women sitting around, refusing to talk to anyone who doesn't look like a Vegas playboy.

"The men are worse. They used to wear maroon sports coats and Rolex watches. Now it's Armani suits and big gold bracelets. And you must have a black Mercedes, even if you live in a dumpy apartment."

Dear LaRue—

The last time I visited Russia was 1986. The Soviet government held firm control. Talk of "Glasnost" was just beginning to bud. Tours were conducted through the propaganda-heavy, government tourism agency Intourist.

I remember the first words of the guide to our small group of college students. "Ladies and gentlemen, my name is Olga and this is your bus driver Yuri. You Americans should know the name Yuri . . . Yuri Gagaran, first man in space."

Driving in from the Moscow airport to our Stalin-era hotel on that cold, gray March afternoon, I remember being stunned by the Third World condition of the roads, projectlike apartments, and city in general. How could this be the world's other Super Power in anything other than defense systems? Long lines stretched everywhere. The few open stores stocked bare shelves and barely any products. Russians walked the streets with hands in pockets, heads firmly fixed down.

The most energy I saw was in the faces of the expert black market traders, easily spotted as the only Russians wearing expensive Gore-Tex coats and Nike shoes. I laughed to myself as they fleeced several of my tourmates, trading cheap rabbit fur hats for Walkmans and new Levi's.

Some friends and I snuck out one night to a small building on the outskirts of town to experience Moscow's first underground dance club. A man played scratched records on a twenty-year-old stereo. They taped a small disco ball to the ceiling. It was inspiring to see smiles and excitement from young people eager to embrace something new. We stayed all night, catching the morning-commute metro back to our hotel just in time to join our group for breakfast.

The most memorable moment of the trip was spending a day in jail after being arrested for the then-crime of sharing a beer with a Russian who wanted to practice his English. No "fra-ter-niz-a-tion," the gray-cloaked policeman sneered at me while pulling the roll of film out of my camera and leading me into an old military vehicle. For some reason (probably ignorance), I wasn't scared. I figured the whole ordeal would make a good story someday.

Moscow is still a huge, corrupt, cold, yet dynamic and exciting place. Picture Mexico City with snow. Police stand at every major street corner waving over expensive cars for no other reason than to extort a bribe. "Your papers are not in order," is an oft-repeated phrase to motorists. The roads are still awful as are the apartments. And a Mother Russia control mentality still permeates everyday life. After being forced along with other fans to sit in our seats for an hour one night after a soccer match we were then herded through a mile-long corridor of police officers until we reached the subway.

But life and energy in Moscow has started to bloom. The city is full of lights now, with billboards and neon signs along the major streets. The lines are gone and the stores are open and full of goods. The clothes are brighter, and smiles and laughter are no longer endangered species.

Best of all, I spent the entire time without revisiting a Russian jail.

Love,
Franz

The morning after John's birthday, we decided to shake off the aftereffects by spending the day at Lena's dacha, an hour outside Moscow. On the way, we stopped briefly at the Izmailovsky Flea Market, a rolling sea of trinket kiosks, salesmen hawking Russian military clothing and fur hats, trick bears and dancing monkeys, wandering gypsies, and babushkas selling their dead husband's belongings on blankets stretched out along walkways, their voices a little more urgent than the others'.

I stopped to stare at the colors more than anything. Brilliant turquoises and golds, Day-Glo oranges and sled reds lit up signs, people's clothes, shops, and even faces. The town had far more energy and optimism. Heads, bowed down fourteen years prior, now looked up with smiles and stares. Curiosity, punished before, blossomed. I could see it in the faces of the young skateboarders and pseudo-businessmen who constantly flashed their PalmPilots to show everyone they owned one.

Lena loved to brag about her dacha. John wasn't so sure when she bought it. Rebar, discarded cables, and construction refuse were spread throughout the one-acre plot near the Bear Lakes, within eyeshot of a collection of enormous, government-owned space satellite receivers. She and John spent weeks removing the garbage and dumping twenty-five truckloads of fertile soil to begin a small garden. They hired a group of Belarussian craftsmen to construct a two-room cabin with a common-area *banya* and a wraparound veranda pointed to perfect sunsets. Moss between the walls served as natural insulation.

John lit a fire in the woodstove while explaining the art of the *banya*. As we peeled off our clothes, he poured water mixed with pine oil and beer over the rocks surrounding the stove. This immediately filled the room with a warm and inviting steam. He then ordered us to stretch out on wooden benches. I could feel the previous night's Gzhelka vodka shots bubble to my pores. John reached in a large oil drum filled with water and grabbed a small bushel of cut branches. He waved the birch in the air, creating a hot wind and a sinus-clearing scent.

"The branches are called *veniki*," he said. "And there's an entire culture centered around how and when they should be cut. Like the intricate rituals for bonsai trees. You can buy *veniki* from any decent grocery store or from women selling them on the side of a road."

John continued with the ceremony, dipping the branches in the water and shaking leaves around our bodies so the scented drops coated our skin. Halfway to sleep, I felt a sharp smack across my back from the *veniki*. I bolted upright and tried to grab the bushel from John.

"Relax, Wiz," John said. "Just want to make sure you get the whole dacha experience."

He ordered me back down on the bench and began to strike me again, more lightly this time, starting at my neck and moving to the bottoms of my feet. Leaf fragments stuck to my skin. I felt the blood rush to my head and to the beaten spots on my body. After a few more minutes, I could take the heat no more. I grabbed a Coke from an ice chest and collapsed on a foldout chair on the veranda.

Then something else hit me. A thought, a realization. We'd been on the road for nearly a month. Yet for the first time on the trip, I felt I'd let go. And it surprised me.

Bizarre. Here, in control-freak Russia, I'm free.

During one-week vacations in past years, I'd sit on the beach or in the hotel room, thinking about work assignments and to-do lists. Despite the distance, I couldn't escape the claws of responsibility. Employers and deadlines penetrated my brain. On those vacations, work consumed me. It was impossible to relax.

Now, after a month on the road, I'd reached a threshold. No longer did I think about the corporate life I left behind. What dawned on me in the dacha was that travel was my job. I finally felt comfortable doing it. Sure, I missed my family and the comforts of home, the small things more than the large—the Friday crossword puzzle in *The Wall Street Journal*, framed photos, Peets coffee, KCRW, fabric softener, and fish tacos. I also longed for conversations that didn't start from scratch, and those Sunday mornings when friends would stumble over to watch NFL football and drink Mountain Dew. None of it mattered. Here in Russia, I was home.

Long-distance runners talk about miles getting progressively easier after you work through the first ones. Miles one and two are a grind, three and four a transition. Five and beyond and you enter a zone. Your body embraces the rhythmic pounding, your lungs settle into a comfortable, almost hypnotic cadence, your mind drifts, and you feel a warming surge of power. I was beginning to see travel the same way.

I'd reached a milestone with Annie as well. I heard through a mutual friend she was seeing someone else, "a doctor from India." Though the news crushed me, it helped me erase any lingering fantasies about another try. No, she was not my future. In the dacha, I knew that. Kurt was, the trip was. It would be a while before I was completely healed. So be it. My focus now was to make the journey as enjoyable as possible.

John joined me on the veranda. I asked him his secrets for living in Russia. Relationships, patience, and immersion were key, he explained. Many Americans came with lofty goals and established lifestyles, only to leave frustrated. The ones who lasted embraced the positive aspects of Russian society—dachas, literature and the arts, wide-open wilderness, rich cultures, resourcefulness, pride—and rejected the negative—heavy drinking, pessimism, and a feeling the modern world had passed them by. The long-termers also tended to embrace Russian spouses and lovers. He invited me to his office the next day to learn more about his life and how the American entrepreneurial spirit meshed with the new economy of Mother Russia.

Housed in Kasakova 16, a decrepit, Stalin-era temple of iron and steel, John's company provided telephone and Internet connections to former Soviet countries, something about using old KGB equipment to enhance clarity. Russkoe Radio, one of Russia's most popular, occupied several floors. The building reminded me of an old Atlantic City structure about to be blown up to make way for a new casino. Cheap ceiling tiles crumbled from water leaks. Elevators idled, broken. The moldy, dark bathrooms had a medieval dungeon decor.

"You didn't use the toilet, did you?" John blurted as I walked into his office.

I looked around at modern computer terminals, busy young professionals, polished wood floors, and ceiling-high windows. His company and others in the building invested heavily in their spaces, filling them with the latest equipment and business accoutrement. Lobbies and common spaces, meanwhile, were left to decay in the government-owned structure.

An engineer banged at a computer keyboard. Another stared at the back of the mainframe and adjoining equipment stack. John explained they were trying to make the machine perform feats well beyond its capacity. The company's female treasurer talked about a friend in the government who planned to sell her a Mercedes-Benz seized from drug dealers. An American consultant showed me an article in the morning's business journal about the Russian government's decision to take back air space for telecommunications after selling the bandwidth to foreign investors for hundreds of millions of dollars.

"Why would anyone invest in this place?" he complained. "This is so typical. The government just suddenly changes the rules."

John placed a call to a potential client in Armenia while the engineers tinkered. He began his sales pitch over the speakerphone. Probably to establish rank, I suspected. Knowing that deals in Russia can languish for months, he stressed the need to finalize arrangements immediately. He gave instructions for the Armenians to hook their computers to his system for the final test run. Then suddenly, a crash. Lights out. They flickered and came back on.

"Shit. Not cool. Shit," John yelled. "The phones are down again. These guys are going to think it's our connection."

The engineers scrambled to reconnect, bypassing the landlines and using cellular phones as an alternative. The conference call resumed. John continued the hard sell to a now wary client. He concluded the pitch thinking he had a deal, but not 100 percent certain. In Russia, you never are.

John and I were late. Lena and Kurt waited for us at the apartment. Kurt's hipstress dancing partner from the disco stewed at a restaurant with a girlfriend. After apologies at both stops, we settled into a corner table at Petrovich and ordered a round of drinks. The underground, exposed-brick restaurant simultaneously embraced and mocked the country's recent history—just as many Russians did themselves. The Soviet kitsch included photos of Khrushchev and Castro, 1940s military phones, shoelace and cardboard menus, and the omnipresent face of the cartoon character Petrovich ("son of Peter"), a lovable old Soviet man trying to cope in modern Russia. Waiters referred to one another as the children of Peter (Ivan Petrovich or Olga Petrovna, for example) while serving dishes with names like "Friendship of the People's Salad."

John's ears perked up when Kurt's date ordered Hennessy and filet mignon. He immediately barked something in Russian to her, before turning to the waiter to change the order.

"Watch this gal, Kurt," he said. "They ask for Hennessy and steak, because they think it's what rich people order and that you have deep pockets. They've seen it on

MTV. I ordered a bottle of vodka and fondue for the table. And let me pour her drinks. It'll save you some money."

Food consumed, a pager rang deep within the dancer's purse. She placed a call, chanted a few words into the cell phone, and explained to John she had an engagement she couldn't miss. Kurt, who had coaxed about ten words out of her all night, wasn't disappointed to see her and her rich tastes depart. To my surprise, the woman's attractive blonde friend chose to stay. She didn't object to John's group orders, added to the conversation, and threw in some money when the bill came around. Walking outside, the woman asked if I wanted to continue the night at her apartment.

Hello!

Kurt could come as well, she said. She had a roommate. So, after a forty-minute cab ride through wave after wave of tenement housing, the four of us sat in her bedroom listening to a Russian pop tune she played repeatedly on her knockoff stereo. She kept jumping up from the bed to rewind the tape, which made me nervous and smothered any embers of romance. Finally, I convinced her to turn off the music, lower the lights, and sit next to me. Kurt massaged her roommate's thigh on the other side of the room. As I leaned over for a kiss, she opened her mouth wide and tackled me on the bed.

"Stay here," she said after a few minutes. "I want to change into sexy clothes."

I tried to steal a glance at Kurt and his friend without them noticing. They didn't. Watching a brother exchange saliva with some random partner isn't one of the more appealing sights in life, I concluded. In fact, it's downright weird. So I stared at the wall and wondered why my friend was taking so long. As the door opened, I started to smile at the . . . two-hundred-pound babushka poking her head in? "What the . . . ?" She scanned the room, then left without saying a word.

My date emerged minutes later, clothed in a skimpy black negligee. "Who's the chaperone?" I asked. She sat down on my lap and told me not to worry about "grandmother." She unbuttoned my shirt and started to kiss my neck. I fought without success to erase the bizarre and competing images of the babushka and my brother trying to disrobe his companion ten feet away.

"Today is my birthday," she said.

"Happy birthday," I replied.

"Are you going to give me present?"

"Uhhh, sure."

"When?"

"How about tomorrow?"

"Tomorrow is not my birthday."

"Later today?"

"You funny."

"Next week?"

"No."

I'd had enough.

"Lemme guess. You want a Barbie for your birthday?"

"What is Barbie?"

"A cheap bottle of vodka?"

"No."

"Cash?"

"I want hundred dollars."

"Hey, Kurt, stop what you're doing. Our friend wants a hundred dollars for her birthday."

"I knew it," he said, nodding his head to suggest we leave.

"I'm sorry," I said as I turned to the blonde. "There must be some misunderstanding. Call me old-fashioned, but I got this thing about not paying for sex. You seem like a nice woman, and I had a nice time. Why don't we call it a night?"

"How about fifty dollars?"

"How about I get you a card?"

"When I first came here, I viewed prostitutes with pity and disdain," said John the next day. "People who chose the easy road, not smart enough to understand the long-term risks and consequences. Now I just pity them.

"You've got to understand they grew up in the collapsing chaos of the Soviet Union, jungle law with corrupt bureaucrats and muscle-head brutes slowly trying to make the transition from thug criminal to quasi-businessman. These girls could stick around and marry some chauvinist alcoholic or go to the big city and try to create a better life. To them, it's a logical choice. Or the only choice. Many have children to feed or aging parents to care for.

"Most of these women aren't full-timers. They have day jobs. But if the opportunity arises for some extra cash, they feel like they need to take advantage of the situation. Almost all would prefer to be the lover of some rich guy who would take care of them. More than anything, they're limited by their imagination."

Putting her arm around me, Lena said she was sorry. "Cheer up. I have two nice friends who want to practice their English and show you two around town. And they won't charge you a ruble."

Distance-runner thin with ash-blond hair and aqua blue eyes, Irina declined food at the pizza parlor that afternoon. She was a Russian folk dancer who performed in tourist shows, on cruise lines, and occasionally abroad. She explained her art as part ballet, part square dance. With work being slow, she had time to wander around Moscow.

Irina was different from most Russian women. She'd traveled outside her country and lived for a short time in Asia. The experiences added context to her commentary as we strolled around the czar's country estate and, later, the Pushkin Museum. She boasted of Russian conquests and contributions to mankind, all said with an infectious smile. She talked about low wages and high costs, and complained about the lack of opportunity in Russia, where PhD holders often waited tables. With her country's natural resources and brainpower, the weak economy still puzzled her.

She explained the quirks of Russian motorists, why they turn their motor off at every stoplight. "Saves gas, though I don't think it does." Or frequently drive at night with their lights off. "It used to be impossible to find replacement lights. So we saved them for emergencies only." She taught me many Russian superstitions, including the mortal dangers of a deadly draft, *skvoznyak,* or that sitting on a cold rock can cause infertility. You should never take bread from a table, she said, because it will stop you from getting rich, and sitting at the corner of a table will prevent you from finding a spouse.

On a walk through the Kremlin grounds one day, we entered a church with crosses and antique religious relics on display. Old women in frayed dresses and peasant scarves lined up patiently to kiss the glass separating them from the ornaments. Husbands with dirty nails and scuffed shoes paced nearby, eager to see the ornate icons as well. I felt a rush throughout my body, seeing the kindled passion for Christ in a country that for generations had gone to extraordinary lengths to stamp out religion. Irina smiled at me like a parent who'd just delivered a present.

When I first met Irina, I didn't think about Russian superstitions or the Kremlin religious artifacts. My initial line of thought was, Would Lena be irate if I tried to sleep with her friend? The impulse ebbed with each day we spent together. And it freaked me out.

What's going on? You've got this beautiful woman on your arm, a dancer, and you're not going to make a move?

Instead, I was content with the history lessons and walks through the city. More than anything, I reveled in the opportunity to spend a few innocent hours with a woman. She fueled me. She gave me warmth as I struggled to thaw. And I made progress. I was able to wait until my second date with Irina before I unloaded the story of Annie and why I was on a honeymoon with my brother.

I'm rusty, I know. And I wish I could give you more.

A few days later, Kurt pushed to pick up his car in Sweden. John and Lena decided to accompany us to St. Petersburg for a weekend before we flew to Göteborg. I called Irina to see if she wanted to go to St. Petersburg as well.

"No, thank you," she said after a long pause.

I pushed.

"I want to go. But it will only make things harder when you leave."

A year later, John told me she married a Danish businessman ten years her senior. He said she called for my phone number before making the decision.

We spent the long weekend in St. Petersburg marveling at the Hermitage Museum's Matisses, Gauguins, and Monets, both for their beauty and the fact that they were hung on simple nails in front of open windows, joining busloads of water pistol–wielding schoolkids at the czar's opulent Petrograd, and celebrating with drunken bar patrons as they cheered their Olympic athletes in shooting, wrestling, rhythmic gymnastics, and other Russian-dominated sports rarely atop ESPN's Plays of the Day.

John scheduled a business meeting the day of our flight. We planned to have breakfast while he worked, then we'd all go to the airport together. He promised to rid our exit of any Russian *bardak*. We packed our bags and waited on a street corner while John flagged down a driver. An old man in a rusty, black Moskvich car pulled to the curb. John immediately began to yell at him. The driver shouted back while waving his arms to dismiss John. The escalating war of words lasted for ten minutes before John stopped and turned to us.

"Okay," he said. "Get in. This guy's going to drive us to the meeting, take you to a restaurant, wait there for you, come back to pick me up, then drive us to the airport."

"What happened there?" I said. "I thought you two were going to come to blows."

"Oh, that? That's nothing. We just debated price. The Russians have been berated and abused for so long, it's the only way they know how to do business. Especially the older generation. You almost have to fight them to come to an agreement. Otherwise they'll think you're weak and refuse to do anything for you."

11

Kurt hovered outside the Saab factory, pacing like an expectant father. We were early that morning in Trollhättan, Sweden. The restored redbrick, turn-of-the-century showroom didn't open for an hour. The sky was clear, the air bracing. A bespectacled lady tapped on the window from the inside, startling me. Kurt sauntered to the door, not wanting to seem too anxious. Through a museum-type display of old Saab models and photos, she led us into a back showroom, and there it was—Kurt's new gray 9-5 sedan with black leather interior, a sky roof, and a Bose stereo eager to swallow the CDs we brought to choreograph our journey to music. Thievery Corporation for the mornings, Mozart in the mountains, Pixies when we needed a boost.

The Saab representative seemed startled when we told her we planned to take the car all the way to the Middle East, but she assured us that the insurance would cover any damages or theft in each country en route. She smiled and asked that we send pictures to verify a safe arrival, though I wasn't sure, as she handed us the keys, if she meant the car or us.

For a half hour we just sat there. In the Saab parking lot. Looking at the dashboard and the lights, playing with the windows, learning what each button and lever controlled.

Ahhhhhhh. Freedom. Freeeeeeeedom.

I leafed through the detailed European road atlas and shouted place-names to Kurt for his reaction. Dots and stars, red lines and green, blue for water. So many places etched in pop-culture memory. Lillehammer and Gdańsk, Transylvania and Sarajevo, Gallipoli, Damascus, Golden Prague, the Blue Danube. A giant computer screen to anywhere. All within reach. Just point and click and go.

We decided to drive through Norway, Sweden, Poland and Slovakia, then back to Prague. Unless, of course, we woke up wanting to go to Denmark. We were alone for the first time of the trip. So we did what comes natural to brothers. We hashed out trivial subjects, sat silent for hours, and we fought.

Prior to leaving America, we'd created Internet programs to check news, e-mail, and stocks. Just an occasional peek, we promised each other. During visits to Internet cafés, we watched the stock market continue its substantial "correction." Kurt had gambled a chunk of his home sale money on an "incorrect" stock. He griped about the decline as we devoured pizza one night during the first week of the drive.

"It's just paper," I said. "It's not a loss until you sell it."

"Unless the stock goes off the board," he shot back. "They say this company could fold. It's not a long-term hold."

"Still, it's just a stock," I continued.

"To you. To me, it's ten thousand dollars."

"Don't worry about it."

"That's easy for you to say. You don't own the stock."

"I own a bunch of others that are tanking."

"It's a lot of money."

"It's nothing."

"I was counting on it to travel."

"Relax. You shouldn't get so worked up over stocks."

He rose to leave.

"Where are you going?"

"I'm taking your advice. I'm going back to the hotel to relax. You pay for dinner. I can't afford it."

Nice job, knucklehead. This is the same guy who dropped his work and flew to California to help you sort through the wedding crash.

I felt sick. Kurt was asleep by the time I got back.

I didn't do that fight-makeup stuff well. Neither did he. Both of us had a serious case of conflict avoidance. Armchair psychologists would say that's because our parents had one of those old-fashioned, Dad-says/Mom-agrees (or at least humors him) relationships. Maybe. All I know is that when either of us heard a raised voice, we'd want to escape. As I walked back to the hotel, I thought about the times my flight-from-fight reflex had postponed resolutions to my problems with Annie. And about how many times Kurt must have done the same. I'd apologize to him in the morning. Instead, he surprised me.

"No more checking stocks," he said. "Someone's trying to tell me to get my head out of the market. I went to bed all pissed off. Then I thought about all the people in Russia with so little. I'm bitching about investments, but at least I have money to invest. Or maybe I should say I *had* money to invest."

I felt relieved knowing the argument was over and seeing the kid who wore my hand-me-downs give me a hand-me-up lesson. I told him I felt bad, and even worse after hearing him talk about stocks. "I'm sorry." We reconnected by the second cup of coffee. He wanted the spat finished as much as I did.

I need to work on this brother thing.

Jonathan Terra placed the tape in his Prague apartment stereo. *"Měla bych tě varovat, umím taky čarovat."* Grinning, he translated the Czech lyrics.

"Oooh, Wiz, you'll love this. She's singing, *'There's something I should teeeeellllll you, I can put a spell on you.'*"

Jana, an aspiring singer and model, giggled from her seat on the couch. Jonathan had introduced us during a group dinner several nights prior. She knew twenty words of English.

"Excellent, Jana," I said, giving her a thumbs-up sign. "Jonathan, tell her we love her singing."

"Speak for yourself," Kurt said. "I think it sucks."

"Don't translate that, Terra."

Jana rose like a performer during an encore. Bravo. She wore a black miniskirt that barely covered the tops of her stately legs, a snug mocha-colored sweater, heavy black eyeliner, and dark lipstick. She was gorgeous, but when she spoke English she sounded like Natasha from the Bullwinkle cartoons. I couldn't shake this image of her pulling out a ball-shaped black bomb with a lit fuse.

Jonathan Terra had been in Prague, on and off, for five years, living off consulting jobs and higher-education grants, inching toward completion of his PhD in political science from Stanford. He'd explained the dissertation to me a dozen times. I never understood. Something about trade unions and privatization in countries that no longer existed—Czechoslovakia, East Germany, and such.

He had a linebacker build and Popeye-size calves, closely cropped salt-and-pepper hair, and wore black-rimmed Los Alamos glasses and scarves in all seasons to round out his coffeehouse look. Chronically late, constantly entertaining, Jonathan would fire off five-page e-mails in the middle of the night about everything from Puff Daddy's rap sheet to the problems of baggage screening at airports to the childhood similarities between Leon Trotsky and George W. Bush. He used words like *philopolemic* and *sesquipedalian*. He'd been a close, loyal friend since Little League.

Jonathan had upgraded his apartment since the last time I visited Prague two years earlier. He'd moved from a dark studio to a three-bedroom flat in the Letná neighborhood near Prague Castle and the open fields where 750,000 Czechs had protested the country's Communist government in 1989.

For dinner that night we settled on DELUX, a culturally confused restaurant with more themes than It's a Small World—Thai curries, Cuban plantains, Czech

Staropramen beer, Italian-style arabesques, red lights from a former Chinese restaurant, and a hyperactive male salsa dancer who kept trying to grab Kurt for a spin. I relaxed with Jana at the end of the table, debating my approach to break her away from the gang.

Before we left California, Kurt clipped an article from *Maxim* magazine detailing "How to Pick Up Women Who Don't Speak English." Using diagrams that resembled exit instructions on old airline safety cards, the article offered such revolutionary pointers as "use eye contact," "smile," and "point to your drink as a way to offer her one." Simplistic garbage, I thought at the time. Yet now here I was, "using eye contact," "smiling," and "pointing to my glass as a way to offer her one." Jana placed a hand on my thigh and grinned mischievously.

I guess that's my approach.

"We're out, gang," I announced. "Going back to Terra's. We're both really tired."

The walk home felt like a stroll through an after-hours movie set. Cobblestone streets glistened from early evening rain. Streetlights beamed a dull, gaslight glow. Coal stains highlighted carvings and curves on expertly preserved buildings, an architectural who's who of cubist, rondo-cubist, gothic, baroque, neo-baroque, and art nouveau.

And, um, I've got a horny starlet by my side.

Back at the apartment, Jana's English improved with each glass of wine. Not much, mind you, but improvement still. Her twenty words expanded to about three dozen. She placed a favorite jazz CD into Jonathan's stereo, and we began to dance. Bodies connected, swaying slowly, she unbuttoned my shirt, then grabbed my hand and led me down the hall to the guest bedroom. I kissed the nape of her neck as she unhooked her skirt and let it drop to the floor.

Focused, driven, she pushed me down on the bed. Jana unbuckled my belt, raised my shirt, and began to kiss my stomach. She looked up to see if I approved. I closed my eyes and moaned softly to show her I did. Cooing, she touched her lips to the insides of my thighs. She arched the small of my back with her hands and slipped off my boxers. I reclined and grabbed the side of the bed for support. Her mouth felt warm and soft.

Mmmmmmmm. It's been a while. Be cool, be cool.

After several minutes I shifted around to pull off her black lace panties. French, I thought. Probably her best pair. She began to grind against my tongue and lips. Slow and deep at first. More intense with each kiss. I cupped her bottom with my hand and felt a slight twitch. She let out a breathy gasp before pushing me back and straddling my waist as if we'd made love a thousand times before—confident, knowing what pleased her, matching her thrusts to mine. She started to whisper something. "*Shhh, Natasha.*" I cut her off with a kiss, and we settled into a long ride. We held each other close and fell asleep, bodies intertwined.

Later, I slipped out of bed and ambled into Jonathan's kitchen. The others hadn't yet risen. I boiled a pot of water and fumbled through his cabinets for a box of tea. Most labels were in Czech, so I picked the one with the prettiest fruit designs. Alone, I sat at the breakfast table, staring out the window over the courtyard, giving myself a huge pat on the back.

Hell, yeah. The kid's back! What I would give to let Annie know I just spent the night with a steamy young Prague model. A thousand dollars to FedEx her one of those Pamela Anderson/Tommy Lee–type videos capturing my grand conquest in Technicolor detail.

I saw my face in the teacup, then my smile disappeared.

Wait a minute. If I'm thinking about Annie immediately after sex, I'm not over her. Not even close.

The tea lost its flavor. I didn't hear Kurt walk in.

"Eastern European gals as good in bed as they say?" asked Kurt.

"Shhh. She's still here."

"She gonna stick around or you think she'll go home?" he asked in a softer tone.

"I don't know. Whatever. She's a nice gal. Brutal English, but nice."

Jana played through, hanging at the apartment the whole day . . . and the next . . . and the next . . . and the next. The second day, I didn't worry too much about it. I thought it might be a cultural thing. Czechs probably just liked to settle in. And I still enjoyed the sex. By day three I began to wonder if she'd ever leave. I'd go out for a jog or to run some errands and come back to find her on the couch, listening to that same jazz CD, motioning for me to join her. When sober, her English vocabulary reverted back to the original twenty words. So I spent all day crafting sentences using the words *good, lipstick, Madonna,* and *Rollerblades.* Day four, I'd had enough.

"Terra, how do I get this gal to take off? The sex is fun, but the hours in between are killing me. The same inane pantomime conversations. Her constant stare. The same sweater and miniskirt."

He asked her several times about her plans. She answered with a shrug and a comment about not having to work for a while. I told him to tell her I wanted to do some sightseeing with Kurt. She told Jonathan she'd show us around. Trapped. No way to shake her. I was stuck with Jana for as long as we planned to stay in Prague. I felt like a kid who, after craving chocolate for months, was forced to eat it every day for breakfast, lunch, and dinner.

"Okay, Terra," I said. "I have an idea. Let's pretend we're leaving. Explain to her we're driving to Turkey this afternoon. We'll take off for a bit, then come right back. That way we don't hurt her feelings."

Jonathan relayed the message, yet still Jana hesitated to budge from her seat on the couch. It wasn't until we carried our backpacks downstairs that she made any move to depart. I gave her a hug, then waved good-bye as we drove away. Several hours later I was back in the apartment, minus Jana, plus a little guilt and an immediate longing for/reminiscence about the sex. A clean getaway.

Jana-free, Kurt and I stretched our legs in Prague. We took long runs through the beer gardens at Letenský zámeček and the adjoining parks overlooking the city, past the platform that used to house the world's largest Stalin statue until Czechs decided to destroy it in 1962. Prague in 2000 felt like a town after a parade. Sure, the city remained an alluring beacon for any foreigner in search of thirty-cent pilsners and more coffeehouses than Seattle, attractive and approachable women, subsidized neo-baroque or art nouveau flats, and scores of like-minded searchers, aspirers, and ex-pat loafers who'd lessen the need to learn Czech. The army of bohemians-to-be had been cut in half since its heyday in the early nineties. They'd packed up their easels, kissed their Kundera-novel girlfriends good-bye, and moved to less-discovered locations like Riga and Sofia. The bookstores and cafés had cleared out a bit by then, leaving the beautiful city in the hands of people who actually wanted to live there.

"It's not really a blending-in type of place," said Jonathan. "Unless you chain-smoke, watch a lot of television, and speak with an intoxicated mumble. Still, the Czechs are mostly comfortable with Prague being a magnet for foreigners. Just as long as they don't bring tanks.

"They're also private and pride themselves on not having a truckload of friends. Friendship is reserved for the relative few. But once you're in the club, it's usually a lifetime membership."

Jonathan talked about the country's short-term love of the sensual. Czechs seconded the sentiment. When we spoke with them about the future of their country, the conversations, without fail, took on an ominous, fatalistic tone. When we saw *Don Giovanni* at Stavovské divadlo or ate fruit dumplings at the top of Petřín Hill, they gushed that their country was of unparalleled beauty and a bargain. They complained about opportunity, but praised the mineral waters at Karlovy Vary, kayaking the Vltava River as it snakes its way through Český Krumlov, and the mountain cottages of Krkonoše. Iron Curtain resentments lingered, even in younger generations, but most Czechs we met felt their history shaped their character for the better, fine-tuning a start-from-scratch ingenuity, fueling brilliant yet subtle offerings in literature and music, sharpening a sarcastic sense of humor that poked fun at everyday drab.

The phone in Jonathan's apartment rang as I walked out of the shower a couple days later. After a few hurried words, he slammed down the receiver.

"Wiz, exit strategy!" he ordered. "That was Jana. She's on her way over. Said she left a piece of jewelry or something. You guys have about ten minutes to pack your shit and run."

"Terra, couldn't you tell her to come over later? That you were busy now?"

"I tried, man, but she was already on her way over. She called me on her cell."

Cursing, we threw our clothes into our backpacks. We planned to leave later that day, but were far from ready. Kurt ran downstairs and positioned himself by the car like a center fielder ready to shag fly balls. I lobbed our belongings from Jonathan's third-floor window—a load of laundry still wet, the bags, a couple loaves of bread and a few apples. A melon slipped through Kurt's hands, probably on purpose. He hates melon. He loaded everything else in the car. Jana strutted around the corner as we sped away. At least that's what Kurt said. I was too busy burying my face in the backseat to notice.

Onward. On. To Budapest. Over the next couple days, we learned the Danube isn't blue. It's gray. Goulash isn't stew, but soup. That Budapest isn't Budapest, but the cities of Buda and Pest and Obuda to boot. We learned the best way to hear about current events in Budapest is to soak in the five-hundred-year-old bathhouses, a daily ritual for many Hungarians and intrepid visitors seeking a cure for everything from sore joints to depression.

We learned Hungarians are among the world's most inventive capitalists after we hopped the fence at Statue Park and saw forty giant sculptures of Lenin, Marx, happy Communist children, and workers of the world uniting. Following the fall of the Iron Curtain, some enterprising Hungarians gathered the statues from around the country, threw them in a field, and sold admission tickets. Only Uncle Joe was missing. Rioters destroyed Budapest's only Stalin statue during the uprisings of 1956.

Onward. On through Romania. The deeper into Eastern Europe, the more dated the surroundings. The scenes transported us to an agrarian Europe centuries prior. Horse carts stacked high with cornhusks shared highway space with thirty-year-old Russian cars. Men walked the sides of the road with machetes, women trailed behind with bushels of grain and sacks of potatoes. Mud-caked cottages and handmade haystacks dotted row farms. The real Disney castles soared above.

Next stop, Bulgaria, where the mountainous countryside was equally striking and quaint, but the roads and poverty worse. We drove past countless crumbling apartments that made American project housing look inviting. Main highways ended without warning in a sea of potholes. The backs of the cart horses sagged a little lower. Abandoned construction sites outnumbered active ones. We shook our heads at the decrepit nuclear power plants and wondered which ones would be the next Chernobyl.

Late one afternoon, two lonely policemen huddling on the side of the road waved their arms for us to stop, a frequent occurrence in Eastern Europe. Through trial and error, we'd streamlined our approach to avoiding speeding tickets. The larger question was why, with nowhere in particular to go, we sped in the first place. Regardless, step one: pretend you don't understand a thing they say, usually the case anyway. Step two: pretend to have no local currency or U.S. dollars. Step three: offer a currency from a distant country. Mexican pesos work well. If all those tactics fail, resort to a simple yet persistent plea for mercy. Nine times out of ten, the officer would wave us away. When forced to pay tickets, Kurt negotiated discounted rates.

This time Kurt pleaded ignorance to the Bulgarian traffic cop, who spoke no English. After a few minutes, the officer threw up his hands and paced back to his police car.

"Okay if we go?" Kurt yelled while motioning his hand out the door.

The policeman paced back to our car and thrust a small card in Kurt's face. It read, in typed English: *You have committed a traffic violation by passing a vehicle on a double yellow line. The fine for this offense is 100 leva. We accept cash or credit cards.*

"Think I could pretend I'm illiterate?" Kurt asked.

12

I sat alone on the roof deck of our Istanbul hotel, staring at the majestic Blue Mosque. Floodlights enlivened the towering minarets from all angles. A piercing voice completed the nighttime call to prayer. Worshipers sauntered in, mostly men, some in embroidered skullcaps and vests, many in blue jeans and polo shirts. I tried to envision Mark Twain's "eternal circus," where "mosques are plenty, churches are plenty, graveyards are plenty, but morals and whiskey are scarce." I soaked in the unworldly scene, but my mind was elsewhere.

Time to think. This is the greatest luxury of travel. Hard-core, maharishi-meditating, clear-all-the-cobwebs-away thinking. One thought, one subject. An idea, an emotion. Pry deeper and deeper and—lo and behold—sometimes find something there.

Here on the roof, I thought about another view I had four years prior. It was at the Republican National Convention in 1996. San Diego. Bob Dole had no prayer of winning the election. Everyone there knew it. Still, it didn't prevent the Republican all-stars from donning their most expensive suits and toasting GOP prospects at swank restaurants and crowded convention halls throughout the city.

Anyone who's ever been to a convention knows status is measured not by the size of the limo or the years of devoted party service, but by the laminated, postcard-size passes delegates and onlookers wear around their necks. While speakers drone on, convention-goers spend all day looking at the number and type of passes hanging in front of ties and blouses. They do this to size someone up and establish his or her place in the pecking order. An acquaintance has a lowly convention hall pass? Move on. Meet someone with a stack of all-access credentials? "Hey, howya doing?"

Before the convention, I wrote a bunch of five- and six-figure checks from The Irvine Company to help the Republican party stage the event. So when I walked up to the check-in table and gave the young Southern belle my name, she looked like she was ready to jump over and smother me in adoration. Smiling wide, she reached into a box and gave me a large envelope. Inside were dozens of passes. Floor passes, center passes, stage passes, press passes, step-aside passes. Every pass the convention issued, I had in spades. I clamped them onto a metal chain around my neck and started to make the rounds. Wherever I walked in the enormous convention center—private suites, media briefing rooms, backstage holding areas—I was met with more smiles from conventioneers and nods from security men.

For the keynote address, I ended up in the Team 100 luxury suite. The people there didn't walk precincts or wave signs. They gave at least 100,000 dollars a year to the party. And they preferred to watch the ruckus from pampered environs on high. I walked past the Matterhorn of shrimp and the blonde trophy wives on the couch and made my way to the bar. The tanned old man next to me turned and smiled. It was Al Haig. He ordered scotch. I copied. Must be the thing to do. He turned to me and said it was great to see me again. I'd never met him before. I walked to the front of the suite and reclined in a leather chair. I could see everything from that perch—the politicians and their aides, the volunteers draped in American flags and Uncle Sam hats, the banks of television reporters applying their pancake makeup before going on the air.

Amid the throngs, a hundred yards away, a young man in a white shirt and rep tie waved up to the booth. He was a friend from the Wilson administration. With scrunched shoulders and open palms, he shot me a "What gives?" look, the same pose Italian soccer players strike when complaining to referees about penalties. He motioned that he'd like to swap places. I pulled out my wallet to signal he couldn't afford it. And I knew then I'd reached another height in the GOP hierarchy.

I thought about that Team 100 suite sometimes when I'd lobby a piece of legislation. The company hired several contract lobbyists in Sacramento to monitor bills and advocate positions. I'd go there for the company's most pressing issues, paying visits to legislators I'd bankrolled in elections. Along with our Sacramento-based lobbyists, I spearheaded approval of many bills that saved the company millions of dollars in taxes and fees. I was a hero at the company, especially with the accountants. They patted me on the back when we passed in the halls. It felt great.

Here on the roof deck in Turkey, the bills, Al Haig, the scotch, and the Team 100 suite didn't feel as good. Here, a half world away from a twelve-year career in government and politics, the bills and the conventions didn't rise to the top of the most-cherished-achievements list. What crept to the top were actions long forgotten—afterthoughts and favors.

Walkie Ray was a developer and friend from political circles. And a Democrat. He went out of his way to invite me to charity fund-raisers and Democratic party events in conservative Orange County. On top of his business and personal projects, he led a volunteer effort to build a science museum in a heavily Latino area of the county. The center needed a final ten million dollars to open its doors. Walkie, knowing of my frequent trips to Sacramento, asked me to put in a good word during visits to legislative offices. He was trying to secure an appropriation on a statewide bond. I told him I'd do what I could. As an aside, I'd mention the science center funding every time I'd pop in on a politician. The legislature voted to put the item in the bond, and the people of California voted to approve the measure, sending ten million dollars to Walkie and the science center. I was glad to help, but still didn't think much about the effort at the time.

That is, I didn't think much about it until he invited me to the opening. It was one of those black-tie and office printer–program affairs with an emcee who says, "Whoever has a birthday closest to today keeps the beautiful centerpiece at the end of the night." Only this one was different. At this gala they opened their doors to hundreds of grade-school children in blue velvet Sunday dresses and clip-on ties. I stood quietly in a corner and watched them all, with their eyes wide open, laughing and learning as they played with giant magnets, earthquake simulators, and other hands-on learning displays.

Eleven years prior, while working as a press aide for Senator Pete Wilson in his Washington, D.C., office, I read an article about a woman from El Salvador, terminally ill in a Los Angeles hospital. The doctors said she had a handful of days left. The woman's final wish was to see her young son from El Salvador. The Immigration and Naturalization Service, fearing her child was a flight risk, prohibited the boy from flying to California for a last visit. It was an all-too-common, heartless government decision based on numbers instead of what's right.

I grabbed a colleague who handled immigration issues and crafted a complaint letter signed by Senator Wilson. INS relented and let the boy in. Before he arrived in California, his mother slipped into a coma.

A few days later, I read in the newspapers that the boy's appearance in the hospital room brought his mother to life. They held each other for long periods, the reports said. Shortly thereafter, she lost consciousness and passed away. She died knowing the feel of his hair, the smell of his skin, and the comforting look on his face.

Our letter was part sympathy/part reaction, something staffers did to help people in our home state, especially since our boss was running for governor. I never met the boy or his mother, and quickly moved on to other projects and stories in the days that followed. In retrospect, the incident mattered. It was important, not just another press conference or an endless policy debate. I'd written hundreds of press releases during my five years as a press secretary, yet I couldn't recall a specific line from any of them. I remembered that boy, though. And I remembered the kids at the science center.

Before the trip, I had an idea that Kurt and I would rework priorities for the future. I hoped our experiences would help shape our goals when we returned home.

How could they not? What I realized on that Istanbul rooftop was that extended travel has a way of reprioritizing the past. Some of my memories expanded and became luminous, others faded away. I was curious about how the upcoming months would shape my recollections.

Kurt walked up on the roof deck. He was a priority to me these days. A huge one. He didn't know it yet, but I was getting there. I just needed to learn more. So I studied him, the way he chose his food or how he would hint, with exaggerated exhales, when he'd had enough museum time and wanted a few hours outdoors. Or needed space. How he bristled during my unsolicited history lessons. Why it was okay for me to borrow his shirts but not his shoes ("Your feet are too wide"). He fretted about the dogs, but not about going home without a job. He seemed to be having a good time.

The more information I stockpiled, the more I worried about him. And it angered me. I never fretted about Kurt in high school. I knew he'd get by. He always did. On the road, his resourcefulness showed. Still, it didn't stop me from the occasional big-brother panic. If he was a couple minutes late from a morning run, I'd sweat about a possible kidnapping. When he said he needed to rest, I'd envision Ebola.

I always loved him. Now I felt a new, powerful commitment to him. Kurt was there all along. I just didn't take the time to know him. I was intrigued by the discovery. I felt I was reading a good novel that had sat untouched on my library shelf for years. I wanted to read more. At the same time, I knew I was just beginning to plow through the pages.

I knew where I wanted the relationship to go; I just couldn't figure out how to get there. We'd talked more in the last couple months than we had in the last decade, yet he still felt distant. I wanted the ability to program the relationship like a computer, take out the viruses and bad files, upgrade RAM and speed. Neither of us was a machine; this would take time. Fortunately, we had that commodity in ample supply.

Kurt sat down on the brightly colored pillows scattered on the roof deck. Today was his birthday. October 7. I scurried around the Istanbul food and spice bazaars that afternoon, buying corn nuts and pistachios, a bottle of rum, Cokes, candies, and a handful of presents. I poured Kurt a drink and saluted his thirty-third. We stayed for several hours and talked about sports.

Dear LaRue—

I bought a carpet yesterday. Make that two carpets. I'm convinced the Turkish carpet salesmen are the best hucksters in the world, topping the scalpers at Fenway Park and the fur hat salesmen in Moscow. As you wind your way through crowded bazaars, affable

Turks stand in the narrow doorways, guessing the nationality of walkers-by, then throwing pitch lines to attract your attention. The standard C-grade line you'll hear is, "My friend, where are you from?" A B-grade line that made me laugh was, "Please, come in and let me help you spend your money." The A line I couldn't resist was, "My friend, five minutes in my shop and I promise you'll send me Christmas cards every year."

Once inside, the ritual begins. Conversations turn to sports, philosophy, and relationships—anything but carpets. The obligatory offers of tea and coffee are next, followed by the appearance of an old waiter who comes, without being summoned, holding a tray of drinks. After a while, two assistants begin to unfold the dozens of carpets usually stacked to the ceiling. Attempts to help them are met with a gentle grab of the arm from the lead salesman and a plea to relax. He gauges your tastes, barks orders constantly, and details the painstaking labor that goes into each masterpiece.

If they don't have your preferred style or size in their store, men appear from other shops holding their goods. Finally, subtly, a price is mentioned. You counter with an offer of half; he throws up his arms. So you thank him for the drinks and walk out. He chases after you with a plea not to be "so hasty." After a couple days of similar routines, you should have the carpet you want. It took me three days and I still probably overpaid. But the carpets are nice trip reminders and much less expensive than in the U.S.

Ah Turkey. The *Orient Express*, fezzes, whirling dervishes—it always seemed like an exotic and romantic place from afar. It hasn't disappointed, though the coastline is more developed than I imagined, and the country more western. The old fishing villages and small remote towns are still charming; it just takes a bit more effort and a few more miles to find them.

We loved the eerily majestic calls to prayer (though I could have missed the sunrise summons) late afternoon visits to lesser-known Roman ruins, grazing through the food bazaars and spice courts, gorging on pistachios, dates, yogurt with fresh fruit, kebabs and crazy-looking pastries, getting shaved every other day by an old-school Turkish barber with a straight razor and a promise that he was "not a butcher."

We could do without Turkish coffee (espresso with mud), Turkish baths (really more of a lukewarm, mildewy steam), Turkish drivers.

Love,
Franz

Friends who'd been to Turkey gave us advice for our travels. Go to the beaches during the day, they prescribed, then see the Roman ruins late in the afternoon. That way we'd have the historical sites all to ourselves. Instead, we did what we often did with travel advice: we ignored it. Instead, we pulled into the Ephesus ruins at noon a few days later. Dozens of tour buses outside forced us to park up the hill. Wading through the throngs of zoom lenses, name tags, and flag-waving guides, I had a hard time envisioning a thriving Roman city. Several hours and miles later, we climbed the hill leading to the Priene ruins, joined only by a young couple from California and dozens of bell-wearing black goats and their shepherd. The late afternoon sun stirred life into the fallen marble columns. Without the masses, the ruins came alive. I saw centurions walking to war and merchants peddling their wares in the agoras. Farther down the road to the ruins, we climbed to the top of the amphitheater at Miletus just in time for the magenta sunset. We were ancient Roman theatergoers, lingering after a show, watching the sun disappear over our fields. Touring ruins late in the day also had the added benefit of costing us nothing. Ticket sellers usually left late afternoon, once the tour buses had pulled away.

Curving along Turkey's southwest corner, past miles of olive groves, countless President Kemal Atatürk statues, and groups of children walking home from school in clothesline-dried white shirts, we adopted a comfortable traveling routine. We stuck to small villages and ten-dollar-a-night pensiones with friendly proprietors and stiff sheets. For breakfast, we had no choice. It was the same everywhere—coffee and juice, cucumbers, olives, feta cheese, bread and jam, and the occasional hard-boiled egg. Runs or reading sessions followed morning meals. Beach time and village strolls were next, supplemented by hikes or boat trips. We tried to drive during the warmest hours, arriving at ruins late in the afternoon. Waterfront cafés capped the evenings.

The days were easy, satisfying, and complete. Or almost. Kurt complained about the lack of nightlife and scarcity of women. I did, too. "There are many women," a friendly carpet dealer explained one day. "You just need to know where to look. And you need to know how to tell many stories. You must turn many pages."

Heading toward the chic seaport of Bodrum one morning, I realized I'd left my notebook at the previous night's lodging ten miles away. I asked Kurt if he minded turning around. He snorted but relented. I started to make a left turn onto a dirt road, then *bam*. A hard jolt from a car behind. I cringed.

Kurt sprang out of our car and began swearing at the other driver. The old man answered in rapid-fire Turkish. I slumped over the wheel. Kurt's new car. His pride and joy. The Saab we picked up at the factory.

Kurt's going to think I just ruined his baby. And put a big ole dent in our relationship as well.

The damage wasn't as bad as I feared. Kurt's car had a ding in the bumper and a nick in the rear driver's side door. It wasn't nearly as bad as the five-hour ordeal that followed.

"Well, think of it this way," I said as we sat in a military police headquarters. "We can now say we've done time in a Turkish prison." Kurt didn't respond.

112

We waited outside a large office as the animated Turkish motorist told his side to the commander of the base. I could hear the driver's hysterics and occasionally see an arm waving through a crack in the door. An hour later, the medalled soldier motioned for me to come in. The room was hot and smoke-filled. Just as I was beginning my defense, he signaled me to be quiet, then jumped back on the phone for another half hour. Finally, he nodded. My version was met with a blank stare. He spoke no English. I asked if anyone else did. He shook his head.

Undaunted, I grabbed a pen from his desk and drew a series of pictures—stick figures in cars, responsible me with hands on the wheel, the Turkish driver with arms flailing. How difficult could it be? In the U.S., the driver who rear-ended another car was at fault. I motioned for him to go look at the dent in the old man's front bumper and our back bumper. Case closed. After staring at my drawings, he handed me a stack of papers in Turkish and pointed me out the door.

I told Kurt the question session went smoothly and that we'd probably be able to leave soon. I lied. The nonchalant commander acted as if he didn't understand a word of my argument despite the drawings. "Fender bender, Turk, see, fender bender, Turk, see." We fidgeted on the bench, staring at the papers, failing to decipher a single word. Our accident partner, meanwhile, made the rounds to other offices, telling anyone with a uniform who would listen about a couple of hysterical American drivers. He waved his arms exactly as I had drawn in the pictures.

Then, a clarion call. A few words of English reverberated throughout the hall. I leapt from the bench and tracked down a tall, chain-smoking Turk with a suit coat draped, Italian pimp–style, over his shoulders. "Our lifesaver!" He contorted his face in confusion. He turned out to be a friend of the commander who'd stopped by to say hello. I guessed, at Turkish bases, you could do that. For the next couple hours, he told our story to the top officer and several of his subordinates. In longhand first, then on a Murrow-era typewriter, he wrote our report and assured officers we were in the right. According to our English-speaking friend, the other driver told everyone we were drinking alcohol and waving a flag out the window.

To counter the man's accusations, I went with a serious young private to a local doctor's office and submitted to the Turkish Breathalyzer—blowing forcefully into the physician's face. The doctor signed a sobriety statement. Kurt, meanwhile, explained the flag as his dirty shirt hanging out the window. And we were free, thanks to the translator. We obtained the police reports and registration information for the Saab insurance company.

"Is there anyway we can repay you for your generosity?" I asked. "A ride? A meal?"

"No, no. Just return the favor to a foreigner in your country sometime," he said as if he knew the opportunity would come soon.

Changing courses, we turned inland. Rugged and expansive with long, straight, two-lane highways plucked from a Wyoming plain, Central Turkey provided some of the trip's most enjoyable and dramatic drives. Compared with the rapidly developing coast covered with cheaply constructed apartment high-rises and charter planes packed full of sunburned Europeans, Central Turkey felt like traditional Turkey. The Turkey of Atatürk. We settled in for a couple weeks, bouncing between lakeside villages and mountainside hamlets and the surreal Cappadocia Valley with its Technicolor cliffs and Guadi-esque sand mountains. We hiked for days amid the desolate moonscape.

The treks and the long car rides in Turkey were an ideal time to talk to Kurt about his divorce, his fears and regrets, or any number of weighty issues I needed to crack if I was ever going to know him. Instead, I used the Saab accident as an excuse to put off those conversations for another day. Probably still peeved about that fender bender, I convinced myself. Wait until he's in a better mood. This was my delayed-wedding-present logic, as faulty then as it was now. We spent the lengthy stretches alone reading *Ivanhoe* and *Don Quixote*, talking about sports, or playing a game we called Worse Case.

"All right, worse case. You can either spend six months at a rest stop or six months straight doing nothing but watching Nickelodeon."

"Can I talk to people at either one?"

"At the rest stop, yes, but in front of the tube, no."

Whatever the answer, we'd spend the next fifteen minutes debating it. We had no problem talking—just as long as it wasn't about anything personal.

I'll get there. Just give me some time.

Driving back to our guesthouse in the village of Goreme, Kurt slammed on the brakes. A uniformed man with an automatic weapon waved us to the side of the road. Two other Turkish military personnel escorted our car to ensure we followed orders. The officers, speaking in clipped, gruff Turkish, pointed us to the back room of a souvenir stand nearby. Our questions about the detainment were met with gun waves motioning us to the room. After a few minutes a young woman asked in perfect English if we wanted tea.

"You guys pulled us out of our car at gunpoint to pour us tea?" I inquired.

She smiled and yelled something to the guards, who began laughing.

"No, we're having our census. Nobody is allowed outside, because government workers visit each house. Turks know this. Tourists don't. You might want to spend the rest of the afternoon in your hotel room. That is, unless you like looking at automatic weapons."

We ran into a snag leaving, but it wasn't because of the census questionnaire or the guns. When we walked out to the Saab, a pack of soldiers crowded around the driver's door, staring at the wood and neon display panel. They yelled among themselves and pushed a man toward us.

"Es et . . . okay . . . for my friend to drive?" asked one of the soldiers.

Kurt froze.

"Uhh, well, uhh, sure," he finally said before turning to me and whispering, "What else could I say?"

The man threw his rifle to a friend and opened the car door. Kurt gave him the keys and pointed to the ignition near the emergency brake. The soldier started the motor but kept turning the key. The engine coughed an ugly grinding sound and died. His fellow soldiers howled and yelled words of encouragement. Again he tried, letting go of the key this time. Shouts continued. With a jerky, hesitant flick of his arm, he then shifted the car into drive and peeled away. After fifteen nervous minutes, a speeding speck appeared at the end of the dusty road. I could see the car swerving, wheels touching the side of the gravel road, all at full speed. It passed us going at least a hundred miles per hour.

"This guy knows how to drive, right?" Kurt, half joking, asked a soldier standing next to him.

"No," said the soldier. "I think it's his first time."

The next week, we returned to the Turkish coast and drove on a winding two-lane highway through pine forests and steeped cliffs along the Mediterranean. Big Sur on a clear day. We stopped in Ovacik and agreed to get an early night's sleep before crossing into Syria the next day. I stared at a map on the guesthouse wall while Kurt chatted with a curly haired motorcyclist in the lobby. The man wore full riding leather that fit a bit too snug.

"Hey, Fritz, come here," he said. "My friend says we need a big insurance policy to bring the car into Syria."

The forty-year-old Czech native explained that many Middle East countries required drivers to place thousands of dollars in an escrow account. The insurance policies were a way to prevent car sales in expensive secondhand-car markets. If the motorist left the country without his car, the government would receive the escrowed money. We huddled in our room.

"Okay, option A," I said. "Drive to a border city, find a place to store the car, and take a bus in."

"No."

"Option B, try to buy this insurance over the Internet."

"No."

"Option C, bribe at the border."

"Now you're talking."

Kurt and I had driven roughly five thousand miles from Sweden, obtained new visas at the Syrian embassy in Moscow for our replacement passports, and sworn we'd reach the Middle East in the car. The chance meeting in Newport Beach with Hazem, the Syrian consul, had me convinced it was destined to happen. No flimsy insurance policy was going to stop us. Option C, bribe at the border.

Desolate and empty, the border crossing on the road to Aleppo was like no other we'd encountered. No car lines. No guards gazing at passports. No well-fed German shepherds sniffing around. Little to no activity at all. Kurt pulled the car up to the draw gate, hoping it would open somehow. Ten minutes, then twenty; nothing happened. After a half hour, a thin man with a pencil mustache walked up to the car with a look of disbelief.

"What the hell are you doing?" he said.

"Trying to drive into your country," Kurt replied.

He shook his head and pointed to a cavernous office building fifty yards behind. That's when we knew the crossing would take a while. He wore a quasi-official-looking identification pinned to his shirt pocket and asked where we were from. Sucker question number one. I said Germany, Kurt said Sweden, and he threw up his arms and mumbled something about "needing many approvals." He scrunched his brow, leaned into us and said he could help. Kurt shot me a stare. He abhorred "helpers," feeling they usually caused more problems than they solved, then charged tidy sums to help unravel the predicaments they created. "How much?"

Our friend didn't answer. Instead, he led Kurt down the florescent-lit hall to talk to an official behind a window. I sat put in a small office. Three cups of tea later, they walked in, Kurt shaking his head and whispering to me, "This is going to be tough." Continuing the maze, we followed our "helper" to a money exchange room and filled out a few lengthy forms.

"Twenty dollars to Hamid, twenty dollars to the director, twenty dollars to Ali . . ."

Kurt snapped.

"Can you please take us to see the big boss, the guy who runs this place?" he said. "We have our visas, I already paid a couple people down the hall, and I'd like to get into the country before I'm broke."

After more arm waves and protestations ("Impossible!"), the man relented and escorted us upstairs to a long rectangular office with black leather couches (*Hey, my couch!*) and large posters of Hafiz and Bashar al-Assad. Our eyes were drawn to the shiny head of a large man staring at paperwork on his desk. Our guide stood by, reiterating the car was the root of our problems. A television blared from a far corner. Glancing over, I noticed it was a CNN broadcast of the presidential debates. *Bing.* I propped up.

"My friend, will you please translate something to the boss? Will you please ask him if he prefers Bush or Gore?"

They both looked baffled, the guide asking me to repeat the question before he translated it to the border chief. The boss still didn't appear to understand. He set down his pen, looked over at the television and paused to process it all.

"Booo-sh," he said emphatically.

Bingo. I rose from the couch and reached for my wallet. A few months before the trip, I had taken Kurt to a George W. Bush fund-raiser in Beverly Hills. Irvine Company dollars put us in a VIP reception beforehand. We chatted briefly with the Texas governor and had our picture taken with him. For some unexplained, yet now clearly inspired, reason I felt I needed to carry a laminated copy with us on the trip. You never knew. I handed it to the Syrian border chief. He stared and pulled the wallet-size photograph up to his nose for a closer inspection before yelling something to the helper.

"He wants to know if a machine made this," he said.

"No. Tell him it's the real deal," I replied.

Still fixated on the photo, the boss started to smile. We nodded in agreement and grinned along. With a wave, he motioned our helper to the desk, grabbed our papers from him, and signed them with a flourish. He gave us bear hugs as we left his office.

"He's allowing you to enter Syria without having to pay for your car," said the helper. "I've never seen this happen."

"I guess I won't tell him that I have an Al Gore shot as well," I whispered to my brother.

Despite Kurt's lingering distrust, we gave the "helper" a ride into Aleppo, on the way passing through a poor village with dozens of poorly constructed cinder-block homes. A large stucco house dwarfed the others, a Newport Beach mansion in the middle of a Mexico slum.

"Wow, who owns the mansion?" I asked our guide.

"The man who just signed your papers."

Dear LaRue—

Now I know what it's like to be Michael Jordan. My jump shot needs a little work, but I can understand the feeling of walking down a street and having nearly everyone stop and stare in fascination. Welcome to the Indiana Jones world of Syria.

It's a bit disconcerting at first. Children run across busy streets to touch your shirt and walk with you. Others sprint up to the Saab as we drive. Veiled women steal glances.

Kaffiyeh-wearing men pat you on the back and say, "Welcome Syria." After a while, your guard comes down when you realize the warmth is a mix of a country starving for more contact with the West and a deeply ingrained sense of desert hospitality.

Some examples:

- The hotel owner who closed shop to help Kurt buy a few bars of Syria's famous olive oil soap;
- Non-English-speaking Syrians who hopped in our car to guide us to destinations miles away;
- The student who saw I was having problems making a long-distance call. He walked me to the post office and made the call for me;
- Countless offers to share food, have tea, visit homes, or practice English.

Most of the "foreign" countries we've visited aren't foreign at all. It's easy to draw comparisons to the U.S.

Syria is foreign.

In Turkish markets, you are likely to get run down by a small Suzuki delivery truck. In the Syrian bazaars and *souks,* you are more likely to get clobbered by a donkey with a back full of goods.

In the Syrian countryside, half-completed cinder-block homes are bunched together across gently sloped terra-cotta deserts. The cities are a jammed labyrinth of run-down, stone-colored apartments, minarets and mosques, billboards of the Assads, and vendors selling their wares on busy street corners. Traffic signs seem to be more of a suggestion than an order. There are no Cokes or McDonald's. The government bans ATMs and Internet cafes. Western music, books, or magazines are difficult if not impossible to find.

Nine out of ten women wear some sort of covering, many masking their face, hands and body with long black coats and scarves. Most of the men still sport the traditional white robe *dishdasha* and, on their heads, the red-and-white-checked *kaffiyeh*. Many walk arm in arm and kiss each other when greeting, once on one cheek then several times on the other.

The Roman ruins are spectacular and empty; the *medinas* (old cities) endlessly amusing; the hummus, stewed okra, and breads delicious; the prices unbelievably cheap (cab rides for less than a dollar, a cup of coffee for twenty cents); and the hospitality unparalleled.

Love,
Franz

DO THE HUSTLE

I used to cringe at the sight of trinket hustlers in foreign countries. You know the ones. The packs of loud women in native dress hawking cheap sweaters. The swarming taxi driver mobs at airports. The Oscar-quality child actors with hands out for handouts.

I used to wince. Then I heard my old high school football coach one day as I tried to avoid a mob of sellers. A bromide of his somehow crept back in my mind.

"The best defense is a good offense," the gravelly voice echoed.

Yes. Yes! Enough dodging and ducking. The hustlers are part of the whole travel experience. Embrace them. From that day on, I've learned to hate the seller-buyer war and love the bombardment.

Here are some of our favorite ways to throw the hustlers off their game.

Kill her with kindness

Learn how to say, "I want to buy a kiss," in the native language. It's a surefire way to immediately drive most saleswomen, and nearly all salesmen, to the other side of the street. If not, you just found a potential new foreign girlfriend.

Self-bidding war

A seller hands you a pair of sunglasses and asks for twenty dollars. Tell him there is no way you'd accept anything less than thirty dollars for such high-quality eyewear. Bid yourself up again, and he'll shake his head thinking you're crazy.

Too rich for my tastes

Expensive is the first word we learn in a foreign country. It's *mahal* in Indonesia, *caro* in Spanish-speaking countries, and *pang* in Thailand. Whatever the quoted cost, yell the word for expensive as if the price pains you. The comment will inspire a torrent of explanations why the items are properly priced and suggestions where you can take your entirely erroneous opinions.

The thespian

Happy kid playing in the street. Mom sees you coming, yells to her child. Suddenly, the boy becomes melancholy with droopy eyes and a pouting lip as he hits you up for a donation. It's an acting scene, so take part. Bury your head in your hands and cry along. Nine times out of ten, the kid will know he's been unmasked and start to laugh.

Misdirection play

When approached by a pack of vendors who speak English, ask for directions to a far-off or obscure location. They'll argue among themselves about the best route and forget about selling you anything.

Define yourself out of a job

"Taxi, taxi. Señor, you need a ride?" Kurt's favorite response to the cab hustlers is to ask them if they are "official taxi drivers." They'll say yes and wave a bogus license or useless driving certificate. "Oh, I'm sorry," he'll then say. "We only ride with unofficial taxi drivers."

Say what?

On the beaches of Brazil, we were pounded by men hawking sodas, umbrellas, and T-shirts. "I only buy from people who think Argentina is the best soccer team in the world," I'd deadpan, spawning looks of horror from the locals. The Brazilians would do anything for a sale . . . anything, that is, except renounce their beloved soccer team. Note: Do not try this technique with soccer hooligans.

Extensive tastes

From the salesman with everything, request the impossible. "Got an Etch A Sketch or a pogo stick?" But be careful for what you ask. Make sure it's way out there. My friend John Dawkins asked for a "falcon rug" as we crossed the border into California from Tijuana one afternoon. We jumped into John's van, laughing. Ten minutes later, a perspiring, panting salesman tapped on the window. He held a large, falcon-crested rug high above his head. Sold.

Language barrier

Learn a few words in an obscure language like, say, Czech. As the hustlers attack, repeat the words over and over. Point to yourself and chant the word *Czech* several times. Confused, they'll shift from English to Spanish to German to French, trying to find common ground. After a couple minutes, they'll give up in frustration and hound someone else.

Better to give

Ask and you shall receive. Someone offers you a souvenir, take it. Literally. Tell him, "Thank you for the free gift." He'll grab it back faster than a Christmas present exchange. One salesman, however, turned this technique against us. "I'm happy to give it to you," he said. "But I was hoping you would give me a gift in return. A gift of a few dollars." Ouch. Out-hustled by the hustlers.

November 2000

Dear LaRue—

Three and a half months, 7,500 miles in the new car, another 8,000 via planes, trains and ferries. Phase One of our sojourn is over. Next stop: Southeast Asia.

Kurt and I have spent the last couple of weeks squeezing the last bits of sun and ouzo out of the Greek isles; lowering fashion standards in Milan, Venice and the Italian Lake District; and soaking in the all too orderly spas of Baden-Baden, Germany.

As we head out to new corners of the world, here's a few lessons learned and confirmed thus far:

- The smiles of the children with nothing are just as big, if not bigger, than their affluent counterparts'.
- Traveler's checks are obsolete. ATMs are the world's currency; just make sure your PIN number is less than six digits. And the US dollar will often suffice. We paid for gas in Bulgaria, tolls in Turkey, and hats in Russia with American greenbacks. Next time I'm in Iowa, I'm going to try to give Russian rubles to a gas station attendant.
- I thought my to-visit list would shrink. It's grown exponentially.
- The notion that the fall of the Berlin Wall was the beginning of more prosperous times in the former Soviet Bloc is optimistic at best. The story you don't hear in the media is that the harsh hangover of the failed Communist experiment will cripple some areas for generations and leave many feeling pessimistic about capitalism as the vehicle for recovery.
- Airports have turned into malls.
- When bribing at borders of Second and Third World countries, stick to cash. We've seen offers of fruit, candy, and booze enrage border officials.
- Duke rowdies, Oakland Raider fanatics, or New York Yankee nuts seem like churchgoers compared to soccer fans. People next to us at an AC Milan–Leeds match felt it was perfectly appropriate to bring roadside flares and M-80 firecrackers, which they threw at the opposing goalie. And we were in the tame section.
- As in America, women do most of the hard work.
- Lower the latitude, crazier the driving.
- Governments cannot spend too much of their available money on infrastructure, open space, or the arts. It's called legacy.
- Open doors are often widest from the people with the least.
- Large drip coffee? Free refill? Still a foreign concept.
- Final tally. Pulled over by police: Ten times. Tickets paid: Two. Total fines: Fifteen dollars.
- And, you're right, LaRue. You never regret travel . . . or time with your brother.

Love,
Franz

13

Kurt grabbed the phone during our weekend in Newport Beach, before we were to head to Southeast Asia. Meanwhile, I examined dog-pee stains left by Fritz and Riley on the hardwood floors. *Damn dogs. No wonder Dad didn't want them.* Looking up, I saw Kurt's face morph into a question and his head nod during the ten-minute conversation.

"You're never going to believe this," he explained. "That was a CHP officer from Crescent City. Someone found my passport at a rest stop in Springfield, Oregon. They turned it in to the CHP after crossing the border into California."

"Someone's trying to impersonate you at a rest stop?"

"That's just bizarre. A rest stop in Springfield, Oregon. I'm going to call Mitch and see if anyone at Windermere knows anything. I can't believe someone would steal them."

"Did the highway patrol say anything about my passport?" I inquired.

"Nothing."

Kurt spent Sunday playing golf with friends while I surfed the Internet for information about Indonesia, Vietnam, Cambodia, and Thailand, our next four destinations. It felt revitalizing to be in California . . . at least for the first twenty-four hours. As soon as I learned the latest work and romance gossip, and visited a couple of the same old pickup bars in Newport Beach, I longed for the road. Immediately. The impulse to flee was even stronger than before. It was as if I'd been given a taste of a drug and now craved it in massive quantities. Kurt came home with a look of frustration late in the day.

"Bad round?" I asked. "You lose money?"

"Naw, I took 'em for fifty bucks."

"What's up?"

"Are you having a hard time talking to people?"

"What do you mean?"

"My buddies—they asked me a question or two about Eastern Europe, then all they wanted to talk about was Raider football."

"Just win, baby."

"I'm serious. It felt like we spoke a different language."

I knew the feeling. "How's the trip?" How do you answer that? *Um, well, I'm beginning to reconnect with my brother, still struggling over the wedding breakup, and I've seen a lot of great ruins and sunsets.* It was impossible to condense several months of foreign experiences and introspection into ten-minute conversations. Most of the time, I didn't even try. I showed Kurt a photo of a rice paddy in Indonesia and we talked about minimizing the next stopover in California between trips. We spent the last couple nights at home with Kurt's dogs.

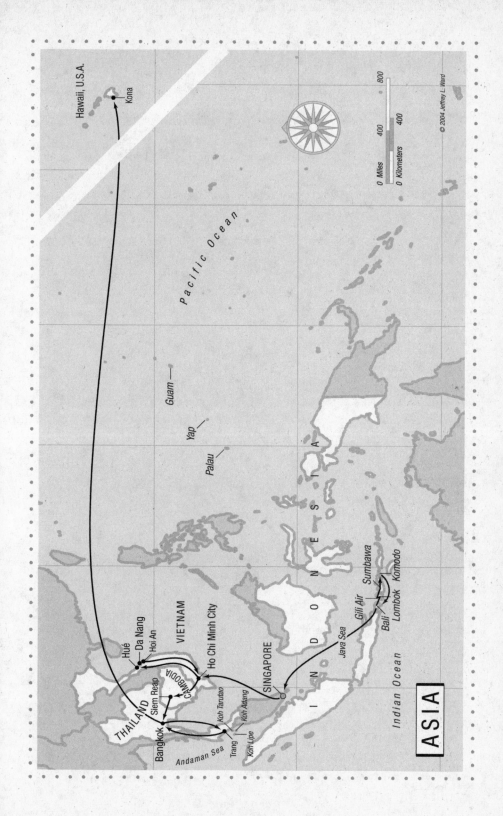

Hawaii, U.S.A.

Kona

Pacific Ocean

800

400

400

0 Miles

0 Kilometers

© 2004 Jeffrey L. Ward

Guam

Yap

Palau

I N D O N E S I A

Sumbawa

Komodo

Gili Air

Lombok

Bali

Java Sea

VIETNAM

Da Nang

Hoi An

Huê

Ho Chi Minh City

CAMBODIA

Siem Reap

SINGAPORE

THAILAND

Bangkok

Koh Tarutao

Koh Adang

Trang

Koh Lipe

Andaman Sea

Indian Ocean

ASIA

14

It wasn't the intricately carved temples or the powder sand beaches with palm trees that bowed out over the water like the stern of a ship. Our introduction to Bali was a cockfight.

Kurt noticed the gathering of people on a back street near our guesthouse in Sanur. Weary from an all-night flight, we explored the neighborhood in a zombielike trance. We'd convinced ourselves that an afternoon nap would permanently reset our internal clocks to those of a couple fraternity brothers, so we started to explore. A large man with low-riding cutoffs and ratty T-shirt motioned us over.

Locals with pantomime expressions and gestures huddled in a makeshift ten-foot-square dirt ring. A couple dozen Don Kings in flip-flops. Owners held their birds by their necks, stroking their backs, and displayed them for locals to inspect. Three other men walked around the ring, rupiah clenched in their fists, yelling back and forth between themselves and the growing batch of spectators. Then the ring cleared except for the owners. The cocks were allowed to roam. Both instantly puffed up, raising their neck feathers like a lion's mane. Their hisses spurred loud chatter in the audience. Before the birds could lunge at each other, the owners grabbed their prizefighters again by their necks and calmed them down with strokes on their heads.

Money from pockets and baseball cap linings began to fly between locals and the cockfight bankers. There were no pencils or notes on paper to record preferences. Shouts and gestures to favorites were acknowledged with nods. I fought back a sneeze, fearful the jerk of my head would commit our month's budget to the fate of a scrawny future fricassee. Other men worked with thread to attach three-inch metal blades to each cock's leg. Another large man standing next to us threw out several bills. It was a showcase of fighters, he explained, similar to trotting horses in front of the grandstand before a race. Expert bettors could spot winning clues or fatal flaws in a few seconds.

Cash exchanged, the cocks again roamed free. They lunged forward like rams butting heads. A split second before the clash, the cocks shifted their weight back and thrust their bladed legs forward. Both struck blood, one on the neck, the other on the side of the face. The crowd cheered the attack, eager for more. Dazed, the cocks lunged a second time. The larger, brown one drew more blood on the top of his opponent's leg. A chaotic flapping of wings obscured deeper damage. With the action coming to a pause, the owners lifted their birds and inspected the wounds. A young man picked away feathers from a large cut. His counterpart sucked the face of the other bird.

"He's trying to get the blood away from the eyes," our potbellied friend said. "Birds that can't see, lose."

Round one.

Amid hoots for more action, the birds were released again. This time they made a halfhearted attempt to strike each other like a couple drunken fools who'd decided to take it outside. Blood and energy trickled from their bodies. Groans stopped the fight. Someone threw a basket into the ring, large enough to hold both cocks. The confined quarters heightened the hissing. When the basket was lifted, the birds stood still, too damaged to fight on.

"It's a tie," the man groaned. "Nobody likes a tie. No money."

It didn't stop the arguments from erupting all around. The cocks could fight again, he explained. Give them a little time for the scars to heal, and they'd be back in the ring soon. He'd seen some birds fight twenty, thirty times. The Mike Tyson cocks took up to a year to prepare. They remained in confined quarters, isolated from other birds, ate the best corn, and were massaged daily to build muscle. By the time they encountered another, they were full of rage and bulging muscle.

Maybe I could be a chronicler of cockfights? Hemingway cornered the bullfighting market. Mailer's got boxing. I'll go to the birds. Write about cockfights in Southeast Asia and Latin America, detailing techniques and champions.

Another clash started within minutes. This one was quick, ruthless, and bloody. A large black bird pounced on the neck of his competitor, nearly shearing the bird's head off with a single strike from the shiny blade strapped to his leg. The crowd roared. The head dangled. Kurt and I looked at each other to see who'd throw up first.

Strike cockfight journalism from the list of potential jobs.

A couple more days in Bali and our interest in the fabled island faded as well. The tiered rice paddies and intricate temples were hypnotic and serene, but the throngs of tourists and beach salesmen pushed us to the string of islands east. We enjoyed Bali's patches of the past, but the overrun artist colonies, neon discos, beer-emblem T-shirts, and tour buses drowned out the romantic image. Kurt pushed to visit the Gili Islands off the coast of Lombok, an island that billed itself as "What Bali Used to Be." On the boat ride over, we learned the flipside of rustic.

Along with a young mother cuddling a baby girl, we hitched a ride on a wooden outrigger motorboat held together by ropes, pine tar, and constant nods from two shirtless sailors. Gili Air, one of the three Gili Islands, was less than a mile away. Gray skies forecast an imminent storm, and swollen seas forecast trouble. The mother looked nonplussed; her baby slept. The young Indonesians struggled for a half hour to jolt the dinghy's rusty engine to life.

How come, no matter what the body of water, it's always a hassle to start a draw-string motor?

Kurt and I jerked our heads when we heard the crack. A stabilizing beam in front snapped, creating a jagged hole that threatened to sink the boat. We were halfway to our destination. I looked at the child in the mother's arms and thought about the easiest way to carry the infant should we all have to swim.

On my back probably. Kurt and I can switch off. Maybe I'll bust out one of those crazy hair tows on her. The kind the Red Cross lifeguards say you should never do unless it's an emergency. This is an emergency. And she has ample hair.

The boy manning the engine yelled to his friend, who crawled out on the beam to hold it in place and curtail the flow of water entering the boat. The mother remained motionless, her child never stirred. Speaking in broken English, the boy told us "not to worry." Alfred E. Newman with a tan. The boat would hold for the remainder of the trip. Between the reassurances, the stabilizer rocked out of place with each ten-foot swell. Kurt and I grabbed empty paint cans and bailed water. Five minutes, I estimated, before the boat would sink.

The sea subsided a bit, though the destabilized stabilizer rippled cracks throughout the rest of the boat. We scanned the vessel after each thwack, searching for more holes. Seeing them, we redoubled our pace and prayed. Somehow, the boat limped into a small bay. We grabbed our backpacks and jumped into knee-deep water while lifting the mother and her baby to escort them to dry land. They looked as comfortable as if they'd stepped out of a limo and onto a red carpet. See, no problem, announced Alfred E. I saw a large cut on his foot and told him it needed a couple stitches. He laughed, both at my diagnosis and the chances of getting medical care on the rural island.

We followed him to a stand of bungalow rentals where he worked part-time. In Indonesia, even ten-hour-a-day jobs were part-time. The island path curved past a series of simple hut clusters. No paved roads, cars, sidewalks, or street hustlers. It was illegal to sell on the island, he explained. Peaceful, remote, and pristine, the

Gili Islands felt more like the Gili-gan islands. I kept expecting Mr. Howell to pop out of a bungalow, martini in hand, and attempt to rope us into a moneymaking scheme.

A group of backpackers in neighboring bungalows reinforced the location as authentic. The packers we encountered had a nose for settling in natural and remote settings. *Cheap* would be the humbug's description. A student from Wisconsin sauntered over to our hammocks wanting to talk. Another backpacker from California joined the group shortly thereafter. A group of Gili children followed him, hands outstretched, tugging at his cargo pants. "No, no, nooooo," then he fished into his pockets and pulled out a bundle of pencils and erasers decorated with farm animal cartoons in aggressive martial-arts poses. One by one, the children received their gift and flew off to tell their brothers and sisters of the newfound booty. Watching it all, I had a panic attack.

Holy shit! Most of the Third World sees America through the actions of backpackers. They're our diplomats in places like this. Our grungy Henry Kissingers. These folks must think we're all drawstring pant–wearing, Hacky-Sacking, white Rasta freaks. We're doomed.

Having heard the news, a new batch of children gathered to receive their gifts. They took one small present each, then hurried off to compare their kung fu cows with the others'. The last little girl grabbed her pencil, and the California backpacker reclined in one of the free hammocks. Bought a shopping bag full of the goods before he left the U.S., he explained. Always had some gifts in his pockets and preferred practical things like pencils over candies. My panic subsided.

If this guy's our foreign representative, we're in decent hands. He left a lot of smiles.

Our foursome dug into backpacker topic number one—spots. The best spots, the most undiscovered spots, the cheapest spots. Backpackers compared notes on hidden beaches and discount bungalows the way brokers swapped tidbits on stocks—sometimes happy to share, sometimes preferring to keep the real gems hidden, the subject usually dominating the conversation.

Most backpackers we'd come across in our five months on the road left a light and positive imprint on the lands they trekked. They strived to understand local cultures, quickly sharing among group newcomers social do's and don'ts. Sometimes with the annoying repetition of a grade-school teacher. "Now you know, in Southeast Asia, it's considered impolite to show the bottoms of your feet," we'd hear daily. They read and swapped the regional literature. Always paperbacks. Instead of splitting bills equally, they divided tabs to the precise costs of each banana pancake or fruit smoothie; and they sounded alarms to prevent shifty restaurant and hotel owners from fleecing others. They rarely griped about conditions, instead taking a perverse pride in having visited places with limited tourist comforts.

"Man, I haven't used a toilet for a month," a packer once told us.

"You must be in some serious pain," Kurt replied.

I looked to Kurt in his torn khakis and mangled flip-flops and had another panic attack.

Holy shit! We are *backpackers.*

It dawned on me that locals looked at us the same way we looked at backpackers. We'd made the conversion, especially since we were now traveling by bus and leaky outrigger instead of driving a Saab. *Members of the Packer Corps, sir, reporting for duty.* Kurt, genius at sniffing out good deals, usually scouted the areas of towns in which packers preferred to congregate. We'd share drinks and meals with them at night, emphasizing Kurt's time in Seattle and Eugene instead of my background as a Republican press secretary. We even went so far as to learn their lingo, talking about "going deep" into a nontouristy area or "cheating" a country by not spending enough time there. For the most part, we'd meld with the group. Unless, of course, they'd ask about how we got around in Eastern Europe. "We, umm, got our hands on a car. Mumble, mumble, mumble." "Duuuuude," they'd coo as if we'd told them our uncle owned a giant marijuana farm in Humboldt County and was looking for volunteers to help with the harvest. In their world of thrice-used tea bags, it was a luxury of which most could never conceive.

Most packer groups had a leader. On Gili Air that week, the general was a twenty-five-year-old New Jersey native named Chad. The others in the pack took his lead on where to swim, what to eat, when to buy hallucinogenic mushrooms from the island boys. He'd traveled for two years, common for Australians and Germans, rare for Americans. Chad had the prerequisite soul patch goatee, stringy hair, tattoos, and earring. He also had the confidence and experience of the road.

"What book are you using?" he asked Kurt one lazy afternoon.

"*Lonely Planet.*"

"*Lonely Planet,*" said Chad. "*Lonely Planet.* Excellent source of information. Use it as a reference, not as a bible."

Thus spoke Chad.

We joined His Honor and his posse for dinner one night at an outdoor patio that would, if enough packers appeared, spring into life as a restaurant. Per custom, he presided over the discussion, the agenda beginning with an introductory talk about adjusting to life in America after years on the road.

"So I had to call the States a couple weeks ago to talk to my bank," Chad said. "It's been two years since I had to deal with bureaucrats. She kept giving me the runaround and using all this corporate mumbo jumbo. I just couldn't handle it. Finally I told her, 'Miss, please. Just talk to me like you'd talk to a friend.'"

"Yeah, yeah." The table nodded in agreement. A younger member of the pack took the comment as license to launch into a tirade against America. In the back-packer world, it was fashionable and almost mandatory to bash the United States as a corrupting force that had spread its evil tentacles into the far reaches of the world (talking point #37). They'd do this in their Abercrombie & Fitch cargo pants and New Balance running shoes, while drinking Cokes at Microsoft-powered Internet terminals, listening to Eminem on their Apple MP3 players, toting their Patagonia backpacks. The most vocal critics tended to be rich and white. Kurt and I usually bit our lips. That night I had enough.

"I love America," I said to stunned silence.

Kurt shot me a look as if I'd announced I enjoyed bestiality. The group groaned and flicked their wrists and chins dismissively. Raised brows condemned the heretical comment.

"Look at the teary eyes of the people in those mass ceremonies for U.S. citizenship. Or those packed boats of illegal immigrants trying somehow, some way to reach America. Do you really think they'd leave their families and risk their lives to come to a country that is as bad as you say?

"I know what you're thinking, that they're just coming for money. Sure, that's important, but it's more than that. Way more. It's a feeling, a fresh start, a dream that keeps you awake at night thinking, 'What if?'

"You guys are judging America by what it exports—fast food, crappy movies, and such. But be honest. Dig in. Explore the negative *and* positive impacts. You know the truth. All this America bashing is hypocritical bullshit in addition to being just plain wrong."

Silence.

Whoa. Where did that come from?

More silence. Stares. I braced for the onslaught but heard nothing except a couple moths doing a kamikaze into a bug zapper. Then Chad weighed in.

"He's got a point. If I owned a company, I'd want an American running it."

The Honorable Chad had ruled. His words prompted others to discard their scripts and begin to offer words of faint praise for the U.S., like how they appreciated the well-maintained trails at natural parks or how you can buy organic produce in most supermarkets. Kurt motioned for me to let the conversation go.

Chad asked the restaurant owner if we could watch *A Perfect Storm* on the island's only VCR. An American movie. A bad American movie. A bad American movie I'd already seen.

Damn Hollywood crap. This is just another instance of America as a corrupting force spreading its evil tentacles into the far reaches of the world. Wait. Rewind. Eject.

Kurt and I finished our fish and told the gang we'd catch up with them the next day. We wandered down the beach, drawn by a faint pulse of drum and bass. The dreadlocked bartender popped up from behind the bamboo counter when we approached. He said he used to be a DJ in London and had recently settled back in Indonesia for a more peaceful lifestyle. We sat alone in the outdoor bar overlooking the moonlit water. We'd be his only customers all night.

"You see how fast those guys clammed up after Chad came to my rescue back there?"

"Yeah."

"Like fish."

"Fish don't clam."

"Whatever. You know what I mean."

"You didn't have to take the bait."

"I know," I said. "I just can't help it sometimes. It's that old press secretary in me. Especially when they take the McDonald's line of attack. For God's sake, be a little creative. At the very least, use Burger King or Wendy's."

"I hate politics."

"No, you don't."

"Hate it."

"Really? But you always talk about politics."

"No, you talk about politics. Democrats, Republicans, to me it's all the same."

"Kurt, I worked in and around government for a dozen years. Trust me, it's not all the same. For instance, you'll never catch a Republican politico in a lavender shirt and you'll never see a Dem at a Lee Greenwood concert. Plus, there's nothing wrong with good, healthy debate. Like all those talks around the dinner table when we were young."

"I don't know. I always walked away."

Our family ate meals in the kitchen under a large metal light fixture hung so low my father would bang his head twice a week, swear, and vow to yank the light out by the end of the day. Breakfast was a free-for-all. Come anytime and grab a neon-colored cereal box from the cupboard. Dinners began a half hour after our dad came home from work. Without fail. Attendance was mandatory, a requirement never questioned.

When relatives joined the mix, we'd shift settings to the big farm table in the dining room, with its large brick fireplace and antique copper ale dispensers and milk cans. As the fire burned down and wineglasses emptied, the conversations usually shifted to politics. That was it, showtime, the moment I'd awaited all meal. I'd sit up in my chair and polish off my food so I could participate in the upcoming debate without distraction.

Now, adding your views to the boiling political discussion was a risky prospect. A wrong fact or ill-advised reasoning would result in verbal reprimands from the rest of the table. Mostly I listened, but the older I got, the more intrepid I became. For hours, we'd plow through topics du jour—taxes, social security, the death penalty, elections, education. A nod or two from an older cousin would embolden me to continue. A stare or a lean on the table from an uncle sent me back to silent observation. The discourse was a trial-and-error process, though with each meal I became more comfortable and more convinced politics was my calling. I was too engrossed to notice Kurt had usually left the table. Until now.

"Why'd you bolt?" I asked as our Indonesian DJ mixed rum and techno beats.

"I dunno. Seemed like it was something between you and Dad."

Ahh, I see.

"I see."

"No big deal."

"You're not angry about that, are you?"

"Nah. The way I see it is you and Dad have spun your wheels and wasted a lot of time talking about issues that never get solved."

Ouch. It's tough to dismiss a career in a single sentence.

"The politics and the lobbying are paying for our drinks tonight."

"I didn't mean it like that."

He stared at his beer and waited.

"You know, Mom used to send me clips of you in the papers talking about some subject as the 'governor's spokesman.' I always thought that sounded so cool. 'Governor's spokesman.' I started to pin 'em on the wall. But then all the guys in the office would want to talk about California politics. So I took them down. Got 'em in a file somewhere if you ever need one."

"Thanks," I said. "I'll remember that. And, hey. I just remembered. George W.'s photo got us into Syria."

"To W.'s photo," he said, raising his glass. "Or Gore's, if he wins."

The heated sessions on *The McLaughlin Group,* the political arguments with Jonathan Terra, the Senate speeches and campaign debates, the discussions over the family dinner table—they didn't seem so important anymore.

Dear LaRue—

One of the first images I saw in Indonesia was a beautiful, sarong-clad woman walking along a country road with baskets of fruit piled high on her head. Her young daughter scampered beside. Without warning, the woman spun around, dipped down, and spanked her child on the hindquarters, all without spilling the fruit. The scene was a decent metaphor for Indonesia today—pretty, delicately balanced, and not afraid to use force (see Timor).

How do you govern a place with 13,700 islands, the world's fourth-largest population, and large divisions of Muslims, Hindus, Buddhists, and Christians? Couple that with a local currency that has plummeted since the Asian financial crisis, and the short answer is you don't. You do what many tourists do here—just ride the legendary waves.

The current leader is a man named Abdurrahman Wahid, commonly known as Gus Dur. In the two weeks we've been here, Gus Dur has been accused of graft, cronyism, corruption, incompetence, and saying naughty things to other Asian leaders. He also proposed to make Arabic the official language of Southeast Asia, an idea that has gone over about as well as a midday Bin Tang beer and plate of *gado-gado* (cooked vegetables with a spicy peanut sauce) during the current Islamic fasting month of Ramadan.

Despite the politics, I love the vivid and exotic images of this nation of islands: the mud-soaked water buffalo pulling men on large wooden rakes through terraced rice fields; Bali's moss-covered, incense-soaked, stone Hindu temples with peaceful lily ponds and chanting priests; or the remote, postcard beaches shared by adventurous tourists, a few cows, and dilapidated outrigger fishing boats. The colorful and crazy town markets clog the roads on the outer islands. Adults sell fish, chickens, and fruits in woven baskets strewn everywhere. Smiling children pile high atop carts and buses, watching it all.

If we ever disappear, you might find us in the Gili islands off the coast of Lombok. They have all the ingredients for the real escape—no cars, no roads, sporadic electricity and water service. The beach shacks cost four dollars a night . . . for two . . . including all the mangos, bananas, and pancakes you can eat for breakfast. And the hammocks help you speed through those books you always wanted to read.

Love,
Franz

After a few more days with Chad and his sycophants, Kurt and I left Gili Air for the shores of southern Lombok. We checked into a small, one-star hotel in the sleepy village of Kuta. I woke one morning, early and hungry. Kurt dozed. I pulled on my shorts and wandered to the common area for breakfast and some coffee. With no one else around, I opened my paperback and began to read. A young woman with a chipped-tooth grin approached the table. In broken English, she asked if she could sit down.

She was twenty-two, though her sun-stained skin made her look a decade older. Her family had been in the area for generations. Her eight brothers and sisters all lived nearby. They survived by working in the rice fields, she said. Twelve was her age when she started. The sun she could deal with. That was nothing compared with the disease-infested insects that thrived in the paddocks, the snakes, or the way her skin rotted after ten hours in the water. She made a dollar each day and brought her own lunch. When the hotel opened, she begged a friend to help her land a job at the front desk. The occasional night shift didn't faze her.

"Now I make two dollars a day," she exclaimed. "Plus two meals. And I work inside!"

Did I have an extra book? she asked. The rice fields pulled her from school at an early age. She'd scrapped together piecemeal English by talking to guests. The books and conversations would help her master the language and advance to other jobs at the hotel, like arranging tours or flights. I wanted to send her on a Barnes & Noble shopping spree. The only book I had was *Don Quixote,* a copy I'd acquired from a hotel book swap, the customary method for refreshing our traveling library. I told her she could have it, then felt like a swim instructor who'd just ordered his five-year-olds to take a few laps of butterfly. Something told me she could handle it. We practiced verbs for the next hour until the guests woke and she had to get back to work. I helped her with her English, but she taught me much more.

Our lessons from the road were different from classroom teachings. They were casual, unstructured, coming in random places from unlikely sources. Still, they were powerful. And I struggled to piece their meanings together. From afar, the rice worker's job promotion would have seemed insignificant and small. Here, as she raved about her new position and showed me the scars on her legs from the fields, I felt the enormous power of perceived opportunity, sustenance on hope and faith. While she gushed about finding a job indoors, I thought about The Irvine Company and all the times I griped about my shrunken office and the loss of my beloved leather couch. I wanted to go yank it out of my successor's office and ship it to Lombok.

Later that same morning, Kurt asked a young South African couple if they wanted to join us for fried eggs and bananas. Vagabonds love company. Especially if they've heard the same story ad nauseam about playing golf with the keyboardist for Steppenwolf (Kurt) or tearing an ACL during a pickup football game but still making the play (me). The man looked depressed, his blonde bride flustered. They declined at first, then changed their minds.

He told us they'd been robbed at knifepoint the previous day. The thieves appeared on a back road and flagged them down on their rented scooters. After one thug pulled a machete, the South Africans readily handed over their wallets and motorbikes. A mixture of anger and fear still lingered. The scooter rental agency refused to give them their passports until the matter was resolved. In the meantime, they demanded the couple pay them one thousand dollars to cover the cost of the stolen bikes. The couple didn't have the money. Without passports or cash, they sat frozen and angry.

We were stunned. The islands and their people seemed Fred-Rogers peaceful. We sensed little crime or political upheaval as documented in the newspapers. I felt

136

as safe in Indonesia as anywhere else on the trip. Even on the outer islands. The South Africans planned to drive a few hours to the town of Mataram to see what they could salvage at a bank and a government agency. They accepted our offer to take them to dinner that night.

Kurt picked a curry restaurant for our evening meal on the other end of the village. Minutes after we ordered, a plainclothes police officer approached the table and announced the bikes and wallets had been recovered. It didn't surprise me. Lombok survived on tourist dollars. Incidents like this were treated with the utmost urgency. The government and police did everything they could to prevent or solve them. Soon we learned to what extent.

Sitting down, the policeman bragged one of the robbers had been shot through the leg, while the other was severely beaten. He explained police went to every house in the village demanding information. They quickly learned the culprits were from out of town and hiding out in a house nearby. "Lucky to be alive," he boasted.

The South Africans, self-professed progressives, reacted at first like right-wingers at a Texas execution. They loved the news and were thrilled to have their money, passports, and scooters returned. As the evening passed, the husband started to question the situation. What if the guy shot wasn't one of the robbers? How much force was used to obtain the hideout lead? He was still happy with the outcome, though less giddy with the means. His wife echoed his concerns, talking about indiscriminate treatment of criminals and the lack of checks against the Indonesian police force. By the end of the meal, they'd forgotten about the scooters and talked solely about the country's thug law.

Friday morning, Kurt and I greeted the day by bickering over dragons—the Komodo dragons. I pushed to go to Flores rather than spend a day coming and going to Komodo Island. Kurt argued it would be a sin to come that far and not make the attempt to see the modern-day dinosaurs, up to ten feet long and weighing two hundred pounds. A couple of packers on Gili Air praised the trek, which strengthened Kurt's determination. So did his memory.

"You've picked every spot on this trip," he said.

"What are you talking about?"

"Croatia, Istanbul, Moscow. You're the one who said we should go."

I didn't know if he was softening me up as he would a street salesman or if he really believed I dictated our ports of call.

"You're full of shit. You were the one who pushed for Moscow. Prague, too. And are you griping about those places? I don't remember you being too upset with that giddy blonde in Russia."

"Look, you're the one who decided when we'd go in the first place. I waited for you until your bonus came."

Bastard. Playing dirty. Next thing he'll bring up is moving down to Newport Beach.

"Fine," I said. "We'll go see the dragons."

We headed to the airport to inquire about flights. No planes to Komodo, the attendant told us. We'd need to fly to Sumbawa Island and take the overnight ferry to Flores, then on to Komodo. The journey would take at least a day longer than we thought. A small plane left in a couple hours. Kurt managed to get us on, while I started a mental tally on the merits of the trip. *Score one point for each of us.*

Arriving in the town of Bima, the taxi hustlers swarmed us. To part the chaos, we started a conversation with a French couple on a dragon quest as well. She talked, he smoked. They agreed to share a cab to the port town of Sape three hours away.

"Impossible!" declared the taxi supervisor. "Sharing taxis is not allowed."

"What kind of a rule is that?" Kurt asked in disbelief.

"Official taxi rules."

"So, Gus Dur can cheat this country out of millions, but we can't share a cab?"

"Yes."

"Okay. Just wanted to get that straight."

I'll take the point.

Kurt motioned me to bypass the taxi hoard, walk outside the airport, and hitch a ride instead. We told the French couple we'd see them in Sape. "Scan-dal!" Before long, an old man with a toothless grin pulled up in a clunker white van. Abdullah was his name. His wife sat in the passenger seat. "Second wife," he bragged when she wasn't in earshot. Second as in "the two don't know about each other" second. He'd give us a ride to Sape for a couple dollars. Kurt said he'd threaten to leak the secret should Abdullah try to rip us off. *The score's back to even.*

"You know the ferry is broken," Abdullah said. "And they're having problems finding parts. Things move slow here."

Two points for me. At least.

"Whatever," Kurt said to me. "We'll find a way. Just another test."

A mile-long line of cargo trucks greeted us at the port, the queue confirming the broken ferry service, down for a week with no sign of resuming. My tally grew. Nothing to do but wait. The French couple, having discovered the same news, approached us. Kurt cornered a young boy and asked his advice. Renting a fishing boat, he stated, was the only option. Within five minutes, fishermen and entrepreneurs looking to charter a boat for outrageous prices surrounded Kurt. Five hundred dollars, they shouted. Six hundred dollars for a boat with beds.

The couple's English was poor, the Indonesians' French nonexistent, so they left the negotiating to Kurt. We all agreed to hire a boat, but only at a lowered price. Kurt set two hundred dollars as our goal. He went to work, inspecting boats, pounding on costs. The salesmen cut their fees, first to four hundred dollars, then to three hundred. It was still a lot of money by Indonesian standards, ridiculous by backpacker standards. We'd grown accustomed to four-dollar rooms and dollar cab rides. A couple hours of hard bargaining later, Kurt threw up his arms and walked away. I was ready to close the roll and tally the votes, almost happy that we were being thwarted because it would strengthen my suggestions down the road.

Why don't you just say "na-na-na-NA-na" and complete your transformation into a fourth-grader?

I forgot that Kurt was a cat who almost always landed on his feet. A half hour later, a man agreed to charter a boat for two hundred dollars. We'd have to leave at 3 A.M., he said, to get there by noon. We'd spend the afternoon in search of the dragons and return at night.

The seas had been heavy of late. They were difficult to manage even during calm periods, one of the reasons why the dragons were isolated to a couple specks of land. An eight-hour boat ride could turn into a twenty-four-hour odyssey. Be prepared, he said. The Frenchman looked at his cigarette supply.

Abdullah, who'd hung around all afternoon to watch the bargaining process and work himself into the deal, took us to the "nicest hotel in town," a rickety wooden shack built on stilts over water. Strike that. Over *sewage* water. The rooms had inch-thick mattresses on the floor, a single bulb on an exposed wire hanging from the ceiling, and broken slats for windows. Our choice was either to take a steam bath all night with the windows closed or open them for a potent combination of bugs and waste wafts. *Two points for the senior Wisner.*

Abdullah kicked the mattress as the hotel owner showed us the place. He suggested we go to dinner to "celebrate" the culmination of his "successful efforts." Other than his nap in his van, telling boat owners how much to overcharge us, and pocketing a finder's fee from the hotel owner, we had a hard time pinpointing exactly what he meant by "successful efforts." And "celebrations," we'd learned, usually meant a gringo picking up the tab.

We were too tired to look for another place. We'd seen few others on the way into town that would top it. Plus, the shack was one hundred yards from the docks. We didn't trust Abdullah to drive us from a more remote location at 3 A.M. Kurt said he would buy him dinner if he promised to give us a ride back to the Bima airport the following day. We shared greasy chicken with Abdullah and wife number two, took baths in an oil drum outside the hotel, and crashed on the wafer-thin mattresses. The closed window did nothing to stem the stench from the water. We opened the slats, rubbed BenGay under our noses, and covered our bodies in DEET. Kurt dozed off. I went downstairs for a pee, only to realize, midstream, I had BenGay all over my hands. I jumped back in the oil drum/bathtub and cursed the names Kurt and Abdullah and wife number two.

The park guide on Komodo Island looked surprised as we walked into the ranger station the next day. The broken ferry meant we had the entire island national park to ourselves. He hesitated when Kurt asked him to lead us on a private tour at the hottest time of the day. The French couple pleaded. Kurt pulled out our George W. Bush photo. Desperate times deserved desperate measures. The guide, Luis, asked if the picture had been doctored.

"We're here to scout future presidential visits," Kurt said. "Bush wants to see the Komodo dragons before he meets with any foreign leaders."

"You're lying," he said with a grin.

"Yes. They want to wait until the results are official."

"I'll give you a tour if I can keep the photo."

"Done."

We had other copies.

Luis led us around the bush for the rest of the scorching afternoon. He explained how the dragons waited for deer to pass, sensing them by smell and with their yellow tongue, which helped them sample the air. They'd then lunge at their victims, pushing them to the ground and tearing them to pieces.

Luis had just finished talking about the large chunks of meat the dragons could digest when we spotted a female sleeping under a tree, well camouflaged within fallen leaves. Kurt nearly stepped on her. She roused and ambled away from us. Luis chose this part of the tour as the ideal time to recount how a couple visitors were once devoured after stumbling on sleeping dragons. I don't think Kurt heard the story. He was too busy quick-stepping ahead of the beast for a photo. The massive and muscular creature snapped her head toward the rest of us and broke into a trot down the side of a hill. Watching this graceful genetic leftover from another age lumber away, I knew Kurt had been right all along. I discarded the point system. For good.

My tendency with Kurt was to freeze our relationship in its childhood form, to view him as someone who wore my outgrown clothes rather than the adult he'd become. The honeymoon and the dragons began to bring us on a more even footing, erasing traditional roles and forging new ones. The truth is, Kurt is better at itineraries. Always has been. He has much keener street intuition, though he thinks the term is demeaning, and a stronger nose for action and opportunity. It just took me thirty-four years and twenty-plus countries to figure that out.

RUNNING WITH THE PACK

There's an army out there. Bigger than Mother Russia's. More tenacious than Afghanistan's rebels. Noses in more countries than the old British Navy.

Lose the wheeled Samsonite, grab an equally expensive backpack by North Face, and enlist in the People's Army of Concerned Kids—the Packers.

They cringe at the thought, but Packer wear is more uniform than military dress whites. Tevas or other rubber-soled sandals are the base. Add socks if you're German. Cargo pants or zip-off Gore-Tex trousers are next. Orange and purple for the Europeans, black and blue for the Americans.

T-shirts, long and short sleeve, are obligatory. Five points if the shirt displays the logo of an obscure product or outdated television show—Brillo pads or *Starsky & Hutch,* for example. Ten points for advertising an organization that cares. Anything with "Save Our . . . " or "Concerned Citizens . . . " will do. Bonus round for shirts promoting a remote destination inaccessible to the tour buses: "The Mystic Mayan Mines of Myanmar."

Bo Derek cornrows and Bob Marley dreadlocks will draw silent, unenthusiastic nods of approval from the community. Rings through noses, eyelids, chins, tongues, and belly buttons barely garner notice anymore. Tribal band tattoos around arms and painted mosaics on lower backs are very prevalent, though usually on the bodies of club newcomers. Henna-dyed hands and faces tattooed like Maori warriors are more cutting edge.

Packer wear is fully androgynous, with uniforms for men and women often indistinguishable. In fact, the men and women themselves are often indistinguishable.

Like officers' clubs and army towns, Packers prefer to bunch together along streets, in neighborhoods, and throughout pack-friendly cities. Most towns will have a Packer-designated section. If you're looking for a cheap hotel near plenty of vegan restaurants and incense stands, just show your backpack to the cabdriver and you'll be whisked there. Used bookstores, Internet cafés, natural food carts, and discount travel agencies comprise the prototypical Packer block. Khao San Road in Bangkok or the Sultanahmet neighborhood in Istanbul are the types of places that make Packers sit back in their hammocks and go "ahhhhhh." But remember, Katmandu is the Mecca. At least one pilgrimage is necessary for exalted status.

Boot camp, or shall I say Teva camp, is the three-month, dozen-country European summer spent hopping trains with a Eurail pass. Packers learn to find the best cots in hostels, wash socks with hand soap in sinks, and look forward to cold Nescafe and stale bread for breakfast. Museums and historical sites are out. They cost money. Instead, Packers learn to glean the experiences through stories of the one well-to-do comrade who can afford to go and is happy to tell all the group while waiting for the next midnight train: "Dude, that Mona Lisa babe is the bomb."

In conventional armies, stars and bars identify rank. The Packer hierarchy is maintained through the first topic broached—years on the road, or, more specifically, "How long you been out?"

Rookie status for three months or less. Year-outs are the equivalent of bank vice presidents—decent title but there's plenty of them. Two years on the road and you're an Australian general, a rank bestowed to honor the concept of Aboriginal walkabouts. Two to five years and you're out on top. More than five years and you're just out . . . out of your mind. Five-plus years and even the backpackers begin to think you should put on a tie.

No five-hundred-dollar hammers or other overcharges in the Packer brigade. Forty dollars for an eight-hour train ride versus fifty dollars for a flight covering the same distance in less than an hour? No question. Hop on the bus, Gus, because time is an unlimited commodity. Kurt says Packers have alligator arms—they have a hard time reaching their wallets.

I can't be too hard on Packers, especially because I often resembled them. And like the Salvation Army, they fight wars every day . . . and sometimes win.

Iran. China. Eastern Europe. Packers are often the first tourists into a country after travel restrictions have been lifted. They're the West's initial, albeit shaggy, diplomats.

An old Packer once told me he received the first visa into Bangladesh after their war of independence. Bewildered guards at the border didn't know what to do with him, so they called the new president. He didn't know what to do either, so he invited the backpacker to stay at his house for two weeks. Great story. Don't know if it's true. But I do know that as soon as a country opens up, the Packer army stakes out positions years before Starbucks picks a street corner.

Kudos are awarded in the Packer community for knowing the language, wearing local garb, or understanding traditions. Locals appreciate the effort, partly for understanding, partly for laughs. The longhaired American who chows down a guinea pig lunch in Peru performs two valuable services: he gives Peruvians a reason to smile and allows the rest of us to skip guinea pig and eat pizza. *Gracias, amigo.*

The Packer push has led to more book exchanges, chai teas, deep-tissue massages, Internet hookups, hemp clothing, last-minute-travel fares, natural juices, and Right Guard sales around the globe.

Whoops. Strike the last one, but sign me up.

15

On one of our first nights in Vietnam, we wanted a good dinner at a Ho Chi Minh City restaurant that served tasty spring rolls, steaming noodle and fish soups with lemongrass, chicken dishes smothered in spicy peanut sauces. We'd prowled around and through the vent-size Cu Chi Tunnels all day, listening to a wiry ex–Viet Cong soldier cackle repeatedly while demonstrating bamboo booby traps designed to impale American soldiers. Enough of the war. We wanted to sit in a local's joint, point at a couple plates, and gorge ourselves.

I grabbed our copy of *Lonely Planet,* the road's most popular guidebook. Despite Chad's warning, we clung to the text for a recommendation. I read a couple descriptions to Kurt, who stopped me on "the one," a place the book described as a find for travelers seeking an authentic Vietnamese meal.

We hopped a ride with locals eager to give lifts on their scooters for a couple dong, the world's most unfortunately named currency. The street scene felt like a fast-forward start of the New York City Marathon. Hundreds of hyper-aggressive motorists scrambled for pole position, bumping into one another and racing like banshees so . . . so . . . well, so they could get to the next light and start the process all over again. Only a handful could afford helmets. I feared for my life at first and asked the rider to slow down. A near-crash sent my mind to the retiree who endangers and enrages everyone around him by driving forty miles an hour on the freeway. "Step on it," I then urged the scooter man. After a couple blocks, I became convinced my guy wasn't any crazier than the rest and actually enjoyed the final stretch.

We walked into the restaurant and froze. An "I told you so" image of Chad flashed as if he were Big Brother on the big screen: *"Use it as a reference, not as a bible."* We saw ten tables, Anglo faces at each one. All had dog-eared guidebooks on their laps, chairs, or placemats. Mass at the Church of the *Lonely Planet.*

"This is ridiculous," I said to Kurt. "Even if the food here is great, I want to go somewhere where I don't feel like I'm at T.G.I. Friday's. Ten bucks says they have a potato skin/green tea happy hour here. Let's bolt."

We walked a couple blocks down the street and stopped to watch a surprisingly good fight between a woman ("She's gotta be around sixty") and a drunken young man. She pummeled him with her purse several times before bystanders stepped in and broke up the brawl. Lucky for him.

"He stole money from her," a pudgy, twenty-something Vietnamese man explained.

"Ouch," I said.

"Yes," Quan replied. "Vietnamese women are very tough."

"Apparently."

Quan worked at a small tourist agency that led backpacker trips to the Mekong Delta and to beach communities along the coast. He had tea-stained teeth and teacup-shaped hands. He began the dialogue with standard questions about our length of stay, nationality, and relationship to each other. We'd tired of these questions by now and had started trying to fast-forward such conversations. Kurt told everyone we were on "official Russian business."

Something about Quan—his calm demeanor, perhaps—told us he was not a typical tour hustler. We griped about the restaurant scene a couple blocks back. Laughing, he said the food was good, but the only reason it made the book was because of an aggressive, palm-greasing owner. He offered to show us a better place for dinner. "Fraaaannhhhk," he called me.

Quan wove us through several crowded streets to a ramshackle, one-room kitchen with steam streaming from the back as if haunted. An elderly, hunched-over woman led us to one of the preschool-size plastic table and chair sets outside on a busy sidewalk. *Hey, these chairs would have been perfect for my shrunken office at The Irvine Company.* Moments later, unprompted, she plopped down a pitcher of beer and a couple plates of spring rolls coated with mounds of fresh basil. Quan lit a cigarette and motioned us to eat, eat. He didn't, choosing instead to smoke and swap comments with surrounding restaurant-goers unaccustomed to Western company.

A limping, unwashed teenage boy positioned a piece of cardboard to sleep on a sidewalk corner nearby. Late-night salesmen pushed their gaslight carts along the edges of the street. A group of beggar girls approached the table selling gum. The men around us tried to shoo them away with threatened backhands. The youngest girl ignored them, staring at me with eyes hardened beyond her years. She held out a pack. I reached for my pocket. Quan cautioned not to give her the money. I handed her a couple dollars anyway and told her to keep the gum. Within five minutes, a dozen more girls surrounded the table. The old woman proprietor tapped them away with a broom. I told Quan I was sorry.

"That's the meal I was talking about," I said to Kurt as we rambled back to the hotel.

"Best spring rolls I've ever had," he said.

"Agreed. Tasted like Fritz and Riley."

"Nahhh," he said, stunned. "You think? Dog?"

"Roll the dice. You never know."

As we entered the room, I grabbed our *Lonely Planet* and hurled it across the bed, knocking over the trash can.

"Fuck that thing," I said. "I'm sick of the cult of the *Lonely Planet*. And I'm sick of hanging out with *Lonely Planet* groupies. Plus, how can this planet ever be lonely if we all congregate in the same cafés and youth hostels sipping our teas and patting each other on the back for avoiding tourist traps?"

"Wow," Kurt responded. "I haven't seen you this worked up since Jana wouldn't leave Terra's apartment in Prague for four days."

"This is no way to travel. Chad was right that it's no bible. But he's wrong about it being a decent reference. I think it's useless. How many times have they been wrong about cab fares or visa options? Plenty. We're not using guidebooks anymore."

The truth was we had already started to phase them out over the past few months. In Eastern Europe, we relied more on friends and recommendations from locals. We referred to the guidebooks mainly for hotels and sights, but preferred to ask around now. I decided we'd go cold turkey.

"Think about it, Kurt. Somebody comes to Los Angeles. The guidebook is going to tell them to go to the Hollywood Walk of Stars and the Santa Monica Promenade, where they can devour the same Cinnabon cinnamon rolls and Jamba Juice found in every other strip mall in America. But let's say that person spends five minutes talking to you. You're going to send him on a hidden hike in Malibu or to a couple killer restaurants in Los Feliz. What's the better experience?"

"I'm with you," he said, laughing.

"Then what's so funny?" I asked.

"It's funny that Quan, a tour guide, would help convince you to ditch tour books."

Talk to everyone; it was a habit we inherited from our mom. From that day on, we relied solely on residents for basic information about everything—ATMs, exchange rates, transportation, cultural do's and don'ts, in addition to recommendations for a "true" experience. The conversations opened us to a different world. If we were specific in our questions and desires, the best recommendations usually far surpassed those found in the books. Like the curbside restaurants in Vietnam that served heaping bowls of tofu soup for thirty cents. Or the expert silk tailors who produced fitted shirts in an hour. Or the crumbling but still breathtaking mountain temples off the tour bus stops. Karma travel, we dubbed it, spontaneous journeys shaped solely through contacts and feel.

I lay awake that night and began to think about life the same way. When I'd forced it to conform "according to plan," it usually felt like the times I tried to cram a dozen museum and church visits into a weekend trip. It was eye-glazing, unrewarding, artificial, and just not much fun. I would have known that had I taken a few minutes to step back. But I didn't. I just plowed through, determined to live according to the guidebooks of life. I was going to marry Annie, despite ample signs it would never work. I had to make vice president, damn it. On one Saturday in London I was going to visit the Tate Museum, War Museum, Parliament, St. Paul's, and Buckingham Palace even if it killed me. It's what the guidebooks said I had to do. From a small bed in a Saigon hotel, I threw it all in the wastebasket next to my *Lonely Planet*.

A friend of Kurt gave us the name of Tom Allen, a Californian living in Saigon. He sounded surprised to hear from an American visitor. At his suggestion, we met for drinks on the roof deck of the Caravelle Hotel, a modern building that looked straight from a Midwest America skyline. A shy, doll-faced young woman named Tu joined the group. Kurt met her earlier in the day and convinced her to come along. She let Kurt drive her scooter to the hotel, but refused to grab his waist as she sat sidesaddle. Didn't want to give her countrymen a reason to gossip, she said.

Tom came to Vietnam for the first time in 1993. He read an advertisement in an American business magazine for medical equipment sales. The Bush administration had recently opened doors for humanitarian trade. Having bombed out of law school, Tom decided the Vietnamese frontier seemed as promising as any. He went with a friend and a suitcase full of brochures and high expectations. Within months, he lost them all. The friend's appendix burst, earning him a foot-long scar courtesy of a stitch-happy, Soviet-trained Vietnamese doctor. Tom, meanwhile, discovered several Japanese companies had already cornered the markets. They offered comparable products at prices well below Tom's. He aborted his plan and returned home.

So he did what many Americans often do after they fail at something—he wrote about it. Despite never having succeeded at business in Vietnam, he published an article about succeeding at business in Vietnam. Suddenly, he was an authority and in demand. A lock company, paint distributor, and mosquito-netting supplier contacted him with offers to peddle their wares. Tom gathered samples, booked space at a Saigon trade fair, and headed across the Pacific again.

This time he left his naivete at home. The first go-around, he saw foreigners come to the country demanding to do business their way. The Vietnamese population didn't trust orders from white males, and the overseas businessmen soon retreated. Tom adopted a different route. When possible, he sold locks and paint to foreign-owned firms building hotels throughout the country. When Vietnamese companies offered work, he made sure he partnered with residents. He talked to us about opportunities and growing pains.

"You have to understand that the top government officials who oversee the economy got their jobs because they were good soldiers. Most had no training in economics. Then after the war, the Russians moved in and taught them their screwed-up ideas about business. Top it off with a heavy layer of corruption and false pride and I'm surprised that the economy progresses at all."

He'd learned from his mistakes and carved out a niche market focusing on locks and doors. His business, like the economy itself, chugged along with steady progress. The bigger gains, he said, had been in his personal life.

Yen caught his eye for the first time at the Intershop, a helter-skelter emporium of kiosks selling peasant shirts, Tommy Hilfiger jeans, Day-Glo candies in glass barrels, natural-remedy aphrodisiacs, and any Western good on which they could get their hands. Yen ran a women's wear booth with a mixture of American and Vietnamese clothing styles. Her silky hair and shy smile—that's what he remembered. He walked by several times before asking her to dinner.

As middle ground, he chose a Japanese restaurant. Yen came in a formal white *ao dai*. Tom liked that. The flowing dress-shirt said she was serious about the date. She didn't want people to confuse their outing as a fling. She'd never eaten sushi, so he chose miso soup and tempura to begin. The next time to the restaurant they devoured sashimi. And each other. Within two months he moved into her small apartment in the Ben Thanh district outside town.

After a year, they moved to a bigger place closer to the city center. She opened another shop selling tailored women's clothing, her joy, while he continued to build his lock and door business. They agreed the small profits from her store didn't justify the long hours, nor would it be good for the family they planned. She closed doors and went to work with him. The relationship, once exclusively a romance, was now a partnership as well.

Tom wanted to get married, but first he wanted Yen to know what she was getting into. In the spirit of full disclosure, they flew to California to meet his parents. He took Yen to San Francisco and Lake Tahoe for some sightseeing, but he thought she was most impressed with a visit to Safeway. She stole glances at the endless aisles of fresh fruits piled like pyramids and castles of canned everything, at the automatic misters in the vegetable aisle, at *Star Wars* scan guns in the checkout line, at the coupon dispensers that talked to shoppers. All the while, she said nothing. Only years later would she relate how overwhelming the shopping experience was for her.

One night at his parents' house, Yen pulled out a hand-embroidered tablecloth. She draped it across a coffee table in the living room and asked his mother and father to sit on the couch. Tom had no idea what she was doing. Yen carefully arranged four teacups and opened a bottle of Vietnamese wine. She dropped to her knees and served his parents. Formal, serious, gracious, she thanked them for condoning the relationship with Tom and asked for their blessing in the future. His mother started to cry.

They got married in Saigon. He wore a business suit, she the traditional red and gold *ao dai*. As customary, the event lasted all day, starting with a brunch and a traditional ceremony at the restored Rex Hotel. More than anything, Vietnamese marriages are considered a celebration between families. The official wedding took place in the old Catholic church downtown on a Thursday at 5 P.M. The astrologers said it was their lucky time. Yen got pregnant on their honeymoon in Bali. Nine months to the day, they welcomed a son. Another followed twenty-three months later.

Tom talked about the luxuries of living in Saigon's District One. Though his business was still small, he employed three maids at home and a driver to shuttle the family around in a Toyota SUV.

"You get spoiled," he said. "Anything you want is a call away. And you can get it delivered. You get used to that."

Yen is a good counter. She sees wealth as communal and insists on giving large chunks of their earnings to the less fortunate. Tom believes in that now.

"I love it," Kurt said. "A perfect Vietnamese romance. You never know, Tu, it could happen to us."

"It's Tu," she said, pronouncing her name "D'ew."

"Tu."

"D'ew."

"How do you spell it?

"*T-U.*"

"That's what I said, Tu."

"D'ew."

"Duh," he fumbled.

"D'ew."

150

"Anybody hungry? Up for some food?"

Tom pointed us to Mogambo, a couple blocks away. With its bamboo furniture, stuffed animal heads on the wall, and Christmas lights, the joint looked like a kitschy mainstay of the Sunset Strip in Los Angeles. A sign above the bar promoted beef from Texas. The bartender poured Budweiser.

"So much for sticking to the locals' joints," I told Kurt after entering.

We decided to go with it. After a month of noodle and rice dishes, a hamburger that night didn't sound half bad. An older American man with graying blond hair and a bowling-ball belly protruding from a black tank top sat in the booth beside us. He lit a cigarette and stared at Kurt. It wasn't his first time here. He wanted to talk. Most single drinkers do. Kurt took the bait.

She was eighteen, he said. They'd dated for a couple years before she moved in. Told everyone he was her husband, though they weren't married. That's because he was already married. Married to a Vietnamese woman closer to his age. He met her during the war and asked for her hand shortly thereafter. He said he was tired of life in the United States. Fuck taxes. Fuck the government. Fuck the women. Fuck. So he sold his house and left his midlevel, pocket-protector aerospace job in Southern California to start anew in Vietnam.

Women knew their place here, he said. One only too well. His Vietnamese wife. She clung to the marriage like a widow to an insurance policy. Scores of attractive, young, obedient women beckoned, he bragged. If he could just convince "the bitch" to sign the papers. He'd offered five thousand dollars. Too low. So he offered ten thousand. Okay, she said, send me the money. He delivered the cash in person, only to find a few days later "she changed her mind." He was stuck. And married. And ten thousand dollars poorer.

And he deserved much worse. The eighteen-year-old pleaded with him to stop the trips to Saigon. She knew he spent his days in the whorehouses and his nights in the bars. Take me, she pleaded. Leave, he said, if you don't like it. There's plenty more willing to take your place. In the last couple weeks, he'd been with one age eighteen . . . and sixteen . . . and, he said with a tobacco-stained grin, "a ripe fourteen."

He should have been with someone closer to his age. Someone like Helga, the retired teacher from Austria. No. Forget that. She was far too good for him. We met Helga on a bus to the Champa ruins at My Son. She moved her small backpack so Kurt could sit next to her in the front row. Best views, she told him. He'd figured that out long ago and was more than happy to join her. Shared peanuts began the conversation. I could see them laughing. When a seat opened up across the aisle, I joined in.

"So your brother tells me you're on a honeymoon," she said. "I think it's a wonderful idea. Good for you."

As she spoke, I heard LaRue.

"Yeah," I replied. "The perfect honeymoon. No complaints about spooning techniques or expensive trips to the shopping boutiques."

"You know, I was dumped, too," she said.

"How so?"

"My husband died a couple years ago."

LaRue's husband died, too. She shifted lifestyles like you.

"Sorry to hear that."

"No. Don't be. He was in terrible health for a long time. I was a caretaker for many years."

"It's not the way I thought my life would go."

"It never is," she said. "It's pointless to predict."

After her husband died, Helga's children suggested a retirement home and a series of hyper-organized trips on cruise lines and trains. The kind with oversize name tags in the shape of the Eiffel Tower and humorless guides who carry flags to herd tour groups. She grabbed a backpack and bought a one-way ticket to Bangkok. She'd been in Asia for four months.

"The kids here are curious at first," she said. "They see this gray-haired woman and think she's on the wrong bus. But after a while they accept me. Especially after I tell them where to find the best deals.

"My biggest problem is I can't find anyone my age to travel with me," she continued. "Don't get me wrong. I love the kids. But these places are too good for them to have it to themselves. I want my generation to see it, too."

LaRue.

"They can do so much more than they think," she said. "They don't need three large meals a day, five-star hotels, or lots of expensive luggage on wheels. Grab a shoulder bag and join the backpackers. They'd love it out here."

The bus pulled into the My Son entrance station. With a head nod, Kurt ordered that we stay in our seats and let the others off first. I was beginning to read his mind better and surmised he wanted the hoards to serve as a block while we skirted around the guards to avoid any additional fees or requirements to take a guide. His plan worked, as a group of Vietnamese men jumped on the teenagers with a barrage of offers and rules for viewing the temples. No digital cameras, one man ordered with a conviction as if Ho Chi Minh had a gripe against Microsoft. Kurt, Helga, and I began the mile hike to the ruins *sans* escorts.

"So before this trip, you didn't do much traveling?" I asked Helga.

"Only in my mind. My husband was just too sick. We had many great years together, but the last one was tough. He was much older and needed me there. I loved him and wanted to be by his side. But I'd be lying if I said I never looked out the hospital windows from time to time and dreamed of being in a place like this."

"Did you feel guilty?"

"No. Because those were my true feelings. You never want to keep those thoughts bottled up. That's not to say you should always act on them. I had no intention of abandoning my husband even though much of the time he had no idea I was in the room. But those impulses are important messages. Listen to them."

"Do you still get them?"

"Every day."

"Like what?"

"I have this strong pull to visit Hanoi right now. To see if the political head matches with the body of people. I'm very curious."

"Mind if I ask you a personal question?"

"They're the best kind."

"Did it feel like the relationship was dying?"

"Truthfully, yes. Or entering another phase. But he gave me so much early on. It was my turn to give him something back."

"How about if the couple were the same age, started on equal footing, and then one faded after a couple years."

"She struggled, didn't she?"

Just then, Kurt caught Helga's attention. He'd strayed from the trodden areas in search of a better photograph while we explored the crumbling temples. "Careful," she yelled to him, before explaining the area was heavily mined during the war and that many explosives remained. Visitors should stay on paths, while cows were encouraged to roam free. The occasional bovine misstep would trigger a loud boom that reverberated against the stone structures and throughout the lush valley. Low-tech minesweeping, Vietnam-style.

I wanted to continue my discussion with Helga, so I asked her to join us for dinner in Hoi An. Maybe she had more answers. She said "perhaps," but we never saw her again. Our dinner guest that night was the thought of her on the back of a Hanoi motor scooter.

Dear LaRue—

My mind filled with plenty of misconceptions thanks to everyone from Oliver Stone to Bob Dornan, my first impressions of Vietnam were more what it isn't than what it is.

It doesn't have that monochromatic, lifeless, cop-on-every-corner feel of other Communist countries I visited prior to the fall of the Berlin Wall. Sure, there are ample billboards with smiling workers and utopian slogans, and the shiny new government buildings occupy prime real estate in towns large and small. For the casual observer, it's hard to see Big Brother impacts or human rights violations through all the neon lights, western stores and media, Internet cafes, and checkpoint-free roads. You don't witness many uniformed kids marching or military vehicles packed with gun-toting soldiers. Yes, Ho Chi Minh's likeness is omnipresent, but the cult-of-personality is nothing here compared to Turkey with Ataturk, Syria with the Assads, or the old Yugoslavia fawning over Tito.

My second impression was that Vietnam is not a country obsessed by what they call "the American War." Ask a local about the war and within five minutes you're talking about the Internet, Madonna, or dimpled chads. There are plenty of propagandized war sites to see, including tunnels, the DMZ, and museums. The tourism industry gives a much heavier push to the beaches and temples.

This is a young country, in which half the population isn't old enough to have remembered or experienced the war. Twenty-five years is enough time for those who were here to begin healing wounds. Today's Vietnam is driven by the dollar. Outdated orthodoxies or relived battles don't sell postcards or cigarette lighters. Learning English and Capitalism 101 do.

This is a nation of "no problem" businessmen and women, whether that means fixing a motor scooter on the road with makeshift parts or stitching together silk pajamas for tourists who want them in an hour. Dirty, dynamic, random, young, haunting, beautiful, green, poor, loud, and warm, both in temperature and temperament—these are a few adjectives that jump out to describe Vietnam.

Roads across stunning, mist-capped jungle mountains flatten out into caravans of smoke-belching buses and garbage-lined beaches. Vietnam today is the young Buddhist monk, draped in orange robes, taking pains to prune a bonsai tree on the grounds of an ancient and decaying temple. It's the aging American divorcee with his pay-per-view Vietnamese "bride." It's the women in their pencil tip bamboo hats, crouched on the sidewalks, hawking delicious noodle soups piled high with bean sprouts and fresh basil. It's the Flying Nun schoolgirls on bikes with their billowy white *ao dai* uniforms and long gloves to keep their skin pale. It's the dragon face long boats on brown rivers that shuttle tourists during the day and sleep families of ten at night. It's warm Cokes and bad karaoke (is that redundant?), a new house for every thousand old steel-roof shanties, bicycle rickshaws carrying dead cows, and bootleg everything. It's fishing nets, war trinkets, and warm baguettes.

Love,
Franz

Kurt and I decided to stay awhile in Hoi An, a picturesque town near the Champa temples. The wooden Chinese bridges, narrow tailor shops, and riverfront teahouses helped retain the town's colonial feel. We took long runs along the market-filled boulevards, talked with the seamstresses about silk, and played a popular game with children that involved throwing sandals at a small cluster of cards, a game with rules that changed each time we played. If the Vietnamese boy hit the cards with his flip-flop he'd raise his hands in the air: "Champion!" If we did the same, the children would strike the Rocky pose again and hold out their hands for the prize money.

"Where you from?" an elderly Vietnamese woman inquired while Kurt and I rested after a run. A group of her friends huddled nearby.

"Laos," I joked.

She furrowed her brow and stared me up and down.

"You no Lao."

Usually we'd tell people we lived in Los Angeles. It was a lot easier than explaining the location of Newport Beach, an hour south.

"Hollywood. We live in Hollywood."

That confused her even more than Laos.

"Los Angeles? You know Los Angeles?"

Silence.

"Orange County?" I said.

"Ahh, Orange County! My brother, he own store. Garden Grove. My cousin. She live Westminster. My uncle, he . . ."

I made a motion that we all sit down at the nearby café to discuss her family tree over tea. Giggling, curious, one by one her friends joined us. None of them spoke English. Hers was poor at best. They all just nodded their heads whenever they heard the words *Orange County*, the world's largest Vietnamese population outside the country itself. Kurt tried to facilitate the conversation by mapping California on a paper napkin that was passed around the group for close inspection. They whispered among themselves and seemed to size us up. Finally, the first woman we met grabbed my hand with both of hers and began a short and impassioned speech to her friends. Others tried to shake hands with Kurt. Then a few of them started to bow. Confused, I looked to Kurt. The women smiled and bowed good-bye. We paid the bill and started the long walk back to our hotel on the outskirts of town.

"What the hell happened there?" I asked.

"I have no idea. But I get the sinking feeling that we've just agreed to marry a couple of Vietnamese gals and move back to Orange County."

"Ahh, maybe that's why that woman kept saying 'pretty, pretty.' I thought she was talking about Hoi An. I kept nodding in agreement. 'Yes, very pretty.'"

"Did you keep that napkin?"

"No. The woman grabbed it from me," I said.

"Did you write our names on it?"

"Yes."

"Watch it be some legally binding contract."

"We could do worse."

"I can't marry a Vietnamese gal," Kurt said.

"Why not?"

"I can't pronounce their names."

A child's yell echoed from a shanty. Another followed. And soon we were escorted on our stroll by a group of children. They weren't selling anything. Just bored. We gave them a round of high fives. "But no, I'm not playing that flip-flop game and losing more money." Then a few started to pinch the backs of our legs. Minions! More pinches. Like a werewolf with exposed fangs and claws in the air, I spun and released a primordial yell. Shrieking, they fled into an empty field. I nodded to Kurt. A job well done.

We paused and listened as their shouts and laughter turned into a serious discussion. An older girl pointed to the smallest among the group, a boy no more than six. Others huddled around and pushed him back toward us. The brave knight. He approached the road with a look of steadfast resolve. "Watch this, Kurt." I cleared my throat and assumed my best *Karate Kid* position, arms stretched high and wide.

Just as I was about to unleash a bloodcurdling yell, the little man broke into a run straight for us. Serious, purposeful, he sprinted to me, extended his arm, and grabbed my penis. Hard. Not a salt pinch. A "squeeze-the-last-bit-of-pulp-from-the-orange" clench. And he didn't let go.

I just stood there. Arms akimbo. Shocked. Not wanting to show the kids I felt like doubling over in pain or vomiting. They yelled and cheered and called the penis-grabbing warrior back to their ranks. He released my member and ran back to them, receiving a round of pats on the back upon his return. The conquering hero. "That little shit!" Kurt couldn't contain his laughter. I wiped the tears from my eyes and told him I needed a nap before dinner.

Rested, recovered, we settled into a catfish dinner at a sidewalk café later that night. A young man at the next table looked straight out of the *Preppy Handbook.* French, I guessed. Pick-the-country was becoming one of our favorite games. And we were getting better at it. I guessed France before the guy uttered a word. All those pink button-down shirts went straight to Paris after America burned through its country club phase in the eighties. I was right. A woman from the States, I guessed, sat a few tables away. *They're the only ones that bring* Elle *to a place like this.*

Drinks ordered, another group of young kids gathered on the sidewalk. I cupped my penis, just in case, then noticed the American woman staring at me. So I played it off like I was just dusting my lap. "What? Doesn't every lap need to be dusted from time to time?" One of the boys pulled a wad of dog-eared postcards from his pocket. He began to give the Frenchman the hard sell, Tony Robbins–style.

"My American friend," he said with a sincerity that made me think they really were friends. "Beautiful postcards. Three for a dollar. But special American price for you. Five for a dollar."

"I'm French."

"Same special price. French, too."

"*Non, merci.*"

The entrepreneur yelled down the street. Five minutes later, a pint-size salesboy huffed up the road holding a newspaper over his head, a month-old copy of *Le Monde.* The Frenchman shook his head no. So the boy shouted again. I half expected one of his young friends to waltz in with a plate of truffles and a bottle of Beaujolais. These guys were good.

"You'll never be able to convince me that these kids are Communists," Kurt said.

"And I love his rap. Guy throws him a curveball and he continues with the same 'special price' angle. Priceless."

"Yo, friend. Come here. I'll buy some postcards," Kurt said.

"You know, people talk about English being the international language of business. Where it's really happening isn't in the big banks or the office towers. It's in the streets of the Third World with entrepreneurs like our buddy here."

"Hmm."

"Hey, I think that gal over there likes me," I said. "She keeps staring."

"She's staring at you touching your penis."

"I was *dusting* my penis. My lap. Whatever. I'm going to invite her over."

She didn't look surprised when I approached her table.

"I was hoping you'd say hi," she said, putting down her magazine. "Do you mind if I join you for dinner? I'm alone."

I shot Kurt a Dudley Do-Right smile. Done deal.

"I heard you speaking English," she said. "Americans, right? I'm Donna."

"Franz."

"Thanks so much for letting me join you. I have to talk to someone."

"Glad to be of service," I said.

"It's this guy I came to Vietnam with," she said.

And she proceeded to detail every single flaw of this poor sap. How he drooled when he slept, staining the pillow. How he splurged on a first-class airline ticket but refused to buy her anything from the silk tailors. How he was a selfish, rude, boring, stubborn, snobbish, scrawny, mouth-breathing, bed-wetting, knuckle-dragging Neanderthal (well, maybe I made up the part about bed-wetting and knuckle-dragging). Vietnam was their first trip together. And their last.

"You're lucky," I said. "Finding this out right away. Some people take nine years, go all the way to the altar, get dumped, then take their brother on the honeymoon."

"Huh?"

"Ignore him," said Kurt. "And please continue with the story. We're both fascinated."

16

Throughout the first five months of the honeymoon, I stayed in e-mail contact with Laura, the woman I dated briefly in Newport Beach before leaving. Nothing heavy. Mostly travel reports from me; work, friend, and marathon-training updates from her. Pick a corner of the world and come visit, I encouraged her. While in Vietnam, I learned John and Lena Dawkins would be in Thailand over the Christmas break. Jonathan Terra decided to escape snowy Prague and come along. Laura sent an e-mail a few days later asking if the invitation was still open. I introduced her to the group via computer and the holiday celebration began. And so did my second-guessing.

Thailand is ground zero for parties at the end of the year. Locals break from work, then head for the beaches. German and Japanese businessmen escape their wives and senses to play around at "golf vacations" enjoyed from massage parlors and strip joints in areas like Pattaya Beach. Backpackers come all year, thanks to the cheap prices and natural environs. In late December, their ranks swell with wannabes itching to partake in full moon parties. The label means nothing. It's about as authentic as *pai gow* poker. "Full moon" is a marketing pitch concocted by hotel owners and tour operators. And it works. Thousands of partygoers from Wall Street to Wal-Mart flock each year to Thailand's version of spring break. Gen-X, dot-com execs also flooded Thailand that year. The bust in the NASDAQ propelled them from cubicles to remote locations around the globe. Southeast Asia was such a popular destination, computer programmers began referring to fired colleagues as having "gone Thailand."

A quick scan of the Internet confirmed the Southeast Asia swarm. Kurt and I saw the situation as a sign. Karma travel. We weren't supposed to be in resort cities. Forget Koh Samui or Phuket, the party epicenters. Go south or north. Go to the rural outskirts and national parks. That was our calling. John Dawkins agreed and pushed for destinations with camping only. Great idea, I e-mailed him, before it dawned on me I'd included a date. I hoped Laura hadn't envisioned the Four Seasons.

We met in Bangkok, a haven for budget travelers, sex-craving/crazed old men, hippies, entrepreneurs, dropouts, transients on their way to other locations throughout Asia, and anyone who didn't mind a little chaos. Make that a lot of chaos. Sidewalk market stands, rickety three-wheeled taxi tuk-tuks, and about nine million people jammed the streets like a permanent carnival. Kurt was in his element. He guided the group on a first-night tour of Khao San Road, the packer favorite chock-full of tie-dye and hemp-clothes sellers, CD bootleggers, Internet cafés, and food carts pushing everything from soup to nuts to deep-fried bugs.

John, our self-appointed travel leader, took the initiative to purchase seven airline tickets to the southern city of Trang. From there we'd make our way . . . somewhere. The number was seven because John brought along his company accountant, Evelina, a self-proclaimed "new Russian" with an aversion to outdoor activities. On the plane down, Kurt struck up a conversation with Julian and Annie, twenty-something New Yorkers in the same boat. Or wanting to be in the same boat should we be lucky enough to charter one. Like our gang, they had no hotel reservations and no reservations about winging it.

Our eclectic group of nine landed late afternoon. We soon learned it would take a four-hour van ride to reach Satun, the jump-off spot for the verdant and vacant islands in the Andaman Sea. Within ten minutes, John and Jonathan launched into a debate about Eastern European politics. The air conditioner belched warm gusts. Bags and bodies battled for space. I looked to Laura with a "This okay?" smile. I looked to the group and hoped it wouldn't combust.

Then, there, just as Jonathan said something rude about Václav Havel, as Julian and Annie decided to tune out the rest of us with their headphones and CD players, as Evelina griped to Lena in Russian, I knew my honeymoon was over. At least for the next two weeks.

These people are invaders. All of them. The road belongs to Kurt and me, not to these poseurs. They can't bitch. Only we have the right to bitch.

At that moment, I knew the group trip would interrupt our rhythm, our rituals. Like our morning coffee sessions. John was an anti-coffee crusader. We'd soon be subjected to his constant badgering about the "evils of caffeine." Jonathan had the habit of turning every innocent conversation into a session of *Crossfire*. The intuitive, often silent language Kurt and I had developed was out, in favor of heated discussions about Polish agricultural policies.

It was fine to visit John and Jonathan in their countries of residence. We were on equal footing in those places. They shared their country, we shared our mission. This was a different story. They could have Russia and the Czech Republic. Kurt and I had staked claim to the rest of the world. We were the road warriors, not them. "Another coffee, please."

To top it off, I'd subjected Laura to the whole spectacle. I'd convinced a woman with whom I'd spent a total of about two weeks to fly halfway around the world, sleep in tents, and listen to John and Jonathan argue about Yeltsin. I looked at her to see if she noticed my fear that I'd made the biggest mistake of the trip thus far. If she did, I couldn't tell. She smiled and rested her head on my shoulder.

"Full, full, full," was the mantra we heard in Satun. The van driver finally found a couple rooms for us that night only. Boats and hotels were booked solid in the days following. No worries. The months with Kurt convinced me never to sweat about hopeless situations. They worked themselves out. Like the passports. Or the entry into Syria.

After a late afternoon nap, Laura and I walked down to the Satun dock in search of dinner, the rest of the group, and a resolution to our predicament. We found all three at a bamboo shack with a handful of wooden tables and chairs planted in the sand.

"Unbelievable," John said between mouthfuls of fire-hot curry. "Pull up a chair and let's drink to our boat. We leave tomorrow morning."

Over Singhas and *satays,* John explained he'd walked the docks for an hour and had come up empty. All boats were reserved or broken. He begged locals for recommendations only to receive shrugs and "I'm sorry." Dejected, he walked to the restaurant to regroup. On the way, he bumped into an ebullient Thai woman who ran a boat out of Satun. Quandy told him a large group from Germany had rented her boat, then backed out at the last minute. Stocked with food, supplies, and diving equipment, the craft rested along the pier ready to go. A cook and crew were on call as well.

John couldn't believe his fortune. So he decided to press his luck. Could Quandy rustle up some fireworks? Sure. Several cases of beer? No problem. Champagne? Maybe, John. He deserved it after having stumbled upon the lone free boat in Thailand for a ten-day tour of the Andaman Sea. I was still having second (and twenty-second) thoughts about the group outing, but at least we had a boat.

Day one, we cut through the blue waters and raced with dolphins in the afternoon sun. Quandy steered us to a small island to swim and snorkel and explore. Dark, full clouds formed on the horizon, approaching without warning, like a desert storm on a clear day. Better stay for the night, she suggested. Only problem was that all the bungalows were taken. The boat's wooden benches or the island's wooded beaches were our only options.

As the rains began, we decided to enjoy the daily magic show otherwise known as dinner. From a single wok and with a handful of spices, Pen, the boat's cook, whipped up one of her signature curries, pad Thais, fish soups, fried mussels, and anything else Quandy could lug from the sea. That first night, the ocean ended the meal on a different pitch. Looking pale, Lena left the table first. Jonathan followed, lunging to the railing to empty his dinner into the water.

"What a waste," I told Kurt and John. "All that delicious fish now feeding fish."

"Terra, play through and have a brew," Kurt yelled.

Jonathan rolled his eyes and bolted for round two. We laughed, then felt bad for laughing. I could remember vivid seasickness bouts.

Cold, windy, rainy, rocky, the environment was far from the ideal first vacation shared by couples. I looked over at Laura. John had her laughing at one of his crazy stories about life in Russia. She fit. With ease. Both with the group and with me. Despite the conditions, I hadn't heard a single gripe. Instead she grabbed a Singha and jumped into one of our random conversations about the worst songs of the eighties (which is, hands down, that song with the chorus of "*I've been to paradise, but I've never been to me*") or Davis nights spent spraying water from a stolen fire extinguisher on hapless pedestrians, the height of our childhood creativity.

After Jonathan and Lena found their sea legs, we all boarded the dinghy for the bumpy and wet ride to shore. Laura and I found our tent in the darkness and bid the others good night. The wind blew its walls like rapid, deep breaths into a paper bag. We joked about the weather and John's tall tales. During a lull between laughs, I kissed her back as she cuddled to one side and pressed her body to mine. The taste of rainwater mixed with her sweat, sweet and sour like a salted margarita. She reached back and grabbed my thigh, stroking my skin and tugging gently at the hairs. I slipped the bikini strap from her tan shoulder as she turned back to face me. The rains stopped, the winds calmed, and the moonlight poured through a small screen like a pinpoint spotlight to expose her body. She looked stunning, her runner's muscles flexing ever so slightly as if she were at a starting block, her head tilted back, her tan lines drawing my eye. My body craved hers.

My mind froze. Naked, relaxed, refreshed by a calm and clean ocean breeze, I froze. A surge of guilt rushed through me. I shouldn't be here, the voice said. She shouldn't be here. Different priorities. Too much time apart. A new focus. Had I changed that much over the past six months? Or maybe I was looking to the coming months of living out of a backpack? Whatever the reason, I couldn't escape the guilt. Just relax, I rationalized, over and over. You don't have to solve everything right away. Sometimes answers unfold slowly. Like Kurt says. These things work themselves out.

I caressed the side of her face and ran my fingers through her hair, wrapping it around her ear in a circular motion. She stroked my chest as I began to massage her body. I kissed the sides of her breasts, then the slope of her navel. All the while I kept my head down. I didn't want her to see my eyes. Didn't want her to see inside and sense something was wrong. Laura was a bright, caring, gorgeous woman. She was the type of woman I should have loved. But I didn't. It hit me there in the tent. It's the trip, I concluded later as we stretched out and held each other close. I've detached from everything in California, including her. We fell asleep entangled. I woke with a jolt a few hours later. I knew the real answer.

I was still in love with Annie.

Thanks to Quandy's navigation, clear skies, available bungalows on other islands, and Pen's cooking, my fears that the group would crumble like an episode of *Survivor* never came to fruition. We'd wake in the morning and point the boat toward a *koh* (island)—Koh Lipe, Koh Tarutao, Koh Adang. Our days were filled with skin-diving sessions through Evian-clear waters, afternoon naps in hammocks, hikes to hilltops and around islands, reading sessions on the boat's top deck. Yet after each swim or stroll, I'd take more pleasure knowing the group adventures would soon end, and Kurt and I would continue. We were a couple college students happy to be home from break, yet happier still to get back to school. Kurt and I were on a mission hard to define. But we'd find it, together, without the help of others.

It was one of the few times on the trip that felt like a pure vacation. So much so, I had to check the date on my watch Christmas morning. For the entire holiday season, we'd heard no carols, saw no decorated trees, and visited no malls. We were about as far removed from the typical celebration as possible. The group spent the day hiking ten kilometers to an island waterfall and swimming hole in the Koh Tarutao National Park. Walking with Kurt, John, Jonathan, and Laura, we dove into the topic of religion and our experiences with faith in different countries, marveling at the similarities all over the world. We talked at length about Christ on Christmas, something I'd never done outside midnight mass and the obligatory nod to the high-voltage nativity scene on the neighbors' lawn. I opened up about my growing faith, stirred by the incredible chain of events that led me to and through the trip. I was convinced the reformations weren't happenstance but the sculpting of a greater hand.

That night we planned a surprise for the group. Kurt and I ducked downstairs on the boat after dinner and slipped into our silk pajamas from Hoi An. He grabbed a bag of gifts we'd acquired throughout Southeast Asia, then Quandy introduced "the Asian Santas." One by one, the group rose to collect their presents. A sarong for Quandy and a scarf for Pen, incense for Evelina and Lena, peasant shirts and books for John and Jonathan. We'd rehearsed a few lines about each person and why that particular item was chosen.

To Laura, I gave batik silk and a hug. I decided to spare her my midnight realization, but sensed she knew things were different between us. My talks about more travel didn't help. To compensate, I took pains to make sure she had a good time, arranging massages for her on the beach, peeling away from the group for time together, making sure she had a couple days in Bangkok at the end of the trip to shop for gifts and clothes. I felt the relationship shift into friends mode. Kurt told me to give it more time. My mind was on the road.

Dear LaRue:

Kurt told me a story about a job he had in high school installing tents at the California State Fair. One day he and some co-workers waited for a delivery truck to show up with tent parts to be installed. The driver was late, and Kurt was a little ticked off. After an hour, the semi finally appeared. It was dirty, beat-up, and stuffed full of tent frames and junk used for other jobs. As they unloaded the awnings, Kurt made a crack about its shoddy condition. The driver didn't laugh. "It's how I make my living," he explained. Kurt said he hasn't made light of someone's job since.

I thought about that story often as we made our way through Southeast Asia. It's a region full of people scratching out a living with dilapidated food carts, improvised shoe repair shops on sidewalks, and beat-up old delivery trucks. Their stories are often inspirational.

Poh was our driver in Cambodia. He's thirty, a chubby five-foot-eight, and speaks broken English learned over the years by listening to tourists and western music. His life goal is to fly. Anywhere. On any type of aircraft. A more immediate concern is to raise 1,000 dollars so he can convince his girlfriend's father he's worthy of her hand in marriage.

When Kurt and I walked out of the small Siem Reap airport, thirty taxi drivers mugged us, tugging at our arms, begging to drive us ten miles into town for a dollar. Kurt picked Poh. His car was closest to the exit. He'd waited all day for a passenger.

We spent the next three days with Poh, climbing around the breathtakingly beautiful Angkor temples, cheering on the rock-tough fighters at a Cambodian kickboxing match, and talking about life.

Late one day, we drove to a monument at one of the Killing Fields commemorating the two million Cambodians slaughtered during Pol Pot's reign of terror. As we stared in horror at a tall glass memorial filled with skulls, Poh quietly told us his father and uncles were among the victims of the Khmer Rouge holocaust. He survived after being hidden by relatives. The living he's scratched out has been on his own.

Quandy and Pen ran the boat we chartered to cruise around the pristine and remote islands of the Andaman Sea in southern Thailand. Quandy is an attractive, tall, athletic woman whose big smile and high-pitched voice mask ten years of service in the Thailand Marines. She jokes she's still single because "I can't find any Thai men as tall as me." She's *The Love Boat*'s Isaac, Julie, and Captain Steubing rolled into one. She pitched tents at midnight on the beach, dove for mussels and fished for dinner, located firecrackers and Singhas in the villages, and showed us her favorite islands, diving spots, beaches, and hikes.

It's only when she wore shorts that I noticed the huge scars on each leg courtesy of several low-tech operations by military surgeons to save her legs following a parachuting accident. Quandy left the military and borrowed money from friends and family to purchase a used boat. The business has been so profitable, she plans to purchase a new vessel next month.

A big reason for her success is Pen, the boat's charming and talented chef. Pen redefined Thai cooking for us with her tasty fish curries, pad Thais, and seafood dishes. Usually stuffed, we always seemed to find a healthy appetite after the first bite of a new dish. It wasn't until the end of the trip we learned Pen lost her husband to a disease the previous year. She only recently took the job as a chef to support her two young children, who stay with relatives while Pen is at sea.

There are many others who have touched us on the trip. In Asia, they included the sea gypsy waiters on Koh Lipe, who wore the same clothes every day and slept on the restaurant floor at night. Or the proud tour guide at the Royal Palace in Bangkok, who talked about his daughter's college education before anything else.

I knew the trip would be a lifetime education. It's been hugely rewarding to turn Trivial Pursuit geography questions into experiences while "shrinking the world."

What I didn't expect is that our main source of education would come not from museums or churches, but from the people we've been fortunate enough to encounter.

Love,
Franz

17

They should call visas cover charges. Because they're no different than admission fees to a peep show. Pay your money and see the sights. Most nations will process a visa within twenty-four hours as long the credit card is valid or money order doesn't bounce. Background checks are cursory, if they're done at all. Many countries adopt a tit-for-tat pricing policy. If the U.S. charges fifty dollars for a visa, they'll charge fifty dollars for a visa.

Our passports, which had disappeared from Kurt's old real estate office in Seattle, had several visa stamps for countries in the Middle East, including Syria, Lebanon, and Jordan. The vanishing act cost us several hundred dollars each for the passports and visas, because countries don't give redo's—just like the peep shows.

"Is there something you want to tell me?" Kurt asked during a quick stopover in Newport Beach after our travels in Southeast Asia and before heading down to Latin America.

"Uh, no."

"Something about you being a stalker?"

"*Qué?*"

A detective in Medford, Oregon, had left several messages on the home answering machine. He asked Kurt to call him "as soon as possible," sounding a bit more anxious with each call. Kurt phoned the officer and apologized for not contacting him sooner, explaining we were on a "worldwide honeymoon." The detective avoided the bait and started to ask him some vague questions about a woman in Medford who had been stalked. Never heard of her, said Kurt.

Continuing the mild interrogation, the officer asked Kurt if he knew the woman's husband, an ex-con who lived in Newport Beach. A month before, the man had broken into her apartment and ransacked the place. When the police went to investigate the break-in, they found overturned furniture, emptied drawers . . . and the passport of a Franz Robert Wisner in a back bedroom closet.

"And there's where you come in," Kurt pronounced, à la Johnnie Cochran. "What were you doing with this scumbag from Newport, breaking into this woman's apartment?"

I pulled his arm behind his back in a wrestling move.

"Kurt, you twerp. Call that cop back right now and tell him I don't know the stalker or how my passport turned up in that gal's house."

"How do I know you're telling the truth?"

He moaned as I tightened the hold.

"Okay, okay."

As I stood by, practicing my next WWF move, Kurt dialed the detective and explained our passports may have been stolen. Did the woman in Medford know anyone at the Windermere real estate office in West Seattle? he asked. The officer said he'd call right back.

"Seems like we have a case of sticky fingers," he told Kurt fifteen minutes later.

He went on to explain the woman did know someone at Windermere, her niece . . . her niece who happened to be the agent at the office that night . . . her niece who brought her eight-year-old daughter with her to the office . . . an eight-year-old with "a case of sticky fingers."

The real estate agent called Kurt shortly after to apologize, explaining her daughter saw the passports on Mitch's desk, then slipped them into her pocket. Having been paged the next morning with a message about the missing passports, the mom turned to her daughter and asked if she'd seen them. "No, Mommy." Panicked, the little girl dumped one at a highway rest stop in Oregon and stashed the other in her aunt's closet.

"I'm sorry, Mr. Wisner," she explained to Kurt after being handed the phone by her mom. "I was only eight back then. I didn't know any better. I'm nine now and promise it won't happen again."

There are few things in life as sad as a rest home on a January day. The Christmas decorations are packed away, relatives returned to their homes and routines. The tree branches are as barren as the visitor logs. Winter flu bouts darken the pall. RNs and orderlies resume their tasks of cushioning death.

But the sun was out and working the day Kurt and I ventured to LaRue's Eskaton. Brighter still in her corner of the complex. She'd replaced the poinsettias with camellias. And a couple of our photographs from Red Square hung in the small display alcove by her door. The ones with Kurt and me in those fur hats Brezhnev used to wear. We decided to drive up to Sacramento from Newport Beach and surprise her with a visit before we flew to Venezuela. I rapped on the door. A little louder than usual. My mom said LaRue's hearing was starting to fade. She was ninety-nine.

"Oh, for heaven's sake," she said, opening the door. "The world travelers. Here to visit an old woman."

The wall-size world map hung in her small family room. I noticed the series of shiny new red pins in our ports of call. Prague, Dubrovnik, Moscow, Budapest, Istanbul, Aleppo, Lombok, Saigon, Siem Reap, Koh Lipe. She'd supplemented them with blue pins to mark her own journeys during a lifetime of travel with church groups.

"Who's old?" I asked. "Kurt and I have more gray hair than you."

"Oh, you hush. I still have to get that hair cut."

Pictures of us at Angkor Wat and the Prague Castle hung over her phone. Our postcards sat on a bureau along with e-mails my mom printed for her.

"Are you boys hungry? I'm ready for some lunch. Homemade minestrone today."

We walked toward the main dining room, the epicenter of activity in retirement homes. A place around which days, lives, are scheduled. Menus for the week were posted on every hall. Seniors debated the best dishes and circled favorite items with red pens.

I wonder if my final thoughts in this world are going to be about navy bean soup.

Before we could go ten feet, an elderly couple stopped to talk with LaRue.

"These are my grandsons," she beamed before they could say anything. "The ones traveling around the world."

"Right, sure," the husband said. "I read your postcards and e-mails from Turkey and Vietnam. Fascinating. Where to next?"

"You remember, honey," the wife said to her husband. "The boys have been in Asia the last several months and are now going to South America."

"Oh, yes," he said. "We've tried to read everything you sent LaRue, and we followed the journey on her map. Great stuff. Keep it up."

"Eskaton is on your trip," his wife added. "We're all traveling through you."

And it hit me. We'd replaced beef Stroganoff as the number-one topic of conversation at Eskaton. Travel is a language spoken by an inclusive club. It's a trigger for memories and a spark for more journeys. It's that warm conversation with the Eskaton nurse from Romania or being able to read the newspaper and exclaim, "Hey, I know that place." Even if the trip is measured in days, its payoffs can be spread through lifetimes. The Eskaton residents showed us that. I began to see our journey in a larger context.

Several residents stopped us before we reached the cafeteria, each wanting to talk with LaRue and meet her globe-trotting grandsons. LaRue basked in the interest. She was the director of an international soap opera orchestrated for the enjoyment of her friends. Kurt and I were her actors. Eskaton tuned in daily. They urged the drama to continue for as long as possible.

Our parents' generation asks when we're going back to work. Eskaton asks where we're going next.

DUMP THE MIS-GUIDE BOOKS

Go ahead. Do it. I know the thought's crossed your mind. Probably the last time you walked into a tourist trap packed with fellow travelers holding the same copy of *Fodor's* or *Lonely Planet*.

Throw the guidebooks away. Or burn them in protest. Either way, your trips will improve dramatically.

Think about it. When tourists come to Orange County, California, the guidebooks point them in the direction of Disneyland or the Newport Peninsula. Is this the best we have to offer? Do those places truly reflect Orange County today?

On the other hand, if the tourists spent a couple minutes talking to Orange County residents, they'd learn about, say, a desolate beach in Laguna, a wonderful Mexican restaurant in Santa Ana, or a pristine wilderness trail.

Still not convinced? Here are some more reasons.

The whole concept of an "up-to-date" guidebook is impossible. Look at the date on yours. If you're lucky, it's only a year or two old. Or is it? Find a ten-year-old copy and you'll probably conclude the book hasn't been rewritten, just edited, tweaked, and spruced up with fancy new photos.

How many people work for a guidebook? One hundred? Two hundred? Even if the number were 100,000, it wouldn't be adequate to scour every neighborhood for the latest and greatest information. For example, I went to Rio and heard about a nightclub jammed with dance-crazy Brazilians. I saw no tourists the entire night. On a return trip, I saw no people the entire night. The Rio revelers had moved to another venue after declaring that one passé.

Of course none of this information was in the guidebooks. The only restaurants, clubs, and bars they promote are the ones that have been around for years—the same types of establishments we avoid at home.

How about basic information concerning an area's main sights? The books do better here, I'll admit. The best ones throw in a decent history lesson or two along with detailed maps. Still, they often miss things like holiday schedules, hours that have been adjusted, discount days, or the best times to view the must-see spots. Besides, all this information can be easily obtained with a quick stop at an information center or through a chat with a concierge.

Another reason to ditch the guidebooks is the practice of paying for print. Though the reputable publishers prohibit payola practices, hotel, tour, and restaurant owners all over the world brag about buying favorable mentions. In Vietnam, a café owner told me he sent money every year to a writer so his establishment would remain in a guidebook. He was angry with his "cheap" neighbor for refusing the bribe, yet tacking up a sign that trumpeted a recommendation.

Think about being forced to get all your news from books—everything from weather reports to stock prices to headlines to sports scores. Impossible, right? Yet this is precisely the rationale of travelers who cling to guidebooks as their sole source of information.

Are you wavering yet? Here's what will happen if you do leave the guidebooks at home.

You'll talk to more people, many of them offering rides, meals, or personal escorts in addition to recommendations. You'll feel like you're experiencing something authentic as opposed to being led through another tourist trap. You'll travel far more spontaneously, taking advantage of gifts and opportunities when they arise. You'll realize you don't need to see everything on a trip. The churches and museums will still be there the next time. You'll probably make more friends with whom you'll stay in contact long after the journey is over. You'll feel like you know a location far better than you ever did with guidebook-dominated travel.

There are whole industries that exist solely by convincing travelers they cannot leave their homes without certain "essential services"—travel clothes, travel insurance, even travel agents in the age of the Internet. The truth is you don't need any of them.

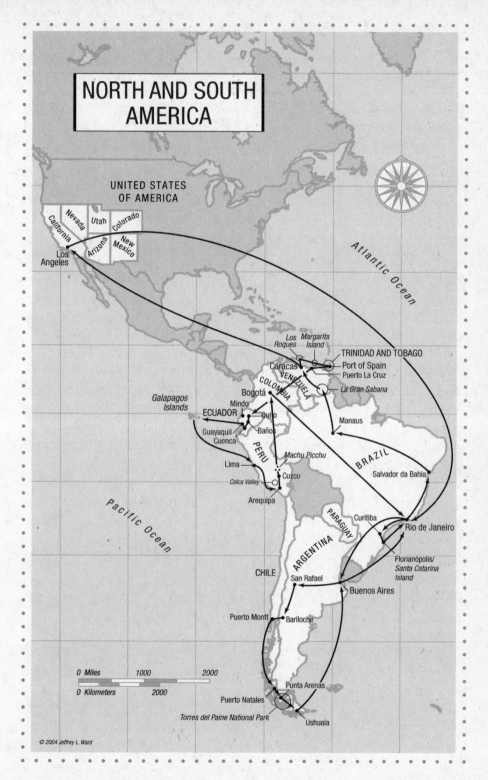

NORTH AND SOUTH AMERICA

UNITED STATES
OF AMERICA

Nevada
California   Utah   Colorado
Arizona   New
Mexico
Los
Angeles

Atlantic Ocean

Los
Roques   Margarita
Island   TRINIDAD AND TOBAGO
Caracas   Port of Spain
VENEZUELA   Puerto La Cruz
COLOMBIA   La Gran Sabana
Bogotá
Mindo   Manaus
Galapagos
Islands   ECUADOR   Quito
Guayaquil   Baños
Cuenca   BRAZIL
PERU   Machu Picchu
Lima   Cuzco   Salvador da Bahia
Colca Valley
Arequipa
PARAGUAY   Curitiba
Rio de Janeiro
ARGENTINA   Florianópolis/
Santa Catarina
Island
CHILE   San Rafael
Buenos Aires
Puerto Montt   Bariloche

Pacific Ocean

0 Miles   1000   2000
0 Kilometers   2000

Punta Arenas
Puerto Natales
Torres del Paine National Park   Ushuaia

© 2004 Jeffrey L. Ward

18

For the honeymoon leg in South America, we had no more planning than a round-trip ticket from Los Angeles to Caracas. And things couldn't have worked out better during the first couple weeks. For one, we were quasi-adopted by a local family we met through a friend from Davis. Pablo and Betty Mancera, and their daughter Luisa, gave us a room in their Caracas apartment and opened our eyes to Venezuelan life. Through them, we experienced the taste of fresh Venezuelan coffee with *arepas* and *queso de mano* for breakfast (corn crumpets with soft cheese). We learned about native arts; 35 percent loan rates for home purchases; and local obsessions with baseball, beauty pageants, and speeding through red lights. *"Come la luz,"* they called it. Eat the light.

The Manceras also introduced us to Los Roques, a national park archipelago off the coast of Caracas. The islands had the feel of a traditional Greek island fishing village, Latin-style, with family-run posadas huddled around a small town square, sand roads with no cars, and more candles than lights. Simple kitchens hid gourmet chefs who'd escaped bustling restaurants in New Orleans or New South Wales. Dogs lounged under hammocks. Fishermen carried their morning take of tarpon and yellowtail in nets draped over their shoulders, then sliced steak-size portions on wood blocks in front of island cafés. Children ran nude on the beach chasing dive-bombing pelicans. Late in the afternoon, the sun dulled and warmed the Izod colors on buildings—blues, deep greens, pinks and yellows.

We had a hard time leaving the islands. Literally. Late one afternoon, a young woman approached us, apologized, then explained our flight had been canceled. We couldn't suppress our grins. The airline, she said, would put us up in their guesthouse and pay for our meals. They even baked a tasty carrot cake for my birthday and gathered the staff to sing *"Feliz Cumpleaños."* Next day, same thing.

She apologized and offered more meals and a catamaran trip. Fly LTA, I wrote my friends. It might take a few extra days, but you'll love the wait.

After LTA finally managed to send a plane, it was off to Margarita Island to join Luisa Mancera and a group of her friends for a long weekend at Pachacuncha, the family's adobe-style hacienda overlooking the Caribbean. Robin Leach would have been proud of the open-air showers, terraced gardens, verandas, pool, and constant TLC from Mayo, the house chef. Her questions *"Más comida o cerveza?"* were as frequent as Luisa's cousin Martin's cries of, "Grab the cards, I'm going to kick some gringo butt."

The neighborhood, far away from the crowded beaches of Margarita, was desolate a dozen years prior. A local artist dared purchase a plot of land to build a hacienda using traditional construction techniques and native materials. Complete with wood-burning stoves, tile floors, wood beams in white walls, and mini canals to move water and cool the air, word of the house spread to artisans and aficionados in Caracas. Mrs. Mancera, a painter, decided to join the movement despite protests from her family. She bought vacant land near the first house and hired local craftsmen to construct a ranchero. After ten years of careful planning and labor, Pachacuncha was *perfecta*.

So good we rarely left the house. We drifted in a sea of Mayo's cooking, cousin Martin's bartending, salsa and sun by the pool, and long discussions about life in Venezuela. Luisa, Martin, and his wife, Marie Angelica, needed to head back to Caracas for work on Monday. They said we should forget Trinidad and stay for another week. Kurt and I looked at each other, tempted by a few more days of paradise.

Instead, we passed up the offer in favor of celebrating Carnival on the nearby island of Trinidad. I knew our luck had changed the minute the taxi driver from the airport dropped us off at the only available guesthouse in Port of Spain, with metal bars on the windows and the front gate, cut glass stacked high on neighboring fence tops, and a sign in front that read *Christian Center for Rehabilitation*. Not that we didn't need some salvation. But a halfway house for wayward souls in a den of sin just didn't seem right that week.

The rooms—with their stained brown carpets, plywood walls, and Boy Scout beds—felt like a low-security prison, devoid of anything that could be stolen. Not even a Gideon's Bible. At least we didn't need alarm clocks. The parking lot next door had several early morning music enthusiasts who blared reggae beats from their cars. They took over from the night shift, which preferred hip-hop. The Christian Center for *Debilitation* was more like it. I suggested we go to dinner.

"See, this isn't so bad," I rationalized as we crammed into a grimy wooden booth in a downtown takeout. Chicken wire separated us from the bartender and kept entrepreneurial customers from reaching for the cash register. "Just a good ole Caribbean dive joint."

Crack. Bam. We spun around to see an enraged man overturning a table and yelling at the floor. Just a drunk, I surmised, before plowing back into my chicken. A little incident like that wasn't going to shake us. The angry man continued shouting and waving his fists. Then I saw a head pop up.

"He's maaahhd at his freend," the heavyset woman in the next booth explained matter-of-factly. She'd seen the show before. "He don't like him smoking craahhk."

A performance, that's what would enhance the island experience. Each night during Carnival the city hosted contests at a large outdoor auditorium. With their showgirl costumes, intricate dance numbers, and Rose Bowl–style floats, locals spent the entire year getting ready for the act. That night included the limbo contest, but first up on the bill was *extempo,* a combination rhyme/rap/ridicule crafted by performers spontaneously. Street beggars who perfected the craft raked in top dollars spoofing tourists.

> You got ya designer glaah-ses
> And your yellow madras T
> But it's your socks and sandals combo
> That say you from Ger-man-ee.

During the competition, *extempo* masters were handed a subject ranging anywhere from West Indies cricket to local political controversies. Singing with accompaniment from the house band, the *extempo* contestants crafted clever and hilarious commentaries in a matter of seconds. We adopted *extempo* as the preferred means of expression for the rest of the stay in Trinidad.

> A hotel on the beach
> A resort room in the winter
> But without a reservation
> Our penance's the rehab center.

Next up were social commentary songs. *Extempo* was interesting. These were "incestering." To the rapt attention of the audience, a woman began a song about intra-family liaisons while actors staged a mini-drama in which a man beat his wife, guzzled a bottle marked "XXX," and proceeded to have his way with his young daughter.

"*Daddy, oh Daddy. Please don't do that to me. Daddy, oh Daddy . . .*"

"Wait a minute," Kurt asked. "What happened to the *extempo* tunes about cricket?"

> The song about incest
> The words and actions linger
> Now we're looking round Trinidad
> For kids with a dozen fingers.

After the competition, we decided to check out the fetes, the legendary, all-night parties/concerts.

"You waahnt to go to fete, go to Cus-taaahms," the bus driver told us. "Eeet's the real thing."

So that night we crammed like cattle through metal gates, trying to make our way into the large field, ground zero for Customs, one of Carnival's most popular parties/concerts. Despite the throng, two of the five entrance aisles sat empty for some reason. Kurt grabbed my shirt and led me over. That's when the cheers started. A VIP, I thought, or maybe one of the evening's singers. Instead, the center of attention was right on top of us.

Amid the catcalls, we looked up at a 250-pound woman peeling away a tight pink lace leotard and exposing her bountiful nakedness to the masses. It wasn't the typical *Girls Gone Wild,* two-second flash. No, the performer, egged on by the supportive crowd, pulled every inch of clothing off her body and began a series of gyrations that incorporated metal poles and the outstretched arms of concert goers.

> The biceps look familiar
> The thighs they ring a bell
> Maybe the Bills or Lions
> But surely the N.F.L.

"*You make me* waaanaaa," blared the energetic singer onstage after we made our way around the hefty exhibitionist. Made our way around her with extreme caution, I might add. "*You make me* waaanaaa."

"This isn't bad," I reasoned. "Kind of catchy."

A slender, young Trinidadian woman ground her derriere against Kurt's lap, encouraging him to join her and her group of friends.

"Brilliant stuff," he blurted.

"*You make me* waaanaaa," shouted the lead singer of the next band as he waved a bandanna in the air. The crowd followed with handkerchiefs of their own. "*You make me* waaanaaa."

"Isn't this the same tune the last band played?" I asked.

Kurt ignored me, continuing his game of techno Twister with the young reveler. I joined with the masses, shaking parts of my body I never knew movable and trying to blend in. I say *trying*, because blending is a relative concept when you are the only white tourists among ten thousand islanders.

"*You make me* waaanaaa," chanted the next band to the delight of the inspired crowd, jumping up and down and chanting the lyrics back at the singer.

After the fifth band played, "*You make me* waaanaaa," I'd had enough.

"I'm sorry," I said. "I don't *waaanaaa* hear that song anymore. This is a great party and I love the energy. But it sounds like any radio station named KISS-FM or K-HITS, the ones that play Britney Spears more often than traffic reports."

Another day, another vote to change our surroundings. It was too late to go back to Margarita Island. Tobago was still an option, as was another part of Trinidad, away from the festivities. Instead, we were moths drawn to the Carnival lights, paralyzed, unable to move on.

There has to be a nice part of town, we rationalized. We found neglected parks, rough streets, and uninviting blocks. There has to be a good beach nearby, we hoped. "Looks nice," we said on the boat ride in. Kurt and I waded to shore first and found ourselves foot-deep in trash. By then the aqua taxi vanished. So we cleared away beer cans and candy wrappers and played cards, using bottle caps and stale potato chips for poker chips.

Scrambling for another remedy the next day, we decided on the steel-drum band competition. The night before, we'd attended a practice session for the Carnival all-star band Desperados, stood in the middle of one hundred steel drums working in unison, some accentuating, some pulsating, some hammering home a groove, some reaching for a height. A combination Mozart symphony, Blue Man Group, Princess Cruise dinner show.

Each pan band had an entourage that rivaled Lollapalooza in terms of size, energy, and substance abuse. They danced, like revelers at a New Orleans wake, around a convoy of flatbed trucks carrying the drummers. They clapped and swayed. They sang and cheered. They stole money from a tourist standing next to us, picking his pocket despite his "theft-proof" traveler's pants, the kind with Velcro and zippers every square inch. The kind you wear for a week on vacation, then stash at the bottom of your closet until the Goodwill truck comes around.

> I'm not mad about the crime
> It's a one in a thousand chance
> My only lingering peeve
> Is that they didn't steal the pants.

We decided to walk the mile from the steel-drum competition to salvation in our "safe" neighborhood. A local drunk decided to join the late-night stroll, forcing us to quicken our pace. He matched it. And like a Tour de France stage that erupts into a full-speed chase, we sprinted down the deserted street half laughing, half yelling commands you'd normally reserve for a dog. "Stop. Sit. Wait. Stay."

"How about the party at the Hilton Hotel?" Kurt suggested the next day.

Great idea. We'd spent an afternoon by their pool a few days before. So we decided to hop the back fence and bypass the twenty-dollar cover charge. Kurt took the lead, jumping over the jagged-edged twelve-foot chain-link fence without spilling a drop from his beer.

"Grrrrrr," roared a beast deep in the bushes after I'd managed my way over the fence.

"What the hell was that?" I asked as we scampered up the hill toward the hotel.

"Who the hell is that?" a large female guard shouted, shining an annoyingly bright flashlight in our eyes, freezing us in our tracks. A growling German shepherd lunged toward us, held back by a thin metal chain.

"We, umm, we're guests here," I said. "Just trying to get back inside."

"Show me your keys."

"They're inside."

"Where'd you come from?"

"California. I mean, inside. We've been inside at the party."

"That's impossible. I would have seen you."

Caught. Guilty. Forgive us our trespasses, we begged. We're just trying to find some relaxing fun during a crazy week. Please, please, please. The lady let down her guard and pointed us to an elevator door.

"You're lucky. Normally the dog is off the leash. I just tied him up for a couple minutes while I was on break."

There were many more guards at the party entrance. After pooling our money, we discovered only eight dollars. No party. Option B was the hotel bar for a drink. "You all look like you're having a rough time," the waitress said. "I'll bring you some appetizers. On the house."

"This is it!" I declared. "Our luck has changed. These free appetizers are a symbol of the turnaround."

She returned with a couple beers and a plate of grilled somethings. They looked like dark sponges that puff up after adding water. We thanked her for the hospitality and grinned until she walked away. Neither of us had eaten since breakfast, yet we were still reluctant to touch the waffle-type food items, let alone eat them. *You first. No, you first.*

"I think it's cheese," Kurt declared after taking the first bite. "Or maybe compressed Sea Monkeys."

"If this is an omen," I said, staring at the brown lump, "it's a pretty stale omen."
We played rock-scissors-paper to see who'd eat a second.

> You can use them as a sponge
> To soak up a sewage puddle
> Or see them at Cape Canaveral
> As tiles on the next Space Shuttle.

"Well, the parades begin tomorrow," I offered.

Two A.M. That's what time the lines of bands, floats, and followers began the two-day romp through the city. After a long nap, we threw on our worst clothes and joined the mass of other parade watchers thrilled to be pelted with paint from float riders. At 4 A.M., we stood on a street corner in the St. James neighborhood, dodging paint balls. Steel drum bands on flatbed trucks drifted by. Dozens of dancers followed each, wearing masks and capes, painted in white face, carrying umbrellas. The rain increased from a drizzle to a downpour. A group of drunken teens urinated ten feet away.

Then *pop, pop, pop.* The rapid-fire blasts echoed from around the corner. We froze at the thought of a shoot-out. But before we could panic, a car peeled out into the crowded street, nearly crashing into the masses. The driver pounded his horn and parted the crowd. A minute later a police car, siren blaring, raced behind.

"You know something," I said. "Drunken revelry is drunken revelry. We glamorize it when it takes place in locations like Pamplona or New Orleans. But it's no different. It's the same as if we were getting tanked with twenty thousand people in the parking lot at a Metallica concert."

For the next several hours, we shot pool at a dilapidated hall and joked about all the events that had gone wrong. I no longer cared about trying to find a good time. I let it go and experienced the best couple hours of the trip.

Man, this is like Annie. Seems like I always failed when I tried to force a good time. "I can make us both happy." It was a line that never proved true.

Just then an attractive, cocoa-skinned partier sidled up next to our table and asked if she could shoot for me. I stared at her slim figure as she leaned over the table to align the cue ball. A teen in oversize jeans and a cocked baseball cap fidgeted behind and whispered something to his friend.

"Careful, man," Kurt advised. "Good news is she's been eyeing you for a while. Bad news is her man has been eyeing you for a while."

"Let's get out of here. The pool hall, the rehab center, the island, the whole thing."

The flight back to Venezuela was delayed for several hours. Kurt and I sat in the airport pizza parlor playing cards. I was down several dollars when I began to laugh. Kurt knew immediately what I was thinking and chuckled along. The crack addict, the supersize stripper, the Christian rehab center—none of it dented the fact that we were back on the road. At that moment, I loved Trinidad. Sure, the time there was far from a chamber-of-commerce stay in paradise. It didn't matter. It was travel. Whether or not trips go according to plan, they're always rewarding and edifying. Before our plane left the country, we'd turned the string of mishaps into a series of stories and strengthened our resolve to see more of the world.

THE WORLD'S WORST CAB DRIVER

His card read, *Executive Taxi Service.*

"Porque taxi ejecutivo?" I asked Victor as he shuttled us down the mountain in his 1978 Toyota to a hotel near the Simon Bolívar Airport in Caracas. A yellowed air freshener in the likeness of Christ hung from the rearview mirror.

He smiled, grabbed his tie, and held it out toward me.

"Exejutivo," he explained with a forced grin.

"Great, Kurt," I joked to my brother. "You picked a cab driver who charges a premium because he sports an ugly tie."

We agreed on five dollars as the price to the hotel. The ride lasted twenty minutes. Dumping our bags, we told him we needed another ride to the airport, five minutes away. He said he'd do it for ten dollars, knowing that cabs stayed clear of the dicey area that time of night. Victor was bad, but he wasn't the worst.

We met Abdullah in Bima, Indonesia. He had an old white van on its last legs with a cheap stereo that blared tinny folk songs. His driving style was fully up to (or down to) island standards; sometimes he paid attention to traffic signs, sometimes he gave way to other drivers, sometimes he kept his head fixed forward. He brought one wife the first day, a second the next, then asked for a double tip to "feed both families." He was bad, but he wasn't the worst.

Haggling is mandatory for decent cab fares, especially outside Western Europe. Lessons learned: Find the going rate, aim for half price, and always agree to a fare before entering the car. Prices are lower at the end of cab lines than at the beginning, and lower still if you walk fifty yards from the official pickup stations. Refuse offers of "free" stops at jewelry outlets, tailors, or souvenir shops unless you want to help your driver make a little money on the side.

We've had many overpriced rides, lost routes, and poor drivers. In Russia, every car is a potential cab; in Vietnam, every scooter. The taxis are a heap in Siem Reap, far from the best in Budapest, and frequently full in Istanbul.

But if you're looking for the world's worst cab driver, touch your finger to a spinning globe and the world will come to a halt on the island of Trinidad.

St. James is the Port of Spain neighborhood where locals point tourists for "nightlife." Smokey and Bunty's serves cold Carib beers through wire enclosures. *No Credit* signs hang on walls. Jerk chicken stands dot the sidewalks. A supermarket up the street advertises *Adult Diapers One Dollar* on a large wooden sign. St. James is the home of Douglas, the world's worst cab driver.

Kurt and I, on a mission to find the best of Trinidad, asked a St. James travel agent for the name of a driver to take us to a beach one morning. Tony laughed at us, saying all the cars and drivers were long taken due to Carnival. Just then, a man walked into the agency and handed Tony a card. "You guys are in luck," he said, surprised. "Here's the name of a driver named Douglas. Give him a call." We jumped on it.

"Doe-Glass," I could hear through the receiver from across the room. Kurt explained we wanted to go to the beach and gave him instructions to meet at our guesthouse/Christian rehab center at 11 A.M.

"I hope he's there," Kurt said after hanging up. "I didn't understand a word he said." Dressed, backpacks loaded, ready to go the next morning, no Douglas. We waited a half hour, then gave him a call.

"Oh, yah, mon," he said as if we had reminded him it was his birthday. "I be dare soon. Jus' need to make waaan stop." Kurt went back to bed. I settled into my book.

Noon, then 12:30 P.M., still no Douglas. We called a few other taxi companies, who told us they were fully booked, so we began making other plans.

At 1:00 P.M., a rusted orange Nissan with missing hubcaps and numerous dents rambled into our driveway. A chubby, thirty-something man with East Indian features and a splotchy black beard rang the bell. He smelled like the previous night's fete.

"Douglas," I said. "We missed you. We were so lonely."

"It's thirty dollars," Douglas answered in suddenly understandable English after Kurt probed him about the price. We groaned and told him much shorter rides were twenty dollars at most. He relented with a sheepish grin.

"We need to make a quick stop at the Brazilian embassy," I said, handing him a map marked with the embassy's location five blocks away. We could have walked. "No prah-blem," he sang.

Large holes spotted the back dash. A makeshift cloth ceiling draped down, resting on our heads. Knees bent to chins, arms around each other, we barely fit into the car. Two minutes outside the guesthouse, Kurt looked at the gas gauge and saw it was below empty.

"Don't you need some gas?" he inquired.

"Ooooh, yah," he said, nodding his head. Did either of us have any money? he asked. Kurt grumbled and gave him a few bucks.

Starting out again, Douglas waved to several people on opposite sides of the street. His eyes darted back and forth as if he were in a front-row seat at a tennis match, scanning for any activity other than what took place on the road.

He stopped and asked someone for directions. The conversation quickly shifted from streets to the street parties that had taken place the night before. After a tap on the shoulder and a couple "let's go" calls from the backseat, Douglas ended the chat and turned the old Nissan onto a one-way street heading out of town.

"Uhh, Douglas," I mentioned. "You're, umm, going the wrong way. It's just a couple blocks over there."

"Ohh-kay, mon," he replied, then spun his car 180 degrees to avoid a few oncoming cars.

We directed him the rest of the way, convinced him to wait while we picked up a visa application at the Brazilian embassy, then pointed him on the proper road to the beach. He kept his head out the window to shout greetings to an endless stream of friends.

"This guy knows someone on every street, yet doesn't know the streets," I opined. "Amazing."

During the half-hour ride to the beach, Douglas pontificated on the must-see-and-do highlights of Carnival. We laughed hard from the backseat, partly at the stories but mostly because we could decipher only about one of every five words. Leaning toward him, Kurt tried in vain to play interpreter.

"Any waahn whaaant a beer?" Douglas asked when we reached the beach. He asked for money again, but promised it would be an advance on the twenty-dollar fare.

"Maybe the beer will help his navigation skills," I rationalized. "Douglas, we'll see you here at five P.M." Or six, seven, or nine, we thought.

We were so fascinated by the Douglas experience, we wound up calling him several times, doing so more for amusement than for transportation. Having no place to go and no deadline to get there, we sat back and enjoyed the rides.

They went something like this. Arriving late, Douglas would ask for a ridiculously high fare. We'd laugh in unison, then cut the price to something more reasonable. Journeys were accompanied by personal errands "to geeeve a mess-ahge to a freeend." Questions about local landmarks or event schedules drew blank stares, then diatribes about obscure Caribbean subjects in his unintelligible Creole-English hybrid.

"You're never going to believe this," Kurt announced late on the one day we didn't need him. "Douglas called to say hi and to see if we wanted to do anything."

"Douglas, you are the world's worst cab driver," I finally told him. He grinned and mumbled something about being "proud to hold de tie-tall."

"No, you don't understand. It's not hyperbole. We've been to dozens of countries and used many, many cab drivers. You are, hands down, the worst cab driver in the world."

He laughed harder, and then suddenly pulled the car into a friend's driveway. "Jus' waaahn mee-nut, mon."

We wanted to say a proper good-bye to Douglas. Unfortunately, he never showed up to take us to the airport. He sent his brother instead, who explained Douglas had partied all night and was still too drunk to drive. Douglas instructed his brother to ask for our addresses in case he ever chose to visit the United States.

I hope he does. My house is open. I just won't have him drive.

19

My bag was the last one to come off the plane in Quito, Ecuador. I grabbed it, cleared customs, and walked into the packed airport lobby. I couldn't find Kurt. So I walked outside, waded through the crowd, and looked for a salt-and-pepper head above the others.

"Chic-lets, Chic-lets," boomed the familiar voice.

A flock of unwashed kids, eyes darting back to my brother, offered packets of gum to the stream of passengers.

"What are you doing?" I asked him.

"They wore me out," he explained. "You were late, so I decided to help them with their pitch rather than get harassed. Plus they gave me a percentage of everything they sell. Want any gum?"

"You get a cut?"

"Yeah, this kid here gave me a couple packs."

"Will he give you the rest of the night off?"

"Hasta luego, amigos," Kurt said to his sales force.

They pleaded with him to stay, grabbing his pant legs and staring at him with puppy dog faces. They should have been taller. They were children of the street.

"Lo siento, amigos."

We walked past the main waiting area, where a large family gathered to meet a flight from Miami. The silver-haired father wore a tattered suit and faded fedora. His wife clung by his side in a muumuu-type dress with a plastic flower brocade protruding where her cleavage began. She rubbed a small silver cross in her hands. Sons, daughters, and grandkids milled around the elderly couple. Twenty-eight in all, according to Kurt's rough count. We stopped to watch.

The doors opened and the travelers poured out. The young kids in the waiting group pushed their way to a front-row view, looking back at their parents, bouncing, excited. A young woman with smooth, tanned skin and dark hair pulled into a short ponytail emerged from the tunnel and parted from the stream. She was already crying by the time she saw her welcome party. Shifting a duty-free bag, she leaned over to hug the screaming children. The adults held back, beaming and shouting greetings instead. They waited for the family matron, who stopped fidgeting with her cross, clasped her hands together, and made her way to a warm hug. The others fell in after, surrounding the woman as if in a football huddle.

Blown away, Kurt and I speculated. Obviously she was family, but had she been away for a long time? Maybe she was the first family member to move to the U.S. for a job? Or school? Or maybe she'd just been away on a vacation?

We'd never seen anything like it. Twenty-eight people. Two or three was the most I could recall for a Wisner pickup at the airport. And our family was close. Not this close. I tried to imagine the circumstances necessary to get my dad to sport a tie at the airport, let alone drag twenty-eight family members to greet me.

It dawned on me that Latin America does family better than we do. A lot of the world does. First calls for outings are to brothers or cousins. Reunions take place each weekend, not once a year at a suburban backyard barbecue. In the U.S., the high school graduate who can afford to leave home and doesn't is either: a., heavily invested in a closet grow room; b., permanently attached to the family PlayStation; or c., so lazy he's started to hear responsibility lectures from slackers. The same kid in Latin America is considered eccentric if he dares share an apartment with friends or go somewhere other than the hometown college. The "gravy train" stretches until marriage. Then it joins with a family caravan for a lifelong journey. Money, sure, shapes decisions. Family ties much more so.

This is a good time. Go ahead.

I put my arm around Kurt. Maybe I left it there a little too long, because he shot me a "What's up?" look before flagging a taxi to take us to a bar near our guesthouse in the backpacker neighborhood known as Gringolandia. He'd heard of the place through a friend in California, and made arrangements through e-mail to stay there.

Now.

"You know the address?"

No!

"Yup. The best part of town. And I think Alberto may let us crash for free."

"That reunion scene back there. Wild. I've been thinking about that. And, you know . . . Well, thing is, I'm sorry if I've been a shitty brother."

"What did you do?"

"Whaddya mean?"

"Lose my Walkman?"

"I don't even have your Walkman. What I mean is that sometimes I haven't been the best brother, and I just wanted to say I'll do better in the future."

"Like when?"

"Like when you got divorced two years ago."

There.

"What about it?" he said.

"Well, I wasn't really there for you. I didn't jump on a plane the next day and help you make calls."

"I didn't need to make any calls."

"You know what I mean."

"I knew that was eating at you," he said.

"Doofus. Why didn't you say anything earlier?"

"I dunno. Guess I was just trying to forget about that part of my life. Get on with things. And mess with you a bit."

"Well, I'm sorry."

"Don't beat yourself up over it. I don't want you crying and stuff for the rest of the trip."

And that was it. There, in the back of the Quito taxi, we buried one of my biggest guilt trips. The *mea culpa* freed the issue for many more discussions in the coming months about his former relationship and mine. Kurt opened up about his failed marriage, admitting it wasn't as simple a case as his wife being too young, the conventional wisdom among family and friends. He talked about panicking on his honeymoon that he had done the wrong thing, about the times he chose golf over discussion, about his struggle to "make it work" while his heart told him otherwise. I listened. The conversations deepened.

Dear LaRue—

Alberto's the mayor of Gringolandia, the backpacker/Bohemian section of Quito. It's not an elected position, but earned through years in the Internet cafes and discount travel agencies housed in the area's rundown colonial buildings.

Originally from Italy, Alberto moved to Quito to hone his Spanish, sharpen his salsa, and add commas to his bank account. The same urges pull thousands of young Europeans and Americans to the friendly capital perched several thousand meters above sea level in the Andes. His shoulder-length dark hair and pencil mustache give him a Gen-X Zorro look. Women knock on his guesthouse at all hours; proprietors of nearby businesses seek his opinion. But Alberto's ready to abdicate his mayoral duties and move to California. Quito can blacken spirits and lungs, like other large South American cities. People talk about the area in the past tense. "You should have been here twenty years ago." It's a recurring conversation about a high school figure or last year's stock market— the focus is on what was.

We caught Quito after a storm, before the buses could fill the high basin with smog. Walking through certain parks or neighborhoods, you can see glimmers of glories past.

After a few days, we escaped to the mountain villages with fedora-wearing, machete-wielding men, women carrying sticks or babies in colorful shawls, and dense forests packed with birds we'd only seen on cereal boxes. Add some snow, swap the ponchos for lederhosen and you'd swear you're tucked in the European Alps. We enjoyed Mindo for the walks and waterfalls, Banos for the *banos* and high valley setting.

The transportation of choice here are four-wheeled markets they call buses. Salesmen we dubbed "buslers" climb on and off like clowns in a circus police car. *Mano-a-mano,* some sing, some beg, most sell. The random selections would make 7-Eleven proud. We saw one busler hawking radio antennas and electronic waist trimmers with one arm, Super Glue and clothes hangers with the other. Territories are nonexistent, with buslers crowding around each other in narrow aisles and over seats. On our bus to Banos, I counted eleven at one time. Balance is a prerequisite since buses rarely come to a full stop for the buslers, forcing them to jump to and fro with goods stacked high.

The buses are cheap in Ecuador. Most things are cheap in Ecuador, more affordable than in other countries on this continent. And while Europe bickers about a single currency, it's already happening here. The Latin Euro is called the dollar. In Ecuador, like several other countries south of the Rio Grande, the currency of choice is the U.S. greenback. We didn't see any local bills. Don't even know if they still print them. Call it a Greenspan, so to speak.

Love,

Franz

Ecuador was the South American equivalent to Costa Rica—it was Americanized enough so U.S. visitors could find a *Time* magazine or their favorite hair gel, yet foreign enough so the folks back home thought you'd been someplace exotic. Americans we met talked about return trips and buying property in the mountains or along the coast. A walk through Quito's La Mariscal neighborhood was a stroll across Harvard Square or Berkeley's Telegraph Avenue. Just add a few more tour hucksters and shrink the height of the locals by a couple inches.

We spent many of our days with Emma, a sunny, adventurous flatmate from Alberto's guesthouse. She'd made the pilgrimage from Britain to improve her Spanish and make a few dollars teaching English, hike the Andes on weekends, eat granola breakfasts and drink fruit smoothies in the colonial-building cafés, and just enjoy a pretty, hospitable, and easy-going foothold in Latin America. She was also on a mission to track down a thousand dollars from an old boyfriend in Argentina the same way the IMF goes after unpaid loans, responsibility lectures included. After she dubbed Kurt a *mujeriego,* Spanish for "womanizer," I knew we could travel in kidding comfort with her. Kurt and I needed a good dose of ridicule and sarcasm at that stage of the honeymoon.

"You guys can skip the exhibit at the equator," she said. "It's tacky."

But, c'mon. How could we skip the equator? That would be like going to Iceland and not seeing the ice. Or like the time I went to Fez, Morocco, a few years back. I didn't want to purchase the red felt beanie. Too many bad memories of Shriner conventions in Las Vegas sitting next to grand pooh-bahs at the blackjack tables and watching them hit on fourteen when the dealer showed six. I fought it and fought it. And went home with a dozen fezes in my bag. Of course we had to straddle the equator in Ecuador.

Plus, I'd begun to send postcards to a third-grade class in California from places I hoped would spark curiosity. The teacher, whom I'd never met, got my e-mail from a friend and contacted me to see if I could help with her geography lessons. I wanted the kids to contemplate the ribbon around the waist of the globe, to go home and tell their parents that toilets flush clockwise north of the equator and counterclockwise south. ("Some man is sending your class postcards about Latin toilets?")

"Amigo, where's the toilet experiment?" I asked the guard standing in front of the high-rise museum at the equator.

A long yellow line split the building and continued into a courtyard of shops and restaurants. *Latitude 0 degrees,* proclaimed the plaque on the wall.

"*Qué?*"

"Toilets. You know, *servicios?*" I explained, making a twirling motion with my hand.

After a contemplative stare, he nodded his head and pointed to an area several hundred yards away.

"How can they be over there if the equator is here?" I said, pointing to the yellow line beneath my feet.

"Thees no the line."

"This isn't the equator?"

"*Sí.*"

"And this tall building here doesn't sit on the equator?"

"*Sí. Sí,*" he said with a grin.

"Ecuador built this whole complex away from the line?"

"*Sí.*"

"I like it. Just go with it. People will never know the difference unless they ask."

"Nobody es perfect."

"Nobody is perfect." I nodded in agreement.

Kurt asked the Banos guesthouse waitress for more coffee. I asked her for a pillow. For my derriere. It still smarted from the five-hour bike ride through the lush and lumpy canyons outside town the day before. The rains didn't help either. Or the cool temps. I pushed for a nap as the best way to start the day. Kurt stared at the town's main waterfall pouring over a rocky cliff nearby.

"Do you have any cortisone?" I asked him.

"An hour in the baths will cure whatever you have," interjected the man at the next table.

He had the compact, wiry build of a runner, black hair like a Brillo pad, and the steely gaze of the street. Dean's the name, he said, pulling his chair up to our table. He wanted company. We obliged with a quick recap of our honeymoon story (now whittled to a minute) and a boast about being on the road for eight months.

"How long you been out?" Kurt asked.

"Twenty-five years."

Ouch. Humbled. We're in the presence of Yoda.

"Whoa," I said, before realizing I sounded like Keanu Reeves.

"Started right after Vietnam. That was thirty years ago. Then subtract the years in prison. So yeah, right around twenty-five."

Ohh. Yoda's got some baggage. And he can probably fashion a shiv out of those toothpicks there. Note to self.

Still, we were curious, especially Kurt. At his urging, Dean began to tell stories of backpacking in countries "before the word *tourist* existed. They didn't even know what to call me." He talked about his close friends, the monks in Nepal and the royal family in Cambodia, about living with rebels in Afghanistan and being held for months against his will after they realized he knew how to farm. He escaped by telling them he needed to brush his teeth by the river.

See, I'm right. He probably turned the toothbrush into a shiv.

Kurt pressed him on the best stops off the beaten path. Laos and Burma have temples that rival Angkor Wat, Dean said. Check it out on his Web site. Ecuador is nice, but "are you guys going to Bolivia?" I flagged down the waitress for a pen to record his suggestions.

"Have you ever heard of Rainbow City?"

"Where's that? Bolivia?"

"No, no."

Pause. Dean looked around to see if anyone was eavesdropping.

"It's five hundred miles inside the earth," he said. "I'm planning to go soon."

Waitress, forget the pen. Check, please. Yoda just led us on a trip around the bend.

Dean continued to talk about Rainbow City . . . and million-year-old arks he'd touched . . . and time travel . . . and the astral plane. Kurt baited him to continue. My arse still smarted, but I'd given up on the nap. This was far more interesting.

Just when we thought Dean was 100 percent crazy, he'd make things even more interesting. He'd snap out of his mystic trance and shift to something sane. Like literature. He jotted down a list of twenty books we "must read," mostly classics. With each suggestion he'd launch into a mini-lecture about the brilliance of Borges or the metaphors of Nabakov. I scrambled to separate his words from the astro plane. He elaborated on a couple of secluded Andes retreats in our next destination, Peru, spots that sounded a little more reachable than Rainbow City.

And we were in. We clung to Dean and his ramblings for the next couple days. In the town's natural springs and grilled guinea pig cafés ("No thanks, I'll stick with the cheese sandwiches"), we listened to Dean pontificate about prison ("They released me after I unearthed some very damaging information, which I don't want to get into at this time"), Vietnam ("At one time, the most beautiful and most ugly place on the planet"), relationships ("If you have any lingering questions, it's not love"), spirituality ("You already have the answers. They're just buried under a ton of debris."), and mostly, the occult ("I don't believe in reincarnation. I know reincarnation."). Who knows what was true? It was fascinating. All of it.

A year ago we probably would have ignored him. Here we fueled off him. He caused us to pause, to chew on a thought. Other than Rainbow City, that is. And he made us reevaluate notions about sources of knowledge. He proved it could come from unlikely fronts.

Like those unwashed prophets in the Bible. Wait. That's going too far. Stick with the unlikely front stuff.

At the end of a lasagna dinner on our last night in Banos, Kurt asked Dean if he had any final words of wisdom.

"Do what's right," he answered without pause.

Pow. Simple. Sane. Stronger than a self-help book or a twelve-step program. Dean didn't bother to elaborate. He tore off a chunk of bread knowing there was no room for misinterpretation.

As we left Banos the next morning, Kurt unzipped his bag and grabbed a hotel towel. He stared at it, then threw it on the floor.

"Goddamn Dean," he said. "I won't be able to lift anything from hotels again."

Most people go to psychologists and counselors to cope with pain and loss. I was beginning to realize we were receiving our couch sessions from characters like Dean, Helga, and Douglas. They showed us ethics, reinvention, and chutzpah, respectively. Sure, they weren't perfect. In Douglas's case, the education was often along the lines of how-not-to. But together the lessons were beginning to add up.

We wanted to go. West. Toward the Galápagos Islands, one of our only predetermined destinations on the continent. The journey started by hitchhiking a ride with two Americans driving from New York to Tierra del Fuego in a heavily customized Nissan Pathfinder with multiple alarms and secret storage compartments. Kurt met them in the baths at Banos. Proving a global cliché, they turned out to be gay. So we helped them find a gay-friendly hotel that night. In most of South America, "gay-friendly" meant any place willing to rent a room with one bed to two men.

We swapped the comfortable Pathfinder the next morning for an all-day bus ride to Guayaquil, the jumping-off point for the Galápagos. An unshaven, deodorant-free man with a *cerveza* belly sat next to me. His gut erupted beneath his T-shirt and onto my space. Kurt smirked. A young schoolgirl with a doll on her lap fidgeted in her seat next to Kurt. His self-satisfaction grew.

A half hour and a dozen U-turns later, I was the one smiling. Minutes after departure, the young girl emptied her breakfast entrée on the floor with a side order on Kurt's shoes. My grin vanished as soon as the smell flooded the bus. Windows opened in New York City Rockette unison. Only after a hard stare from Kurt did the girl's mom budge. She threw a newspaper sheet over the heap of used food and gave it a swipe with her foot. And as the bus wound down the mountain, the girl gave repeat performances, thankfully now in a plastic bag held by her mother.

My seatmate on the airplane to the Galápagos, a salesman from Chicago, didn't vomit. He just spewed a ton of questions.

"How long's your vacation?"

"A year. Maybe longer."

"A year? What did you do? Win the lottery?"

Most Americans we met on the road, or at least the ones without nose rings, had a hard time fathoming the idea of a year's travel. Australians and Germans would nod in "of course" approval. Our countrymen would fixate on language barriers or some hideous tropical disease. They'd talk about the nightmare scenario— a Third World appendectomy and not being able to tell the doctor to use clean needles.

With his tour name tag (*Jed M.*) already pinned to the crisp golf shirt (*Something Pines*), my seatmate was also perplexed why we didn't have reservations on the boats, which toured the islands by day and slept visitors by night. It was the way nearly all visitors toured the islands. He'd paid 2,500 dollars for two weeks, not including airfare. To a skeptical jurist, I explained our experience during the last eight months had been to save money by eliminating tour operators, travel agents, and middlemen whenever possible. Deal directly with boat operators, guides, or hotel owners, I argued, and cut your costs in half.

"Honey, this guy's gonna try to hitchhike his way on a boat," he shouted to his wife across the aisle.

And we did. Kind of. After an afternoon of haggling, we jumped on a boat half-full, the *Amigo II* (Astroturf deck, park-bench dining room, eighteen-inch television with no VCR or reception), agreeing to pay five hundred dollars for ten days, a fraction of the standard prices advertised in the travel agencies and guidebooks. In the U.S., if a boat or a bus is half booked, it leaves as planned rather than face the ire of passengers. In Latin America, and throughout much of the world, trips don't depart until they are 100 percent full. Make that 150 percent. Travelers expect as much and rarely complain as buses circle towns continuously before departing.

The *Amigo II* was comfortable, save the moody AC, the group adventurous, and the crew friendly and proficient. Yet something was wrong. It wasn't the daily traipses through the living rooms of iguanas, sea lions, tortoises, frigate birds, and boobies. They welcomed us like a wedding party, posing for pictures, shuffling aside as guest after guest sauntered by. All these people have to be hurting the environment, I'd think, as I added my harmful footsteps to theirs. The tours, photos, and eco-love didn't seem to inhibit the wildlife's daily routine. They recreated, vegetated, and procreated as if we didn't exist. No, that wasn't it.

And it wasn't the Marine World snorkel sessions. Mornings spent chasing schools of fish were followed by afternoon bombardments from sea lions. They'd dive, spin, stop, dart, roll, inspect, bump, shoot away, and chase back better than an ace barnstormer. The sea-wrestling matches made me laugh, which wasn't advisable underwater. The comedy routines forced me to resurface, clear my snorkel, and take a quick peek to make sure Mr. Alpha Male sea lion rested comfortably onshore. Other dives featured cameo appearances from sprightly penguins, colorful eels, methodic turtles, and ominous hammerhead sharks. Still, something was a bit off.

"It's our guide," Kurt said day two. "He sucks."

"Give him a chance, amigo. He seems knowledgeable enough. And his English is decent, though I'm having a tough time pinpointing the accent."

Short, muscular, and serious, Raul was an Ecuadoran who'd completed the prerequisite years of higher education to qualify as a guide. A part-time researcher, he filled in for vacationing guides like a substitute teacher. We tried to crack his stern demeanor, on hikes and during meals, without success.

"Theeeese es marine eeeguana," he'd bark during a morning hike, and then launch into a two-sentence explanation of how the creature came to call the Galápagos Islands home.

"Theeeese es lava leeezard. . . ."

By day three we'd had enough pat-and-packaged descriptions. I baited Raul off the talking points with specific questions about evolution and natural selection.

"Theeeese es marine eeeguana. . . ."

"He's a machine," I declared. "Or a politician during a debate. No matter what the question, you'll get the same answer."

We gave up on Raul and gleaned sufficient information to satisfy our curiosity through the boat's library, conversations with other tourists, and by cornering guides on different tours. The accent, the demeanor, the scripted answers—Raul was an enigma. On our last day I cornered him and asked about his background and training.

"I went to university in Russia. Lived there for many years."

Ahhh. Lightbulb. We'd managed to climb aboard with the world's only Galápagos guide with Soviet training. Problem solved.

Another lingered. As hard as I tried, I couldn't shake the realization I had in the middle of the night in Thailand. I still loved Annie. More than anything, it frustrated me. If there's any place on the planet that should be able to distract attention, it's the Galápagos. Yet I thought about her often during the afternoon treks and those hour-long snorkel sessions on my own. As I floated with penguins and seals, I often drifted back to our days together, replaying the road to our crash over and over.

Mate, you got seals doing Cirque du Soleil moves all around you and you're thinking about that blown weekend in Carmel? Don't you realize there's nothing you could have said? The relationship was doomed. It was only a matter of time. You know that.

I'd emerge from the waters mad at myself for spending so much time thinking about the past. Not that I wanted to abandon the trip, move back to Orange County, and try to rekindle our relationship. My friends would have used a straitjacket to prevent me from doing that. Make that a crowbar and a dark alley.

No, I knew our time together was over. And I knew it was okay to feel lingering emotions after a decade-long relationship. I just wanted to stop dreaming about her. That was my personal-recovery gauge. I'd go to bed each night praying she wouldn't pop into my head. At the very least, I wanted someone else to share the REM stage.

20

"You want to hike to Machu Picchu?" asked an attractive, Medusa-haired woman standing outside baggage claim at the Lima airport, waiting for our flight from Ecuador.

Sensing a tourist fleecing, Kurt was far from enthralled with the allure of our pretty travel agent. He worked her over on a deal for a "five-star hotel" for the night with a promise we'd talk to her the next day about travel packages. (Note: Don't be fooled by hotel ratings in Latin America. Best to treat them like army generals after a sex scandal . . . remove at least two stars.) She got us a good price at the Miraflores Park Hotel, so we found ourselves in her office in the morning bargaining for plane fares, a trip to the Colca Valley, hotels in Arequipa and Cuzco, and a trekking expedition to Machu Picchu.

"I thought we'd given up on prepaid package deals?" Kurt asked me mid-negotiation.

"I know, I know. But this one seems like a good deal."

"She's clouded your judgment."

Kurt agreed to buy the airline tickets and Colca Valley package, but to leave Machu Picchu deals for later.

"How much you pay for this tour?" he asked a German traveler during a coca-tea break on our drive around the stunning and serene Colca Valley a few days later.

"Nineteen dollars."

Kurt almost gagged on his coca leaves. The price was less than half of what we paid, a cardinal sin in Kurt's code of travel. He shot me an angry stare and mumbled something about not wanting to know how much we'd overpaid for the flights and hotels.

"Never again," he said adamantly. "I don't care how good-looking she is."

We sucked it up—the prices, the thin air, and being lumped with an all-too-serious group of young Germans with perfect English and perfectly no sense of humor. Middle-aged at twenty-five. At least the surrounds were inviting. Hang-glider dream cliffs, *Sound of Music* meadows, and siesta villages centered around white stucco churches with wood beams and cracked bells made Colca a low-touristed, highly rewarding experience. We spent the days on prep hikes for Machu Picchu and prep rests in natural mineral baths.

Cuzco, the well-preserved colonial town and launching pad for Machu Picchu treks, was also the starting point for Kurt's revenge.

"Our hotel sucks," he told a representative of the tour company. "We need an upgrade for the rest of the trip or else we won't book the hike."

An hour later and we were in a new hotel with a large fireplace, two-chair balcony, and cable television. That was just the beginning. Without telling the tour representative, he led me on a trek to find the cheapest trek. Two hundred, 150, 125 dollars: the price dropped with each office we visited. Kurt would tell the operator we had reservations for a ridiculously low price, and they'd lower their fees accordingly.

"It's all the same," he said. "These tour operators just sign up people for the same treks going out. The higher the price, the larger their profit."

It was the way most tours in Latin America worked. And in the rest of the Third World. The operators didn't operate tours, they just booked them. The actual work was left to someone else, someone receiving the end crust of the fee. At the end of the day, we paid 115 dollars each, which included the fifty-dollar entrance to the park. To reverse the pecking order, we decided to tip big at the end of the trek.

As we fumbled through our belongings at the beginning of the trail, I noticed a small group of hikers with American accents. They assembled expensive North Face backpacks, skyscrapers of aluminum rods and Gore-Tex that towered a foot above their heads. One sported a water bag with a scubalike tube to his mouth. Matt, their leader, pulled out ski-pole walking sticks, swearing they enhanced his endurance. With Arctic-ready sleeping bags, Power Bars with scientific equations on the Day-Glo wrappers, military-issue flashlights, the threesome from Connecticut had it all.

Our equipment would have made Edmund Hillary wince. We crammed a couple days clothing and four pairs of socks into my borrowed backpack. Running shoes, one raincoat, and a poncho between us ("we'll rotate"), our plan was four days of pain and pray for no rain. "We'll just dry the shoes out by the fire at night if we get drenched." If temperatures dropped, our backup plan was to shiver.

The week we chose to climb Machu Picchu wasn't optimal either, coming at the tail end of the rainy season. A foursome from France told us in Cuzco they'd just completed the trek in four rain- and fog-filled days without ever seeing the lost Incan city in its entirety. Showers, showers, showers, read the forecast on the Internet.

So what. It had to be done. Too many old-time hippies told us of mind-blowing religious experiences at the ancient ruins to pass it up, though I forgot to ask them if they had the same experiences at Woodstock or after each time someone passed them a bong. We had cut short our time in Ecuador to do it and admitted we were "cheating Peru" by spending only two and a half weeks there.

The second day of the trip was, by far, the hardest. The morning climb continued at a chalet-rooftop angle. Up to nearly fourteen thousand feet. A quick lunch in a valley past a peak, then another four hours of tough, uphill climbing awaited us. We were in decent shape after eight months of walks and runs, but still found ourselves stopping every ten minutes to catch our breaths and reload coca leaves that numbed our mouths and eased our panting. I resisted the leaves at first because of the bitter taste.

"Give me a wad of that stuff," I barked after an hour of level 200 StairMaster climbing. "Maybe this is what the hippies were talking about."

Still, we were doing pretty well trekking along the stone-path Incan highway, through landscapes that changed from jungle overhangs to Scottish glens to treeless tors. At least we thought we were doing well until we saw our group's fifty-year-old porter, clothed in thrift-store dress pants and dime-store plastic sandals, lugging a fifty-pound propane tank and portable stove, breeze past us as if we were a scooter on the Autobahn. Show-off. We picked up our pace and plowed ahead.

"You mind if I ask you a question?" I said.

"You just did," Kurt replied.

"Another one?"

"You just did."

"Do you still love Claudia?"

"The altitude is messing with your brain, bro," he said. "We're divorced, remember?"

"I know, but you can still love her."

"I don't."

"Really?"

"Well, not in the way you're asking. I suppose I still love her as a friend and wish her well. But I don't ever dream about getting back together with her."

"What do you mean by dream?"

"You're not still dreaming about Annie, are you?"

"No. I mean, yeah. And it's driving me crazy. But don't panic. I'm not going back to her. Or quitting the trip. It's just that every now and then I fall asleep and wake with her plastered across my mind."

"That's nothing. I still get those once in a while. That stuff's just residue."

"How long until they're a rarity?"

"For me it was a year or so."

"I'm overdue."

"Don't worry about it. You'll meet someone, and Annie'll take a backseat in your head. Just don't expect her to leave. Old flames have a way of lingering."

"Thanks."

"Or maybe try some more of those coca leaves. They could change your dreams."

At the end of our talk, we reached a summit. Kurt handed me a bland Peruvian granola bar and we continued on to the midday camp. I felt relieved knowing he'd struggled with the same issues, better still sensing the hardest part of the climb was behind us. We drank watery bouillon provided by the porters, stretched out in a large tent to escape the off-and-on rain, and watched the others make their way into camp.

"There's Matt with the walking sticks," I mentioned a few hours later, after a nap.

"And there's a half-pint carrying his buddy's bag," Kurt replied.

I stared in disbelief as a prepubescent Peruvian girl lugged a pack equal her size into camp. She dumped it near Matt's pack, nodded, and took off back up the incline.

"Matt, what happened to your friend?" we asked our exhausted companion.

"He, ahh, paid some twelve-year-old girl to haul his gear. He'll be here soon. Hopefully. Just don't ask him about it. He feels awful."

Altitude entrepreneurs, that's what we called the young porter and her partners. They shuttled packs and pocketed money better than resort bellhops. The youngsters waited at the base of the trail's steepest portion before offering their services. Sweat-drenched climbers would hesitate, then swing their bags over to the industrious kids in torn T-shirts and taped-up sandals.

The hippies, young and old, prophesied correctly. Machu Picchu was a religious experience, if for no other reason than our bodies felt like we'd spent four days sleeping on a stiff wooden pew. We loved every bit—the stone and dirt paths through forests and wide-open expanses, the serenity of a walk in the park and the dizzying exhilaration of a marathon, the well-choreographed music of the wind, the dance of the trees, and the light of the valley crevices.

On the day after we reached the fabled lost city, Kurt and I snuck into the park at 4:30 A.M., perched ourselves on an overhang, then sat back to enjoy the show. We had the entire place to ourselves at first light. The dulled, stone temples, draped over the mountain ridge like a saddle, warmed to life as the sun peeked its head. Two hours later, and it was all downhill as the buses unloaded group after group of tourists in spotless hiking boots and freshly pressed safari shirts. We prowled around for the rest of the day, poaching information from high-priced tour guides and explaining to visitors from America that we normally didn't look or smell this bad.

Exhausted after four days of gasping and gawking, we wanted to sleep. Throughout the hike I fantasized about a remote control and a mattress that didn't require Tylenol PM. Once in Lima, we crashed hard at the Miraflores Park Hotel again, then found ourselves on poolside lounge chairs next to two chatty, preppy American women with Southern accents.

They were there "with Jimmy Carter, here to monitor the election," answered the one with the expensive bob haircut and chipped French manicure. The other bright-eyed Beltway ballot bouncer explained in detail who would win the presidential election. They debated only projected victory percentages. And, of course, there would be no fraud in this one. They had all the answers. Except for the fact they were completely wrong.

Now, I long admired former President Alberto Fujimori. He inspired us wannabe politicians with foreign-sounding names. I didn't want to change mine to Frank Wise if I ever ran for office. But I never understood how someone with co-Japanese citizenship could win an election in Latin America. The answer, we found out, is that he didn't. At least not in his last election.

Fujimori was a pioneer. He didn't simply buy and steal the election like his predecessors. He combined old-fashioned theft with modern-day drug-money payoffs while capturing the whole show on videotapes that would make even Rupert Murdoch blush. The morning papers reviewed the videos à la Ebert and Roeper, critiquing the ham-fisted performances of Fujimori and his henchman, Vladimiro Montesinos, as they prodded politicians with cash. Like studio executives after a flop, Fujimori and his cronies fled the country to avoid the aftermath.

So Peru had a special election. We couldn't escape it. Cartoon advertisements were painted on remote village walls, plastered on most billboards, painted on rocks in the middle of rivers, stuck on cars and curbs. The candidates were measured along a right-to-left spectrum—right in line with common corruption standards or left the country like Fujimori. *Menos corrupto* was a common phrase heard to justify a candidate: "He's a good guy. And less corrupt, too." The contestants included a former president previously forced to leave office, a woman viewed by opponents as a Fujimori puppet, and a Harvard-educated populist drenched in drug and paternity scandals. The tired, hired, and mired trying to replace the fired.

During walks around town we were bombarded by election officials in white windbreakers explaining the do's and don'ts of the upcoming election. Kurt kept trying to hand them money, a joke that sent them fleeing to the company of others. An older man in a white hat tracked me down to explain they couldn't kid about favorites since the "top bosses were watching."

"You guys are good," I reassured him. "You might even put Jimmy Carter out of work." He scrunched his face in confusion.

Peruvians are amazingly honest, I thought, as I walked into the small market next door, purchased soft drinks and candy with a fifty soles bill (the equivalent of fifteen dollars), and left with a wad of counterfeit money that I didn't realize was phony until we got to Brazil.

Continuing on the campaign trail, we added our bodies to a packed political rally in the Arequipa town square a few days later. They were there to hear Alan Garcia, a contender for the Fujimori post. He was the "tired," the scandal-drenched former president seeking to reclaim lost glories. It was an old-fashioned whistle-stop tour. Thousands of Peruvians danced to one of the omnipresent Gypsy King pan flute and guitar bands that bust into *"I'd rather be a hammer than a nail"* faster than you can say *"El Condor Pasa."* They rah-rahed with sleepy enthusiasm as if Jerry Garcia was taking the stage. This one looked fit and inspired and tan. He hugged the band members, gave kisses to several women onstage, grabbed the microphone, and recited a litany of more promises and "I do's" than a mass wedding of Moonies.

I didn't notice the man walk up next to me. Kurt tapped me on the shoulder. I looked around and still didn't see him. The Peruvian couldn't have been more than five feet tall. He wore a white Oxford shirt with the sleeve rolled and carried large water buckets in each arm. I glanced down. He stared up at me. I glanced. He stared. He placed his buckets on the ground, shifted his hands to his hips, and nodded at me to begin a conversation. I had no idea what to say. Especially in the fifty words of Spanish I'd acquired over the previous months. We had the following conversation in Spanish:

> Me: You are a little man.
> Pause.
> Amigo: Yes, but I can clean a lot.
> Pause.
> Me: Okay, then give me a hug.
> Pause.
> Amigo: Okay.

We hugged for thirty seconds, and then he picked up his buckets and walked off.

"What was that all about?" Kurt howled.

"I have no idea. After he told me he could clean, I couldn't think of anything to say. So we hugged."

"That was a long hug."

"I know. Maybe he's really into Alan Garcia or something."

I turned to another man next to me and asked if he planned to vote for Garcia. He took a step back before I could finish my sentence. I think he saw me hug the little guy.

"No, señor. Mas corrupto," he said as if everyone felt that way.

Of course. He wasn't there because he loved Garcia. Political rallies were de rigueur. You attended them regardless of political views. I thought about the countless times I'd pleaded with my former colleagues to join me for a half hour at a cushy cocktail reception for Senator Big Wig or Congressman Big Hair.

In Peru and in many of the Third World countries we visited, there was a much higher level of political activism than in the U.S., yet a much greater level of distrust. Indonesians, Peruvians, Russians, Cambodians, Venezuelans, and Turks all cornered us to explain how their politicians "put the money in their pocket," making motions to hide bills in their pants. These were the same people who packed rallies, devoured political stories in newspapers, and detailed platforms of office seekers. The greater the participation, the greater the mistrust. I hoped it wasn't a causal relationship.

Alan Garcia. In many ways he was symbolic of world leaders and candidates whose countries we toured during elections, with their scandals and efforts to advance their agendas. He inspired me to sit down that night and jot a few basic rules about foreign politics for my friends still involved with government in the United States:

- Be suspicious of national leaders who wear medals, army fatigues, military dress, swords, or emblem-crested hats with feathers.
- If the foreign leader plasters his face all over the local currency, don't hold your breath for democratic reforms.
- In the cult-of-personality game, billboards and statues are singles and doubles. Embalmings are home runs. And for embalmed-dictator fans, the winning trifecta is Lenin in Red Square, Mao in China, and Ho Chi Minh in Hanoi.
- If government policies are usually the lead stories on the front page of the business section, the country probably isn't the best place for your investment.
- No matter what Jimmy Carter says, if a candidate reportedly receives more than 70 percent of the vote, the election was rigged or stolen.

- The world must be using the same blow-dryer because all the candidates are starting to look the same.
- With apologies to Great Britain and many other countries, I still don't trust systems in which politicians can set the date of their own election.
- Countries that dismiss, abolish, or send home politicians for bad behavior don't quite have the democracy thing down.
- It's the infrastructure, stupid. The most effective leaders we witnessed were the ones who stuck to the basics—roads, power, water, and schools—and left the extra-credit stuff—global treaties, goodwill missions—for others.
- Baby Doc, Uncle Joe, Gus Dur—red flags for world leaders with nicknames.

THE REAL DANGERS OF BRAZIL

For years I believed the conventional wisdom. "Don't go to Brazil," the experts said. "It's too dangerous." The guidebooks warned of hooligan militias, while travel agents said, "Beware, beware, beware." Better stick to someplace safer. Like Branson, Missouri, or Conway Twitty City.

After a training regimen that included numerous John Wayne movies, karate classes, and Power Bars, Kurt and I flew to Rio. And I was furious . . . furious it took me thirty-five years to unearth one of our planet's most exhilarating places.

Forget about petty theft, because there are plenty of other pitfalls lurking. Here's a list of some of the real dangers awaiting visitors to Brazil.

It's dangerously fattening. I knew I was in trouble the first time I walked into a famous Porcão restaurant. The sign in front featured a giant, smiling pig's head. The waiter inside handed me a card colored red on one side, green on the other. "It's to let them know when you've had enough," a friend explained. Great. They see my stomach as a multilane freeway. Like an accordion car wreck, the barbecued steaks, pork, chicken, seafood, and anything with a prior pulse began to pile high on my plate. Put another fork in that and then put another fork in me.

It's treacherously fun. Be careful or you'll be plowed over by a mountain biker or a seventy-year-old man clocking his daily ten-mile run. Rio's beaches are packed like an FDR Supreme Court, jammed with paddle ball maniacs (still don't understand how someone wins that game), heated soccer and volleyball matches, and an endless parade of stunningly beautiful women in less-is-more bikinis. They make your mind skip like a scratched João Gilberto album—*tall and tan and young and lovely . . . and tall and tan and young and lovely . . . and tall and . . .*

For men's swimsuits, there is a double danger. Wear your knee-length, California surfer shorts and risk ridicule from local women who abhor tan lines. Sport a skimpy Speedo and risk having your friends take a picture and post it on a dating Web site for pale men.

Hand signals can also get tourists into trouble. Many locals end conversations with a thumbs-up. It feels like being trapped in a *Happy Days* rerun. "Um, it's Franz, not Fonz."

And make sure to lose the A-OK sign. Here it suggests an intimate act with oneself. An A-OK can result in a KO if you're not careful. Wish I picked that up sooner. I ordered meals and drinks for the first few days with the sign. Thanks, waiters, for not serving the food on my lap.

Wearing the wrong soccer team colors in a locals' bar before a match can be hazardous. Kurt's black shirt in a room full of red went over about as well as my wisecrack to a group of Argentine soccer enthusiasts about Maradona being a drug addict. "Joking, I'm joking. Anybody know the word for joking?"

And I don't care how many *caipirinhas* (see "high-octane margaritas, Brazilian-style") you've downed. Do not try to samba. Leave it to the locals. Stick to the gringo two-step. Chances are you'd just throw out a hip and spend the rest of your trip in a hospital. Yes, Brazil's most famous composer, Antônio Carlos Jobim, said there are only three countries in the world that "swing"—Brazil, Cuba, and the United States. Trust me on this. He didn't mean you.

But the most risky aspect of Brazil is the likelihood of addiction, a charge of which I am guilty. Completely and remorselessly. It took me three and a half decades to find my way. I'm here for another month, but already looking forward to the dangers that await on my next visit to Brazil.

21

A week after I wrote that piece, I was attacked at knifepoint on the streets of Rio de Janeiro.

Wait. Forget I said that. It was a small knife. More of a pocketknife, really. The kind you'd use to open a letter. A tiny letter. And I could have kicked the little guy's butt. If it wasn't for his two big buddies, that is. But no problem. I rarely carried more than change, which was easy to do after ten months of siphoning my bank account. When the local, *Carioca*, pulled the knife, I just emptied my pockets of their measly five reais. So just forget about the whole thing. I don't want it to distract from the fact that, despite its plethora of problems, Brazil is one of my favorite foreign lands on this planet.

Despite the assault, I remained in love with Brazil. And for many reasons beyond those sacred threads of clothing they call bikinis. The marriage between elevation and shore made Rio (and other cities with similar geographical blessings—San Francisco and Cape Town, for example) dramatic and easy to view. Neighborhoods with distinct character and feel nestle in flat areas and on hillsides. In Rio, they included numerous shantytown *favelas* that clung to patches of real estate both expensive and/or unwanted. Giant ribbons and expanses of open space—the Parque Nacional da Tijuca and the Serra da Carioca surrounding the city—tied the whole package together with the warm Atlantic serving as a blue bow on top. A gift from Christ himself, Corcovado.

During our time abroad, Kurt and I found ourselves gravitating toward the planet's cultural crossroads, meeting points that blended everything from architecture to skin color. Places like Istanbul and Indonesia (or New Orleans and Los Angeles, for that matter). The restaurants tended to be a little more interesting and spicy, the people more exotic, the dress more colorful, the rituals more showy, the gathering places a maze of present and past. Rio is all that, with a mix of African, Portuguese, North American, and Latin cultures. Like the six-foot-tall black samba dancer with her jeweled skirt and Revlon makeup or the *boteco* owner who served the rain forest's *açai* shakes and *guaraná* drinks, hamburgers, Cokes, and *pão de queijo*.

As important as physical attribute in Brazil is attitude. I loved the optimism despite an economy in shambles, staggering crime, and chronic lack of opportunity. As long as the Brazilian soccer team was playing well, that is. I loved the way *Cariocas* from sixteen to sixty attended the same concerts and how everyone sang along. How the tattoo artists from the *favelas* peddled their designs on the beach and shrugged off bullet scars as if they were bug bites: "No big deal." I loved the irony of the *Ordem e Progresso* motto. It would be like Singapore stitching the words *Wacky and Carefree* onto each flag.

I loved the way plus-size women sported skimpy bikinis at the beach, unafraid to showcase their shapes. How when you're getting ripped off, it was only for a couple dollars, and that movie theaters didn't force you to go to the ATM every time you wanted to buy some popcorn. I loved how the Brazilians hated global conflict but obsessed over ultimate fighting. Or how conversations about getting rich weren't fantasies about ski lodges and sailboats, but dreams for earning enough to pay for a cousin's tuition or a family vacation to Florianópolis.

I loved the inventiveness, which usually came with a smile. "One hundred dollars U.S.," the police officer deadpanned after pulling us over in a rental car. He explained in Portuguese to our friend Tina, a *Carioca* we met at a restaurant, that we lacked the proper permits to drive in Brazil. Avis had assured us that all we needed was a valid U.S. driver's license, so Kurt shook his head no. The junior officer trudged back to his boss in the police car behind, then returned after a heated conversation. One hundred dollars, he insisted. Rules had been broken. Kurt fished into his wallet and handed the man our photo with George W. He jogged back to confer with his boss again. A few minutes later, the now jovial officer started a warm conversation with Tina. She had a hard time containing her laughter.

"He wants to know if you two can get him a job as a New York City cop," she said as the man bobbed his head in agreement.

"No problem," Kurt said.

He and his partner escorted us the rest of the way to Corcovado.

Sure, Rio was overripe, an overly sweet piece of fruit past its prime. Black-and-white-tile sidewalks in sixties mod design peeled away like sunburns. The downtown skyline lacked modern skyscrapers found in other cities its size. I found further confirmation on a quest one morning in search of Carmen Miranda. "Ahh, Carmen Miranda. What a beauty," the locals exclaimed. Like Rio itself. But they couldn't tell me the location of the museum that bore her name. A bus ride, a cab ride, a dozen requests for assistance, and I still couldn't locate the Brazilian bomb-shell. The best I could do was a young pharmacy clerk who set aside his broom, floated on the thought of the icon, and pointed me in a general direction.

I understood why so many people were directionally limited when I finally un-covered the one-room structure that resembled a Miranda hat plucked of its gems and feathers. A couple of weathered posters (*Down Argentine Way, Week-end in Havana*), a handful of her decadent outfits on mannequins, and faded black-and-white publicity shots left me feeling like I'd missed something. Maybe it was the Lady in the Tutti Frutti Hat. Maybe a couple of decades. Maybe Brazil at its prime.

We didn't care if Rio had seen better days. Our Rio was just fine, still beauti-ful, elegant, sexy despite the constant reminders of "you should have seen her when."

Deborah was another reason why I fell in love with Brazil and Rio. Marina, a girl-friend of Kurt's, introduced us at a café. I was lulled by her flawless teeth and easy-going manner, only to be jolted each time she crossed her long bare legs. In heels, she looked me square. We shared a steak sandwich, a stroll around downtown, then several days after. Her words echoed others.

Deborah was in her final year of the ESPM advertising school, an A student all her life, but someone who still had a hard time finding internships or summer jobs. The advertisements for women-only positions turned her off. She longed for her country to adopt sexual harassment standards like the First World and felt, on a societal level, that Brazilian women had evolved farther and faster than their male counterparts during the post decade.

"You don't understand," she said. "In the United States, if you get good grades and graduate from the best schools, you're guaranteed opportunity. Here, you're guaranteed nothing. You do everything they ask and come out with nothing. It's so frustrating."

Yet, at the same time, she was conflicted about ever leaving Brazil. The two years her family spent in the United States were a mixed bag, she said. Her father had a navy job that paid for a home in Bethesda, Maryland. She liked the amenities and neighborhoods, but found the high school cliques hard to penetrate. "I couldn't figure out if I was a geek or a jock." She and her twin sister, Cláudia, ended up spending most of their time with the sons and daughters of foreign nationals. Maybe the integration would have been easier if she'd stayed longer, she reasoned. The trips to New York City were energizing, but she missed her culture, packed deep inside. The desire was quenched only on occasion at the weekend gatherings of fellow Brazilians abroad. She couldn't understand how the country with every-thing didn't know how to celebrate.

"And I always thought it was so weird when politicians said, 'God bless America,'" she said. "Doesn't God bless everywhere?"

After her years at Walt Whitman High School, Deborah returned with her family to Brazil. The money her father earned was enough to upgrade to an apartment in a nicer and safer part of Rio. The Sony televisions, two computerized microwaves, Persian carpets, and wall-size stereo console made the trip as well. As did their optimism for increased opportunity in their homeland.

But the Brazilian economy is a massive, lumbering heavyweight that has never reached its potential. The sisters enrolled in public universities and pushed for office jobs with as many as five hundred applicants. While they waited for second interviews, Deborah and Cláudia donned orange Afro wigs and worked as Fanta models, handing out soda samples in malls. They also sold sunglasses over the Internet and, like stockbrokers, bought and sold goods on the Brazilian eBay.

I liked Deborah immediately. Long before I finished that first steak sandwich. She had a warmth and ease about her, and a simplicity, in the positive sense of the word. It was as if she'd discarded life's superfluities and decided to focus only on what mattered. As with most other young women of the Third World, she'd matured as soon as she realized the handout wasn't coming. She'd managed to do so without hardening. I liked the fullness of her lips and how she rode me for giving her "20 percent" of the affection she needed. "Gringo," she'd say dismissively. She showed me the hidden corners of her city—sleepy music bars that exploded with samba on certain nights, the best places to eat pizza at 3 A.M., choice beaches a short drive from town.

The best gift she gave me wasn't a restaurant recommendation or a tourist tip. It was her appearance in my dreams, taking the place of another.

Deborah invited me to her parents' apartment for rice and beans one afternoon, coaching me as we walked there through her Copacabana neighborhood. Fluminense was her father's soccer team, so I scrubbed any positive references to their heated rivals, Flamengo and Vasco da Gama. Her mother didn't speak much English but could understand plenty, she warned. Note to self. Cláudia was engaged to a Norwegian, she told me. *(Let me get this straight. She's moving from Copacabana to Norway? Isn't that a Disney movie? Or a punch line?)* Her older sister, Ana Carolina, also lived at home. I brought Kurt for backup.

The late lunch began according to plan. Her father reminisced about onion bagels and the Tyson's Corner shopping mall in suburban Virginia. The only snag, though slight, came when Kurt mentioned something about his favorite football team, the Washington Redskins.

"I do not understand this 'football,'" he said. "How can you call it football? You use your hands. We play football. You play handball."

He set down his fork and digested his words before speaking again. "Wait. You can't use that name either because it's taken. So think of something else."

"We'll, ahh, jump right on that," Kurt said.

I stepped in and began to praise the city's traditional sights. Corcovado, the beaches and Lagoa, the Modern Art Museum, Pão de Açúcar, or Sugarloaf.

"We loved Pau de Açúcar," I said, pronouncing it like "pow day ah-Sué-car." "Took the tram up there yesterday afternoon for the sunset. Beautiful, just beautiful, Pau de Açúcar."

Claudia began to chuckle, prompting Deborah to shoot her a glance. I assumed my pointless story had fallen short, so I carried on.

"Do you all see it often? Pau de Açúcar? It's stunning."

Her father grabbed his plate and started back to the kitchen. I thought I heard him laugh as well. I know I heard Claudia giggle some more. Ana Carolina, too. Deborah grabbed my arm, pulling my head below table level for an emergency conference.

"Do you know what you're saying?" she whispered. "You're telling my parents you think your penis is stunning."

"What did I say?"

"You said *pau* instead of *pão*. *Pão* means bread. *Pau* means penis."

"So *Pau de Açúcar* means sugar penis? I've been raving about my sugar penis?"

"Yes."

"So what's the problem?" I said before she slapped me on the arm. Hard.

Kurt and I were on one of our daily runs by the beach. We'd begin in Arpoador, jog along the bike paths through Ipanema and Leblon, rest at the pull-up bars where the sand ends and the hills to the *favelas* begin, then turn around and do it again. We were winded, both from the run and the buses that emptied their exhaust toward the sea, but we felt strong and renewed.

It dawned on me that after nine months of travel and countless conversations both meaningful and frivolous, I knew, finally *knew,* my brother. I accurately predicted he'd do three sets of pull-ups and three sets of sit-ups on the wood bench while I rested. Of course he wore the golfing socks with the holes. The longer ones grabbed the muscles around his ankles, he felt. I'd have wagered anything he had ten reais stuffed in that small pocket on the inside of his running shorts to buy a cold Skol beer at the end of the run, but only if it was from the kiosk with the man who'd give him the locals' price. Most days he'd run for a few miles after I stopped.

Probably not today. He looked like he wanted to run fast, then finish in front of our hotel.

As we ran, I thought more about his quirks, how he ordered ginger ale on airplanes but nowhere else, procrastinated with his rental housing repairs and in delivering bad news, walked with his right foot slightly askew thanks to the car accident in high school, and believed with a passion that if you killed a fly and left it on the dinner table, other flies would take notice and avoid buzzing your food for fear of a similar fate.

More than his tendencies, I now understood his makeup. He was inquisitive and kind, protective, and comfortable in routines. Apt to forget birthdays, he still remembered the detailed tastes of one-time acquaintances. He was likely to side with busboys over waiters and to dismiss most bosses as corrupt. Cheerful most of the time, he was prone to the intermittent quiet spell or occasional huff, especially if you disparaged his dogs. In Brazil, his confidence grew. I noticed it in the elevated voice he used when meeting people. I saw it long before he told me it was the most comfortable he'd been around women since his divorce.

Together in Brazil we hit a groove. By now, we knew how to travel, how to dive into a country and swim around in its offerings with few wasted motions. In Brazil, the waters were warm and inviting. Professional ultimate fighters invited us into their run-down gyms to watch training sessions. We spent weekends in Búzios and Parati, lingering on the beaches and at the seafood restaurants. The Fluminense soccer hordes at Maracanã welcomed us into their bars for prematch celebrations, happy to add a few gringos to their ranks.

Words were no longer necessary. We knew where the other was heading on instinct. The silent language began at the hotel desk after we dropped our bags. Kurt would pound and plead for a special rate, while I strolled the surrounding blocks for restaurants. We'd meet in the lobby ten minutes later with a bargain room and a plan of action. Together we'd devour the city, pulling in locals for guidance and laughs, seeking out specialties and routines hidden to tourists, fighting the masses for that authentic slice of "ahhhhh."

Kurt had become my ideal travel partner. And my new best friend.

I checked my e-mail on one of our last days in Brazil. URGENT, screamed the heading.

Shit! Fritz knocked up that mangy mutt down the street.

Instead, it was a message from my neighbor in Newport Beach, informing me of a situation that demanded my "immediate" attention. The fence separating our houses had become a bit flimsy. And the cause, he said, was my melaleuca tree. The roots stretched beneath the wood structure.

"We only have a small window of opportunity," he wrote, as if we were talking about hurricane season in Kansas.

Men were coming to remove the tree on my property the next day, with fence repairs slated thereafter. My share of the damage should be no more than a couple thousand dollars, he reassured me. *Great.*

"That," I said to Kurt, "is the ultimate wet blanket. Here we are, chilling on the beaches of Brazil, and this guy is making Desert Storm battle plans to attack my tree and fences. Someone's telling me to sell the house."

SOCCER

Forget the stuffy museums. Or the useless guidebooks. If you really want to understand a country and its culture, leave your valuables at home and join the fellow hooligan masses at a professional soccer match.

Disclaimer. During the trip, I've seen countless games on television, in packed bars, and live among the crazies. Despite the dozens of loyalists who've explained the subtleties and fueled the fervor, I still don't love the game.

Sure, I enjoyed watching the U.S. women win their World Cup (or maybe it was just Brandi Chastain removing her jersey). And I remain hopeful that with millions of soccer shrimps occupying every inch of grass in our country that someday we'll be able to reach soccer's elite status.

But, c'mon. Admit it. The game's dull. There's less scoring at a soccer match than at a Saudi Arabian Junior High School. And the only drama occurs after a foul, when a simple tripping turns into a Merchant and Ivory production.

So forget the game and watch the real excitement—the soccer fans.

Soccer in Brazil is like *forro,* a rhythmic, colorful, fast-paced, cross-cultural, and at times erotic form of dance and music. Brazil's zydeco. The name is derived from picnics thrown by Ford Motor Company plants in Brazil "for all." It's also a good way to describe matches in Rio's Maracanã stadium, the world's largest. Ice cream vendors and truck drivers, lawyers and land barons, students, vagabonds, and work shirkers cram, wiggle, shout, moan, sway, and pray for victory. They dance and sing like the culmination of Carnival.

Crumbling economy? Who cares. Disappearing rain forest? Don't have the time to worry about that. Not when Brazil is playing. And heaven forbid a loss.

I had a Brazilian friend in college who locked himself in his room after a World Cup defeat. "Give me a couple days alone," he said as I tried to coax him out for a school party. "This one is going to take a while to stomach."

Italians are passionate about their soccer as well. It's just a more fashionable passion. Men blend team-color scarves with Armani jackets and Versace sweaters. Even the road flares and fire bombs thrown on the field match the banners and flags overhead.

Kurt and I earned numerous stares at an AC Milan match. It wasn't because we were out-of-place Americans or obvious soccer novices—calling it soccer instead of football alone qualifies one. It was our blue jeans and gray sweatshirts. They didn't quite fit the style palate.

Italians sang boisterously to encourage their team and waved their arms after each penalty whistle, 75,000 divas in an Italian opera.

During halftime at a match between AC Milan and Leeds, a young Italian enthusiast berated his English counterpart a deck below with an emotional diatribe accentuated with *momma mia* wrist waves, fingers bunched together. The Brit took a more direct approach, acting out a pulsating hip thrust that looked like a prison love scene with the Italian as his imaginary cellmate.

Verdi versus Sid Vicious.

I think there were thousands of cheering fans at the Spartek Moscow game. I just had a hard time seeing them through the tens of thousands of police and military personnel who ringed the field, lined the aisles, and formed a mile-long human tunnel from the stadium to the metro.

In Russian soccer and society, the authorities love to exert control. So we ended up spending almost as much time waiting to be excused to leave as we did watching the orderly, ordinary match. Dance of the Russian soldiers.

Also like the country, the stadiums are massive, poorly constructed, and cold; the food bland, though improving; and the people surprisingly warm and friendly.

Intricate, precise, old-fashioned yet enjoying a renaissance—soccer and tango in Argentina share much in common. Both cling to past glories. Both worship their icons, Diego Maradona and Carlos Gardel, respectively. Both view themselves as being more European-influenced than the rest of the continent.

Kurt and I have a British friend living in Buenos Aires. She's married to a local. One night over wine, we tweaked him about siding with the enemy.

"They can have the Falklands," he said. "We have the World Cup," a championship Argentina grabbed after defeating England with a controversial goal that deflected off Maradona's hand. Argentina residents call it *la mano de Dios,* the hand of God.

I don't need a Gallup poll to know that most Argentines would choose cups over rocks without hesitation. And, based on the soccer fanaticism we've seen around the globe, the rest of the world would probably agree.

22

My parents bought into a time-share cabin in Truckee, California, in the 1970s. The place hadn't been remodeled or refreshed since then, long enough so that it was now back in style. Lots of baskets on walls, faded posters of Squaw Valley without snowboarders, and orange and green everything. The best attribute of the place was its size, big enough to hold our immediate family plus any relative or friend who chose to join us. Kurt and I, along with a group of family members, made the place our weekend base before a cousin's wedding in nearby Lake Tahoe. We were back in California long enough to sell my house, a process I hoped would be swift so that we could soon explore our final continent, Africa.

"Okay, who wants to go win some money at the casino?" Kurt said to the group after a steak and potato dinner.

Silence. Lisa and Doug shook their heads and said they'd tend to Elizabeth. Aunt Shirley preferred bed. More silence.

"Lakeside Casino," Kurt continued. "Who's in?"

"I'll go," chimed LaRue.

Nice, LaRue.

Wait a sec. Is it cool to take your ninety-nine-year-old step-grandmother to a casino? Plop her in the middle of the RVers and college kids playing dollar-a-hand blackjack? Then again, what if she wins?

"LaRue's in, I'm in," I said.

"Then sure, me, too," said Mom.

Once inside, Kurt chose the slot machine, a fruit-themed, nickel-a-chance one with a button option to spin the wheel instead of pulling on the lever, far from the slots with airbrushed Playboy bunnies and Harley Davidsons in the back of the casino, along a low-traffic row. This was serious gambling here. Kurt didn't want

LaRue distracted, as if she were on a stroll through the halls of Eskaton. We handed her a small bucket of nickels and told her to go at it. Simple.

Except for the fact that LaRue had never gambled. Ninety-nine years and she'd yet to set foot in a casino. I began to feed the machine a couple times and showed her how to spin the wheel with the button. Three strawberries, that was good. Three BARs, even better.

"Don't worry about these credits and cashing-out buttons," I said. "We'll be here all night helping you out. And on nickel slots, I mean all night. Just grab the coins in the bin here and root for fruit."

"Well, for heaven's sake!" she declared after an inaugural jackpot of a couple dollars. "I haven't had this much excitement in years."

"You feel like pulling the lever?"

"Sure."

"Right here. Like this."

An apple, a wheelbarrow, a farmer.

"No. We didn't win that way. The button is better luck."

Ah, the logic of a wizened gambler.

The lights on top of the machine flashed and spun every five minutes or so. Just about the time LaRue drained the pile of nickels in her tray. Lights for a dollar jackpot, a siren for the five-dollar ones. Those nearly knocked her off the stool. We'd cheer each one, attracting the attention of several gamblers nearby. They'd saunter over to see the big winner, realize the jackpots weren't enough to feed a parking meter, then shuffle off to find their riches. While LaRue focused on the fruit, Kurt fed the kitty with more nickels. At the end of the evening we escorted her to the cashier's booth and tallied the booty—six dollars and thirty-five cents.

"Make sure to use the push-button machines," she told my uncles the next day at the wedding. "And stick with the fruit."

She beamed through the entire afternoon. But a few days later, she had a "come to Jesus." Literally. The more she thought about it, the more the earnings gnawed at her. LaRue was a spiritual woman, so she decided to talk to her minister.

"How much did you win?" he asked after hearing a detailed breakdown of the night's events.

"Six dollars and thirty-five cents."

"LaRue, the Lord is okay with six-dollar jackpots," he said with a reassuring smile. "Now, anything more and we might have a problem."

Truth is I'd debated selling the house for months before I received the "urgent" e-mail in Brazil. The local real estate market was hot, I needed the money, and I had little use for the place while on the road. The only reason I hesitated was because of a sentiment, albeit a faded one. Part of me still saw it as the place I'd settle into with a family and someone special. Kids' rooms, jungle gyms, a work den—I rearranged the house over and over from afar. The e-mail shook me from the dream. I contacted the neighbor and told him not to touch a leaf of my beloved melaleuca until I returned or else I'd activate an army of Earth First protestors to move atop the row of trees between our two houses.

Kurt made arrangements with a realtor to list the house for a reduced commission. We sanded out the dog pee stains, put a couple daylilies in the flowerbed, shined the brass knob on the front door, and put the house on the market. After nearly a year on the road, my bank account was rapidly approaching empty. Of the 77,000-dollar Irvine Company bonus, I'd spent about forty thousand on my monthly mortgage payments and insurance. I needed another ten thousand for the next year's taxes. By sticking to the Third World, we'd traveled to and around thirty countries for considerably less than the 27,000 dollars remaining in the tank. But Africa beckoned. As did some semblance of temporary sustenance if and when we ever stopped traveling. I had to sell.

The timing was optimal. The house I bought for 550,000 dollars three years earlier sold for 810,000 to a family of four wanting to live closer to the beach. Perfect. The profit, minus commissions, would be right around the 250,000-dollar tax-free homeowners exemption. Immediately, I upgraded our class of preferred hotels in Africa. I didn't even complain when the buyer showed up for a routine inspection with a bunch of guys straight out of the Chernobyl cleanup and with a Hollywood-style film crew to videotape every inch of pipe and crawlspace in my house for further nitpicking. All right, I told him. Take another ten thousand off the price. Just get me on a plane.

Kurt and I held a final garage sale to shed the last vestiges of our lives in Newport Beach, the junk we didn't sell or give away the first time we cleared out, things like the large terra-cotta pots and broken ironing boards. And Kurt's enormous wedding photo in an ornate frame that hung above their fireplace—the kind photographers hang in their display windows to alert the world to the endless possibilities of staged poses. He sold it to a lady whose son planned to marry soon. He sold it for a dollar. She didn't want to take the photograph, but he insisted. Wouldn't sell it otherwise, he said. The rest of the stuff we gave away to the endless stream of gardeners and housecleaners working in the neighborhood. People we'd never met would knock on the door and say their friend sent them. We'd load up their cars (Baja California plates) with boxes they didn't bother to open before driving off.

We rented a U-Haul with plans to transport the remaining goods—carpets from Turkey, beds and couches, computers and televisions—to a small storage unit in Santa Ana. The plan was to wake early on that Tuesday, load the belongings in the truck, spend a few hours cleaning, and leave our lives in Newport Beach. We'd drive to Davis for a few days with family before heading to Africa. Escrow closed at 5 P.M. No problem. We'd have ample time. Escrow closed at 5 P.M., Tuesday, September 11, 2001.

I first heard the news while picking up a couple of morning coffees at Peet's. By the time I got back to the house, Kurt had taken the television off the truck. Numb, we watched along with the world. Like everyone, I thought of loved ones in New York and prayed for their safety. *Please, Lord. I mean it this time.* The numbers meant little until we started to see the faces, mother after mother, child after child. And I knew amid the chaos we'd lost our innocence as well. Never before had I felt that level of hatred in my heart.

Later in the day, my mind wandered to the penniless villages of Indonesia and Turkey, to the innocent and neglected corners of the globe that relied on tourism as their life support. I thought in fast-forward to the empty planes and hotels, to the increasingly desperate vendors and guides, to the families who would soon go without meals, to the peaceful Muslim enclaves like Sumbawa and Bodrum that would feel the backlash. I thought of Cuzco and Hue and Koh Lipe and Bahia, tourist destinations that had never heard the words al-Qaeda, yet soon would suffer along. The aftershocks in most of the world would come later, well beyond the reach of Western news cameras.

The escrow company took a few hours to return my call, but informed me the sale was still on. September 11 or no September 11, we needed to vacate the house by the end of the afternoon. So we left the television on and completed the move in near silence, speaking only to bark orders or swear a little too loud after we cut a finger or put a ding in a wall.

It wasn't until after we padlocked the storage space door that we discussed how the day's activities would impact the honeymoon. Was the world, our world, now a different place, one not as hospitable to a couple of curious brothers? Would security measures and terrorist alerts end travel as we knew it? Would we soon be at war? Those questions, we decided, were ones we couldn't answer. So we set aside the world's problems for a moment and focused on our own situation. We'd purchased plane tickets to Africa. The question was, would we go?

Kurt pushed to continue. Finish the year, he argued, and visit our final continent. Don't let the terrorists disrupt our lives, though we both thought that logic seemed hollow as the death counts continued to soar. I craved family and was happy we were heading to Davis for a few days, and I agreed with Kurt that the thought of ending the trip prematurely didn't seem right.

After Brazil and the house sale, Kurt and I hit a lull for reasons beyond the swirl of confusion and anger that followed September 11. We'd been on the honeymoon for more than a year, the time we'd said we'd stop. But all those career inspirations and lifestyle revelations we'd heard about from other global wanderers had yet to hit us. Instead, we spent our days babbling about ways to combine Third World relief work with moneymaking schemes. We were adrift, lacking motivation, stonewalling friends and family who wanted to know our plans. Our lives felt like a replay of the year after college graduation, minus the Top Ramen and *What Color Is Your Parachute?*, that is.

"How about this?" I said. "We open a Cheesecake Factory in Brazil. Do it like Ben and Jerry's. Lose the tie-dye. Donate part of the proceeds to the rain forest."

"You don't even like cheesecake," Kurt said.

"Kind of."

"No, you don't."

"Doesn't matter. Everyone down there does. How many times did someone tell us it was their favorite dessert?"

A screwup from Seattle diverted our attention. Saab had shipped Kurt's 9-5 to Seattle rather than to our home in Newport Beach. Our friend Matt Welch, the high-rev manager of Carter VW/Saab in Kurt's old hometown, said he'd be happy to hold it at his dealership until we finished the trip.

"I got an idea. How about we go to Seattle for a week, crash at Matt's, and fix up my rentals?"

"How much you paying?"

"You have any better plans?"

"Done."

Day one, we visited his Sanford and Son properties in West Seattle and drew up chore lists. For his first house, the to-do's looked something like this:

1. Remove weeds engulfing Chevy Impala in back yard.
2. Clean bong water stains in living room carpet.
3. Replace batter-rammed doors.
4. Remind tenant not to breed pit bulls in garage.

The place also needed an exterior paint job. So Kurt gave me a scraper and asked me to prep all morning before the professional painters came to give it a spray. He took off to work on a duplex down the street. I didn't mind the work. It's not as if I had any meetings or strategy sessions to attend.

While I ate a bag of pretzels for lunch, a twenty-something good ole boy named Roy pulled his white Ford van into the driveway. He had that dark mustache, eighties porn star look, and a slouching, sleepy demeanor as though he'd just completed a scene. He said a quick howdy (accent on the *dee*), then began to organize his tools like a surgeon, a messy, paint-spotted surgeon. I continued to scrape yellow enamel from a wall and started a series of dead-end conversations with him about travel and geography.

We need a new topic.

"You have a girlfriend?" I asked Roy as he cleaned his paint gun with a hose.

Suddenly animated, he dropped the sprayer and dashed to his glove box in search of something. Several minutes later, he called me down from the ladder and thrust a Polaroid in my face. A pale woman in a Day-Glo bikini half squatted with a hand on her hip, bottom thrust forward. She was large.

"Wow, she's hot," I lied.

"Yeah. Best thing is she ain't a slut, but she looks like a slut."

I bit my lip to stifle a guffaw.

"You've got to show that picture to my brother when he gets back. He's a big fan of sluts who ain't sluts."

A few hours later Kurt stared at the shot as Roy hovered proudly.

"What's that on her ass?" Kurt asked.

Roy's grin vanished.

"Aw, that's nothing."

"No, dude, on her ass."

"It's some old tattoo. We're going to turn it into a butterfly or something."

"Roy, that's some kind of lettering. What's it say?"

"Something about being someone's property."

"What?"

"It says, 'Jeff 's property,' " he relented.

"She tattooed 'Jeff 's property' on her ass?"

"Mmmm."

"Who's Jeff?"

"Her ex. But that's cool. 'Cause when I'm with her in bed I'm like, 'Hey, Jeff, how's your property?' " he said, pulsating his hips as if he were riding a barroom bronco.

Yes, we were in a mini-rut. Kurt and I had explored dozens of countries, cornered nirvana at Angkor Wat and Machu Picchu, gleaned life secrets from travel gurus, and it had all led to this—stripping paint from low-income housing, listening to Roy explain away tattoos that portrayed romance in real estate terms.

Shouldn't I be marching on the capitol now with Richard Gere and a group of Buddhist monks in orange robes, demanding that Congress overhaul the nation's immigration laws? We have the same hair. Richard and I, that is. It's a start.

That's when I noticed the new VW camper van.

"That a loaner from Carter VW?"

"No, it's mine."

"For the week?"

"For good. I traded Matt the Saab for it."

"Nah."

"You'll like it. Less bulky and more horsepower than the old ones. Feels like a twenty-first-century hippie mobile."

"Fitting."

"I figure we can take a couple U.S. road trips while we get our act together, before we head to Africa."

Kurt called the American Southwest "-N-"country, as in Bait-n-Tackle, RVs-n-Campers, Biscuits-n-Gravy, Lube-n-Latte. (True. You can check for yourself. Bullhead City, Arizona.) The whole thing was a blur to me—the faded tepee inns off Route 66, the graying Harley riders, outpost trading shops, French families in their rented Winnebagos. I couldn't stop thinking about careers and lives after the honeymoon was done. At least Fritz was into the trip across the Southwest. He watched it all from the front passenger seat. I'd push him back repeatedly for the first hour of each day, then give up and go lounge with Riley on the dog pillow in the back.

"How about we open a B-and-B in Thailand?" I said.

"You want to make granola and herbal tea for backpackers every day of your life?"

"Nah. We'll make it a high-end place with a staff. Open it half of the year, then rest for the other."

"Call me during the second half."

Fritz began to bark at a cattle herd outside. Riley sprung from my stomach to better witness the provocation, adding his yelps to Fritz's. Kurt pleaded unsuccessfully with two dogs that had never finished a training lesson in their lives.

A few weeks after September 11, my check for the house sale arrived. That was the good news. The better news was its amount—810,000 dollars.

Forget employment, I'm king! Maybe not of Brazil or Vietnam. But at least some island kingdom in the South Pacific. Yeah! Someplace where the American banks won't be able to touch me once they find out they gave me an extra half million dollars. This is an ending scripted by Grisham.

Wait a minute, I thought. This had nothing to do with "giving." As soon as an auditor discovered the overpayment, and that I was deep in the heart of Africa, my file would go straight to the Treasury Department. Or to the local bounty hunter. I imagined the agents tracking me down on safari.

I called the escrow agency and told them I still owed the bank around

450,000 dollars on my original loan, and that the check they sent me should be for about 250,000 (810,00 minus the loan debt, commissions, and fees). The polite, if somewhat panicked, agent told me, "Don't cash that check!" She'd call back as soon as she double-checked everything with the lending bank. An hour later, the now relieved agent told me that everything they'd done was correct. According to the bank, I'd already paid off my loan. The check was mine to spend.

Topless women. The island nation would definitely have to have topless women in batik sarongs. And thiamine-enriched rice so I wouldn't get beriberi.

Then reality. Once the bank discovered the error, not only would they snatch the money from my backpack in Africa, they'd probably charge me interest for hoarding it or hit me with some outrageous pirate/money-laundering fee. Their lawyers were better than my spin and Kurt's jive any day. I'd be the one to pay the price for this screwup. I called the bank directly. The clerk punched my account number up on the screen.

"No," she said, "our records show you've paid off your loans in full. You don't owe us anything."

"Can you double-check?"

"I just did. You're fine."

Okay then, if you insist. Now I just need to make sure I don't buy one of the "paradise" islands that just happened to have doubled as an A-bomb-testing site for fifty years. The kind where kids' teeth glow in the dark even when it's not dark. I'm king, damn it!

One last try. I called the same bank agent the next day and asked, with apologies, for her supervisor. After fifteen minutes of elevator music (surprisingly good, by the way), she told me the same thing as her underling. As far as they were concerned, the money was mine. Before hanging up I gave her my mobile phone number. Just in case. She called me the following day in full terror mode.

"Have you cashed that check?"

"No."

"Don't, please! Just rip it up! Oh my God, this has never happened. When you refinanced your house, we never attached the new loan to the property as collateral. You could have gone to China or somewhere and we would have never discovered it."

"Africa, actually. Southern Africa. Safaris and such."

"You sure you didn't cash that check?"

Before leaving for Johannesburg, we paid a visit to Justine Amodeo, a friend and editor of *Coast Magazine*. A transplant from New York and a cancer survivor, she brought a cosmopolitan outlook and a healthy perspective to the lifestyle publication. She credited part of her cancer triumph to a California mentality, so it was common to see things like aromatherapy candles, wooden massagers, and giant exercise balls in her office. During the trip, she'd turned my e-mail missives into a semiregular column and encouraged me to do more.

For years, I'd written for others. Press statements for Governor Pete Wilson, speeches for executives at The Irvine Company ("No, I'll let you say *strategic,* but I'll fight to the death over *synergy*"). Now, during the trip, for the first time in my life, I wrote for me. When I wanted. On what I wanted. Whenever I felt the urge, I'd grab a pen, scribble a few notes, plant myself in an Internet café, and send a few thoughts or observations to family and friends.

After seeing a couple of my random rants, a newspaper editor in Orange County asked if he could start publishing the e-mails. No problem, I wrote him back. Just take out the dirty words, clean up my spelling, and don't pay me a thing. I insisted on the final proviso because the last thing I wanted was for the writing to feel like a job with deadlines and editorial controls. He started to publish my pieces along with photos from Kurt. And the e-mail list grew, doubling to 150, then again. Other papers asked to publish materials, and I agreed, with the same ground rules. Soon, articles appeared in the *San Francisco Chronicle,* the *Los Angeles Times,* the ABC News Web site, and *Coast Magazine,* among others.

"You want to go to Yap?" Justine asked. "Do you have time before you head out to Africa?"

"Umm, sure," I replied. "We can make time. Just one question: where's Yap?"

"You go to Guam and take a left."

"Can Kurt go, too? He's my photographer."

"Sorry," Justine replied. "I tried. But the invite is only for one."

All right, how do I do this without making him grumpy? Maybe tell him later that the junket is key to taking more trips together. That we need to get our foot in the door on this kind of thing.

"Go," he blurted. "If I was the writer, I wouldn't hesitate to go without you."

"Thank you. Or the hell with you. Take your pick."

Wait a minute. You can't write about hotels, restaurants, and beaches. That's a complete sellout. What happened to all the talk about editorial freedom and a lack of deadlines?

"I don't know if I can write the kind of story they'd want," I told Justine. "I'm horrible at that stuff."

"Write about anything you want," Justine replied. "Write it like you do your e-mails. Just throw in a few more adjectives."

"I don't know."

"Look at this," she said as she unfolded a large brochure filled with color photographs of divers exploring coral reefs, smiling women with leis that covered their bare breasts *(Hey, that's the island I almost bought!),* and crescent-shaped beaches.

"How does luxurious and lavish sound to you?" I said.

"Leave," she said. "I have work to do. And your lifestyle is pissing me off."

"Usually we fly first-class instead of just business class," a writer from a ritzy Florida magazine complained to me. "You should see some of the other trips."

"Yes, you're right. I should see some of these other trips."

The travel writer junket game went something like this. A public relations firm selected the publications. The cushier, the more upscale, the better. Forget hard-hitting journalism as long as the publications had plenty of large glossy color photographs. These magazines had names like *Brentwood Today* or *Palm Beach Society.* Tourist bureaus coordinated visits, spreading the word to restaurant and hotel owners to spiff up their places and be on good behavior. Airlines offered comp tickets.

From the minute the plane rested on the tarmac, we were shown the best the area had to offer. Chartered boats waited to whisk us away to isolated bays and beaches. Five-course meals loaded with fresh fish and giant crabs appeared on cue at lunchtime. Hyper-friendly hosts scurried reporters around to skin-diving sessions, umbrella-cocktail parties, and sightseeing excursions.

With Yap and neighboring Palau, they could have saved their money. I would have written something nice about them even if they'd given me a hammock and a can of tuna. The islands are enchanted and blessed (and luxurious and lavish), made more so by the people lucky enough to call them home. The adjectives came easy.

Let me get this straight. I'm being flown to a gorgeous corner of the planet to tell people that it's a gorgeous corner of the planet. I can do that. Moral dilemma solved. And an idea planted.

QUINCY

Quincy was having a hard time. Maybe it was the humid, ninety-degree temperatures, or the long line of former warriors at the podium. Maybe it was just being on
a small island in Micronesia that had exploded with some of the fiercest gun-
slinging in the Pacific phase of World War II for a couple weeks in 1944.

Peleliu was essential, the generals declared. Capture the island and protect
McArthur's flank before he returned to the Philippines as promised. Fifty years
ago. Quincy hadn't been back.

As the ceremony rambled on, Quincy grabbed Joe, an islander helping with the
event. Can you get me a van, he asked, or a ride out of here? Too many memories
long repressed, too much pain.

There, that's the beach, Quincy declared. Orange Beach. Pull over. Joe followed
behind as the fragile, silver-haired old man walked to the sea. Resting on a stone,
he peeled open his heart and confessed his tale.

Arthur was his best friend from Canton, Ohio, Quincy explained. They'd en-
listed in the war because it was the right thing to do. Arthur was athletic, Quincy
bragged, and handsome.

Alive and well after the battle of Guadalcanal, they stole a bottle of Jack
Daniel's from a commanding officer. We'll drink it after Peleliu, they decided. A
celebration before we head home.

Arthur didn't make it out of Peleliu, Quincy mumbled as tears dotted his shirt.
Crossfire on the beach landing ended their lifetime of plans. He was a good man.
He was a good man.

With care, Quincy pulled the same Jack Daniel's from his bag. The fifty-year-
old bottle had the original stamp and seal. Quincy rolled up his khaki pants and
walked out in the knee-deep bay. He paused, opened the whiskey, poured half into
the ocean, took a generous swig for himself, and started to cry.

Many World War II buffs come to Peleliu and the islands of Palau to inspect the vine-covered battle sites and well-preserved ruins. Children retrace the steps of father-soldiers. Wives uncover chapters of heroism previously untold. Divers inspect bombed ships and downed Japanese Zeros that now serve as homes for kaleidoscope fish and Technicolor coral.

"Respect," says Tangie as he guides history seekers around the lush island strewn with tank shells, artillery guns, and caves occupied by Japanese soldiers years after their country surrendered. "That's the most important part of the tour."

Quincy collared Joe again at the hotel the next day. Thanks for the understanding and help, he said. He was better now. Just needed a quiet moment with an old friend.

I'll be back to your beautiful islands, he promised. Where can I reach you, Joe? I'll be back next year.

The box arrived one year later along with a letter from Quincy's daughter.

My father spoke warmly of the afternoon you shared. He fought another battle that day—a battle with cancer, a battle he recently lost. In his will, he left instructions for his remains to be sent to you.

I believe you'll know where to scatter them.

23

Before we left for Africa, Kurt and I stopped by Eskaton to visit LaRue. She'd moved from her apartment to a hospital room in another wing of the complex after taking a spill "on that nice, plush carpeting." Her smile was still the same, though she looked pale. Kurt opened a window to dismiss the stagnant smell of sickness. I noticed a small wooden cross tacked to the wall near her pillow.

"So where are we going next?" she asked.

"The casino," said Kurt.

"Africa," I countered. "We're going to see the elephants and the lions."

"Oh, just like my hair," she said, touching a lock over her ear. "Tell me how the lions are wearing it these days."

"You don't need a haircut, LaRue," Kurt said. "You just need to get out of this room and back to your apartment. Then we'll go hit the slots again."

"As soon as I get my strength back."

"They treating you all right?" I asked.

"They're spoiling me. Stana brings me desserts from the dining room."

"You deserve it," Kurt said.

"Will you keep sending postcards from Africa?" she asked.

"Of course we will," I said. "We'll do you one better. Kurt and I have talked about it, and we've decided that the honeymoon is coming to a close. We're going to end it on your one-hundredth birthday this summer. We'll fly back from Africa in time for the party."

After protesting that she didn't want the trip, or the postcards, to end, LaRue talked in inflated tones about the party for the rest of our visit. I knew she wanted us there. There'd be music, she promised, and a big cake that she'd decorate with roses and stars. I looked at her small body, swimming in the hospital gown, and knew the

Happy Birthday icing would be inscribed in a hand other than her own. My mom would find a cake. It wouldn't taste as good as LaRue's, but my mom would find one.

Kurt wanted to pick up sandwiches at the corner deli in Newport Beach. We were there for the day before catching a flight from LAX to Johannesburg. He stood in line for BLTs while I wandered to the glass refrigerator in search of drinks. Cokes? No, he'd want Gatorade. One of the new, high-tech varieties. The kind with words like *mist* and *power* and *rain*. Especially a sports drink after the morning run. I should have joined him. Yeah, but I hated those early workouts . . .

And then I noticed her. And then I noticed them.

I set down the neon blue Gatorade and inched to the window to make sure it was who I thought it was sitting at one of the small tables on the patio. Yep. She wore a tailored, taupe-colored business suit, he sported a rolled-up shirt and loosened tie. That's them. Her hair was streaked blond. I liked it, then kicked myself for liking it.

Okay, brave man, people have asked you for months what you'd do if you ever saw Annie again. Now's your chance.

"Give her a hug," is usually what I told people on the road after they asked. Annie had liberated me from another life and set me on the path with Kurt to the world. But that hug didn't feel so easy to offer right now. Here, face-to-face, my immediate reaction was to flee. Her table was directly in front of the door. Either we could linger in the store until they finished their lunch or grin and bear it. I went to Kurt for help.

"Where are the drinks?"

"Forget the drinks and take a look outside. Recognize the blonde?"

"No way."

"And that's her dude. The Indian doctor she married in that Hindu ceremony in Palm Springs."

"He's an improvement, but still . . ."

"What should I do?"

"What do you want to do?"

"Teleport myself."

"I can bring the van up."

"I'm going in. Come out in a couple minutes and rescue me. Give me CPR if I need it."

I left Kurt to the sandwiches and walked slowly to the front door having no idea what I'd say.

Unbelievable. This is a replay from the night she dumped me. Walking into a lion's den with no plan of action. What happened to all those scenarios you worked out in your mind? All those great speeches and subtle put-downs that she'd realize days later?

"Annie," I said, hovering over her table.

Her man raised his eyes only briefly before returning to his sandwich. Her eyes locked onto me with the gaze of a child. I could tell she had no idea what to say. *Great. Makes two of us.* I let the silence linger. I'd already done my part. Then after a few more seconds, I did it again.

"Annie? It's me, Franz. Remember me?"

"Of course."

"How ya doin'?"

"I'm sorry, I . . . I . . . I don't know what to say."

"Then give me a hug," I said, holding out my arms.

Her awkwardness gave me confidence. Suddenly, I was the composed one in the conversation. I gave her a big squeeze, partly because I said I would and partly because I wanted to feel her new breasts. I'd heard she'd had the operation a couple months after the wedding crash. And it bummed me out. She always seemed so comfortable with her flat chest, joking with people that she'd already had a boob job. I loved her breasts, the way they'd rub against my chest and look pert and erect after she put her negligee back on. I hugged her and concluded they were a C cup. At least she hadn't overdone it. She sat back down and we again reverted to silence.

"I'm just so surprised to see you," she said.

"Yeah, we're on our way out of town. Just stopped in to pick up a few things from our storage unit."

"I'm stunned. I thought you were traveling. Africa or somewhere."

Ah, you're keeping tabs on me. Must be getting my e-mails from someone. I knew it.

"We're wrapping things up."

Before I could continue, Kurt walked up to the table and said an icy hello, not bothering to shake their hands or dole out any hugs.

"Sorry to interrupt, but we should be going."

He held the sandwiches in a bag and carried a large bottle of blue Gatorade. *I knew it.* I knew him. And I knew he'd be cold to her. She was the one who'd struck down his brother. He would never forgive her or mask his feelings. I loved Kurt for that.

"Well," I said. "It's good to see you. Tell your family hello."

"Yeah, you, too."

And it *was* good to see her. She looked thin and older, still pretty and graceful. But as I neared Kurt's van, a wave of resentment rippled through me. And it had nothing to do with Annie. No, this was all internal.

As Kurt fiddled with the CD player and Fritz started barking at a passing bicyclist, it dawned on me how distant she seemed, like a movie I cherished at the time but with a plot I could no longer remember. While abroad I'd continued to fit feelings for Annie into compartments long shut. Those emotions were the only I'd known. When I finally saw her, I realized how obsolete they'd become. That longing, that burning desire to be with her—*saudade,* as the Brazilians say—was no longer there.

As I climbed into the van, I felt zero impulse to look back to her table or ever to see her again. And that triggered a slow, growing anger from within. I felt a palm-slap-to-the-forehead frustration, the kind of feeling you get after you do something foolish and avoidable, like burning your tongue on hot coffee. Seeing Annie for five minutes immediately erased the countless times on the road I'd reconstructed the relationship in my mind, playing the what-if game ad nauseam.

I should have flown back home to confront her months ago. Right after that night with Jana in Prague. Before she stalked me for four days, that is.

When I finally did see Annie, the dreams died. Quickly, easily, without ceremony.

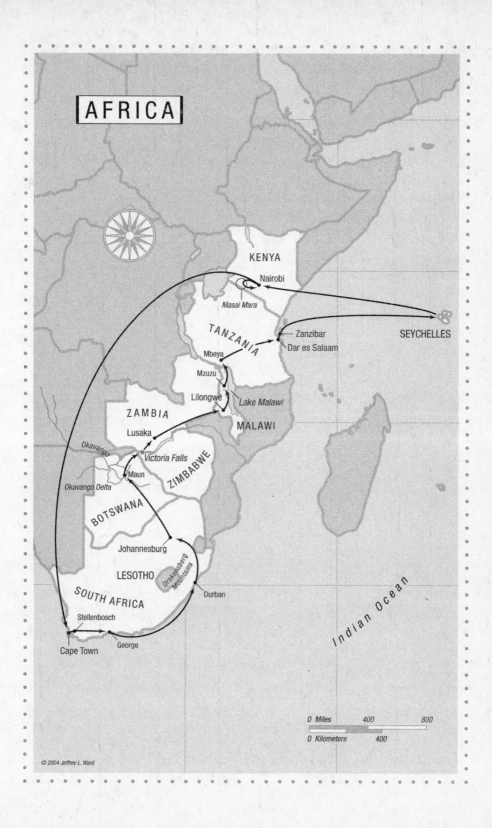

AFRICA

KENYA
Nairobi
Masai Mara
TANZANIA
Zanzibar
Dar es Salaam
SEYCHELLES
Mbeya
Mzuzu
Lilongwe
Lake Malawi
ZAMBIA
MALAWI
Lusaka
Okavango
Victoria Falls
Maun
ZIMBABWE
Okavango Delta
BOTSWANA
Johannesburg
Drakensberg
Mountains
LESOTHO
Durban
SOUTH AFRICA
Stellenbosch
George
Cape Town

Indian Ocean

0 Miles   400   800
0 Kilometers   400

© 2004 Jeffrey L. Ward

24

So we were all set for the final leg of the honeymoon. Four months in Africa. And it made perfect sense. All the signs of karma travel pointed toward our journey's end. Or so we reasoned.

Africa would bring us to two years from the beginning of the worldwide journey. Two years to the day. And two years to niece Elizabeth's birthday. Maybe a stuffed zebra would do the trick for a gift, with several photos from a safari to tide her over until then. Lisa said she stared longer at the animal photos than the uncle photos. *Ouch.* She was a person now, a little girl. A little girl whom we'd seen grow mostly online. Kurt and I justified missing the early months. "She's a blob. A cute blob, but a blob." Now we wanted her in our lives.

Two years on the road would also bring us to LaRue's big celebration in August. We swapped e-mails with our mom to plan the affair according to LaRue's wishes. Though stalled in her recovery, LaRue stirred with each mention of the party. Mom said she talked more about the wooden cross on the wall. She worried LaRue wouldn't last until August.

You'll make it. You're LaRue. And even if we have to cram everyone into your little room, we're going to have a party. We're coming, LaRue. We're coming. Hang on. We're coming.

Africa also seemed like a graduate degree for travel, a place where you'd go only after extensive practice in other countries. Hard-core travelers we had met described Africa as the ultimate high. If travel was a drug, they said, Africa is heroin. We were ready. For Africa, that is. We were ready to challenge our accumulated travel skills—Kurt's negotiating, my diplomacy, both of our ingenuity and improvisation—in mostly overland journeys in the southeastern portion of the continent. We bought round-trip tickets to South Africa and planned to make our way up from there. Bring it on.

The money from the house sale gave me time before I needed to work again, but I wanted to set most of that profit aside as a down payment on another house in a California housing market that refused to cool despite the Silicon Valley crash and a prolonged economic slump. We'd splurge for one more trip before settling back into employment of some sort.

Where we would work was a tougher question. Kurt and I were as far from figuring that out as we were from home. A final four months away should do the trick, we convinced ourselves. Africa was the ideal place to find career enlightenment, or at least to give us perspective if we ever found ourselves in a cubicle, wearing a pager, or griping about the speed of the company's Internet connection.

The travel writing helped. I sent a batch of articles to several PR agencies in New York and, presto, large pieces of our costs were covered, including safaris in Botswana and Kenya, hotels in Cape Town and Johannesburg, train rides and likely more once we arrived. Kurt upgraded his camera, and I brought a small thesaurus to conjure up adjectives. *Coast Magazine* and a few other California publications said they'd run anything we sent back.

The honeymoon entered its final days.

Laura, the friendly public relations representative at the Westcliff Hotel in Johannesburg, said she'd meet us for high tea in the Polo Lounge. *High tea in the Polo Lounge.* The pink hillside hotel complex was a tastefully converted residential development in one of the city's ever-shrinking upscale neighborhoods. Valets and doormen wore blue safari shirts and white pith helmets. Maids delivered warm laundry in picnic baskets complete with flowers from the garden. Our friends and family in California thought we were roughing it in the bush. Truth is, the only struggle we had at the Westcliff was learning how to work the towel heater in the bathroom. Kurt and I threw on our best (a.k.a. only) pairs of khakis, ironed a couple shirts, and rushed down to play the role of serious travel journalists.

Laura's breezy manner and refined accent meshed with the highfalutin surroundings, the lady of the manor directing everything just so. She paused before accepting a bear hug from each of us. We couldn't help it. We were in the *Polo Lounge for high tea*. From a corner table overlooking the vanishing-edge pool, she flashed a few discreet hand signals to the wait staff. Moments later they carted out a giant, tiered, birdcage-shaped silver platter overflowing with finger foods that oozed cream, balanced stacks of meat, and beckoned "come and get me." I pulled out a notepad and pen to feign the appearance of work. Kurt dug into the smoked salmon.

"Ah, yes," Laura said. "Here's our guest of honor. Lorraine, meet the honeymooning brothers."

Must be the general manager or the food and beverage director, I assumed.

Either way, we should be on our best behavior. No fifth helpings of the eclairs. I flipped open the notebook and readied for the interview as Lorraine launched into a friendly commentary about South Africa and Johannesburg, stressing its luxury comforts at bargain rates thanks to the tumbling rand. Without looking up, I hurried to record it all.

"The wineries in Stellenbosch, spas in George. And for dinner tonight, there's Ciro's, or a steak at The Grillhouse. All of which makes the perfect setting, of course, for our Surgery and Safari program," she concluded.

Surgery and Safari program. Got it.

Hold it. Did she just say Surgery and Safari?

"You two are from California, right?"

"Correct."

"And where is your magazine published?"

"Orange County. Perhaps you know Newport Beach or Laguna Beach?"

"Of course, we've had many women from Orange County in the program. Some of them come over here without their husbands even knowing."

"Knowing what?"

"About their plastic surgery. And our doctors do such a first-class job, many husbands still don't know even after their wife's procedures. Plus, the costs are half of what a nip-and-tuck costs in Newport Beach. The men glance at the Visa bill and it looks like a duty-free purchase."

"What does?"

"The *nose jobs,* darling. Are you sure you're a journalist?"

"And the safari part?"

"Whenever their wounds heal or as long as they want."

"So let me get this straight. Women come over here for a rhinoplasty, then recover with the rhinos."

"Men, too. Nose jobs, rhinos, breast jobs, baboons, peels, lions, skin tucks, whatever."

That's it! The perfect way to entice Orange County socialites to come to Africa—plastic surgery. Maybe someone will read my stories now.

"Fascinating."

"But you can't use the rhino-rhinoplasty line for your article. Someone already did."

Kurt interjected, "Has any reporter received plastic surgery while doing an article?"

"Now that's a marvelous idea," Lorraine boomed, half-serious. "We can schedule a consultation tomorrow. What do you want done?" she said, looking at me.

"Cankles," Kurt said.

"Pardon?"

"Cankles," he continued. "You know, thick ankles, calf-ankles, cankles."

"Now that would be two firsts."

"I don't have cankles," I said.

En masse, the eyes of the table shifted to my feet. Kurt tried to lift the khakis above my shoes before I kicked him in the shin. Lorraine pulled out a stack of press clippings with nice things to say about the burgeoning program and continued her spiel. All the while, I had this panicky vision of being trapped in the bush with a couple dozen rich, gauze-wrapped housewives asking the camp waiters to puree their ostrich fillets and serve them with a straw. They'd pass me magazines and ask how my cankle recovery was progressing. *They're ankles, not cankles. I don't have cankles!* Time to refocus.

"This will make a great sidebar story, Lorraine," I said, cutting her off, "but I think my readers would also like to hear about the joys of a normal safari. You know, ones without mummies."

"No worries," said Laura. "The people who run our safaris are here on the premises. You can leave whenever you want."

"There, that's settled," said Lorraine. "Now we had this flat-chested woman here last month . . ."

I signaled for the waiter to bring over a second bottle of wine.

Dear LaRue—

Most tourists seeking to shoot big game (with cameras, mind you) head with the hordes to the herds of Kenya and Tanzania. And the game there is plentiful. So are the caravans of Land Rovers lining up to see lions or leopards eat their dinner. The whole experience can feel like a crowded drive-in at In-and-Out Burger—a large group of vehicles waiting to get close to meat.

Enter Botswana with all the beef and half the filling (of tourists, that is). And the location of choice for zebras, elephants, giraffes, baboons, Cape buffalo, lions, cheetahs, and almost every other star of your favorite childhood picture book is at the confluence of the Quito and Cubango Rivers, otherwise known as the Okavango Delta.

We explored the Okavango before the prides, packs, and gaggles were at their height. May through August are typically the peak months for game. Still, the area felt like a scene from *Jumanji* with hippos grunting, elephants trumpeting, giraffes grazing, hyenas laughing, lions dominating, and monkeys constantly throwing tantrums.

"Very few admirable qualities with the baboons," our camp director warned during check-in. Keep your rooms latched shut, he warned, or the monkeys will trash everything and devour your toiletries. A woman with severe back pain came back to her room a few days earlier only to find the quarters ransacked and her month-long supply of prescription pain medication devoured by a baboon—a very sedated baboon.

"How will we know if a lion is near?" I asked our guide one day during a walking safari. My question was amplified a notch or two given the fact he didn't carry a gun.

"The baboons will warn us," he replied.

Wonderful. I'm entrusting my life to some baboon that's high on Demerol and craving my Right Guard.

I won't tell you much about our accommodations (felt more like a Ralph Lauren show-room than a middle-of-nowhere safari), because I want you to be under the impression that we roughed it. Don't want to completely ruin our backpacker image.

Love,

Franz

"Watch for the hippos," our pilot said as we pinballed our way around a half dozen clouds in the see-forever Botswana sky en route to our safari camp in the Oka-vango Delta. "Hopefully they're still around the water and not eating grass on the runway."

That one could use a little lipo. Mental note: talk to Lorraine.

Rogers, our camp guide with an inviting I've-got-a-secret face, met us on ar-rival and tossed our bags in the back of his open-air Range Rover with seat cush-ions as thick as a sofa's. The open-arm treatment continued upon our arrival at camp, with the staff of twelve welcoming us with song, fresh orange juice, and of-fers to escort us to our "tents." At Savute Elephant Camp, the definition included hardwood floors and teak writing desks, chaise longues on view porches, air-conditioning units, queen-size beds, and showers large enough for the hippos. Two large women followed with our backpacks balanced on their matted-down Afros. Rogers shooed vervet monkeys from the front door and warned to always keep the tents zipped shut or fear their wrath. The late afternoon drive would leave momen-tarily, he explained. What would we want for the sundowner?

Ah, the sundowner. Love the concept of the sundowner. A cold cocktail on the sa-vanna, herds migrating in the background as if cued, maybe an end-of-the-day kill by the lions. Perfect.

"Pretty nice setup," I said to Kurt. "And you notice how polite everyone was to us? All those smiles?"

"Maybe they know we're reviewing the camp."

We slapped on some insect repellent, anything with the letters *D, E,* and *T,* and hurried to join Rogers in the Range Rover for the drive. Kurt planted himself in the elevated backseat. I joined a demure housewife in the middle row. A ruddy-faced man with silver hair and mustache, Boy Scout shorts, a pressed pink dress shirt, and knee-high wool socks presided from the shotgun seat, acknowledging our presence with a *hrrrrmmph* and a nod. As Rogers pulled out into the bush, I decided to start a conversation with our titular head.

"So, are you on vacation?"

"Sir, I am an Affffrrrrican," he said, both rolling and clipping his words in an exaggerated fashion à la Schultz on *Hogan's Heroes*. "Some Affffrrrrrricans look like me. Others like Rrrrrrrrrogers. Ernst's the name.

"And you, sir? Which continent do you call home?"

His theatrics pulled Kurt closer. Ernst's wife slumped a bit more and forced her attention toward the plain.

"America. That's my brother, Kurt. We're on a honeymoon."

"Come again?"

"Slip of the tongue. I meant to say we're here to write articles about safaris."

"Well, if you wrrrrrrite about nothing else, wrrrrrrite how the Indians are rrrrrrrruining Afrrrrrrrrica."

"Come again?"

"They take all the world's donations," he said, "and fail to pass any on. You will not find a single brrrrrrridge, school, or hospital named after an Indian. Isn't that rrrrrrright, Rrrrrrrrrogers?"

Rogers just grinned, only I couldn't tell if it was out of politeness, fear, or ridicule. But I knew then why everyone else in camp had smiled on our arrival. It had nothing to do with journalistic deference and everything to do with lumping a couple of gringos with a dwindling species that unfortunately refused to die—*Bigotus South Africanus*. Meals, drives, sundowners, we were stuck with Ernst.

"You can take the ocean, Mr. California. I'll take the bush," he said before nodding off. I could smell the scotch through his pores.

The rest of us, meanwhile, scoured the wilderness for signs of the so-called Big Five—lions, leopards, rhinos, Cape buffalo, and elephants, the latter being the easiest to spot since our camp fanned around their favorite local watering hole. The others were much more difficult to locate. After a few hours, the loudest roars we heard came from Ernst's snoring.

"Rrrrrrrrogers, you won't find any cheetahs here. The grrrrrrrass is too long," he proclaimed before dozing off again.

"Hey, what's that?" I blurted after noting movement near a bush.

"Red-billed francolin," Rogers said. "They are everywhere. Run on the trails in front of the trucks."

"How about that?" Kurt added, pointing up the dirt path.

"Crested francolin."

Clearly we had yet to master the art of spotting game. Brown dots on the beige hillsides were still brown dots on the hillsides, not cheetahs positioning themselves for a premeal sprint. Black clumps on tree branches had yet to show themselves as leopards sleeping off an impala gorge-fest. The most progress we made was being able to differentiate between the red-billed and crested francolins. Ernst slept, his wife started to knit, and Rogers located about as much big game as we did. Nothing. A call over the walkie-talkie punctured the lull.

"A pride of lions huddled by a pond," the voice cracked. Rogers spun the SUV toward the activity. We arrived late and took our place behind five other vehicles with tourists snapping away at the jungle kings, bloated to twice their size after a morning feast on gnu. Panting heavily, moaning, yawning and stretching, the lions struggled to digest the massive quantities of food. The lions refused to rouse, but Ernst did.

"Look at those damn Chinese tourists," he said in a voice that reached the other cars, including the one carrying the group of bowing, *konichiwa*-ing Japanese tourists. "Typical Chinese, always talking."

In the lead truck rested a killer, as methodical as a leopard tracking a gazelle, with eyes as keen as a bird of prey's and the muffled laugh of a jackal. Only this one wore khakis. He was another Savute camp guide with a Botswanan name unpronounceable to gringos. So everyone called him Killer. He'd spotted most of the big game that afternoon, moving his lucky passengers to the show's front row to enjoy the animal calisthenics and feeding sessions, inviting the rest of us to join the fun long after the main event. We'd arrive to a chorus of: "Oh, you should have been here a half hour ago. That cheetah sprinted for a mile before catching the baby gnu. Then he and his brothers fought off a pack of hyenas. Amazing. You should have been here." I hated Killer.

"Rogers, quick. Leopard feasting in a tree," he radioed a few hours later.

Kurt, always anxious for the head of the line, had enough. He grabbed the walkie-talkie that linked all the caravans.

"Killer, we've spotted a red-billed francolin by the watering hole. Come immediately."

"We'll be right there after this leopard finishes his impala," Killer said, laughing.

Our luck improved as the sun dulled that afternoon. Kurt spotted another pride of lions and we tracked a herd of Cape buffalo with their nasty tempers, brick-house bodies, and center-part horns that rested on their heads like a matador's cap. Still, we knew Killer's group would have far greater boasts at the dinner table. By now it didn't matter. Kurt and I had settled into the safari trance—a rhythmic, hypnotizing, highly rewarding state of mind.

French-press coffee delivered to your patio before sunrise, in the Range Rovers at first light, Ernst in front, chasing Killer's finds soon thereafter, breakfast at a prime viewing spot, late lunches and naps at the camp, a late afternoon drive to check up on the animals, five-course meals followed by fireside cigars—the daily ritual was hugely alluring and addictive. The entertainment was an action serial with a cast of characters we'd tracked for days. The dastardly hyenas, sidekick jackals, star lions, and silent protagonist leopards. Sex, violence, intrigue, betrayal, buildup, and disappointment—*The Days of Our Botswana* had it all. Monday? That meant the lions hadn't eaten in several days. Follow them around and see what's for lunch.

There was also a surprisingly strong personal gratification from seeing the beasts in action. From birth, we'd been fed a steady diet of animal picture books and mobiles, graham crackers, stuffed monkeys, *Z* is for zebra, the twenty-five-cent elephant ride in front of the supermarket, Disney and Hanna Barbera, sports mascots, and Halloween costumes. Now it was all being played out in front of us, the uncut, uncensored, XXX version. As children of the African-animal image barrage, we'd come full circle.

Now I get it. I see the order and our place in it.

Kurt and I learned quickly the best place to avoid Ernst's roar was the backseat of the Range Rover, binoculars up whenever he seemed ready to launch into a diatribe. To do so required him to swivel around in his front seat and shout over the row between. While he didn't mind shouting, he disliked swiveling. Usually he'd doze off within minutes. Kurt and I were free to spot francolins and solve the world's issues the rest of the day. I started with one of mine.

"Got an e-mail from Larry Thomas before we left Jo'burg," I said. "He's back at The Irvine Company. Great gig. Overseeing corporate communications and company positioning. He's up on the ninth floor with all the big dogs. Swank office overlooking the water."

"Good for him. He deserves it. I hope they're paying him a boatload."

"I'm sure he's doing just fine."

"Did he keep the membership at Big Canyon? Love to tee it up over there."

"He said there's been a big management shift. Most of the senior guys retired or left. Including Gary. There's a whole new crop running the place."

"Do you still need a jacket to go to the ninth floor?"

"I'm sure."

"You're more of an eighth-floor type of guy."

"Interesting you say that. Larry mentioned something at the tail end of the e-mail. There may be a spot for me if I ever want to go back to corporate America."

"Do you?"

"I don't know."

I'm thinking about it.

"What would it be?"

Can you tell I'm thinking about it?

"Government relations."

"Would they stick you back in that closet?"

Give me some more here, Kurt. Tell me what you think.

"I don't care about that stuff anymore. He just mentioned the possibility. I haven't even e-mailed him back."

But in my mind, I'd plopped myself back at the company and envisioned how it would feel. I thought about arriving to work, walking past the rows of black BMWs and Mercedes-Benz with the attendants who'd wash your car in the parking lot, stopping to pick up a three-dollar latte from the coffee cart, and making my way to the silent elevators that required a magnetic key to operate. I pictured talking to the secretaries for a couple minutes before reviewing the list of fund-raising calls I'd need to make that day to subcontractors and political allies. The cost of government continued to rise. The cast of characters would be the same.

It's your background, it's what you know. You can do that job with ease. And the money would be enough to buy a new home, start from scratch. What are your other options?

Kurt pointed his binoculars toward a hill and didn't say anything else about it for the rest of the afternoon.

Per custom, we capped our drives with a sundowner cocktail party at a scenic vantage point. Rogers pulled the card table from the back of the Range Rover, and assembled a mini-smorgasbord of dried nuts and fruit, *biltong* (beef jerky), cheeses, pâtés, and crackers before shifting into bartender mode. The crack of the beer can woke Ernst from his slumber.

"Rrrrrrrrogers, pour me a Famous Grrrrrrrrouse," he bellowed before saying a few minutes later, Rrrrrrogers, pour me another.

"You know, I like you Yanks," he continued. "We'll all go out again tomorrow. I'll bring a bottle of gin in the morning and a bottle of scotch for the afternoon."

"Let's get Ernst tanked so he'll sleep through the morning drive again," I whispered to Kurt.

"No problem."

"Rrrrrrrrrrrogers, pour this man another Famous Grrrrrrrrrrouse," I said in my best Afrikaans accent.

YOU CAN COUNT ON IT

Like stomachaches on Halloween or athletes who talk about themselves in the third person, there are constants in life beyond death and taxes. So, too, for life on the road, especially during travels. Here's an incomplete list of things you can expect on an upcoming trip:

- Someone will stand up in the airplane before it comes to the gate, prompting a stern warning from the flight attendant.
- Your best experience will be something spontaneous.
- You'll change your views on an issue thought to be previously unalterable.
- Despite the push following September 11 for major changes in air travel, you'll see that security procedures in most of the world have been upgraded little.
- The longer you're on the road, the less you'll stress about things like traffic jams or lack of hot water.
- You'll feel guilty about not knowing a foreign language, yet believe even more strongly that English is the universal tongue.
- Canadian flags will begin to bug you. You know the ones. They're plastered all over backpacks and clothing by hyper-patriotic Canadians and optimistic Americans who somehow think they will be immune from abuse as long as they have a red and white maple leaf somewhere on their belongings.
- You'll overpay by at least 25 percent, most of the time never realizing it, and the longer you have been on the road, the less you'll care (Kurt excluded).

- After the trip, newspapers will be far more interesting, though you'll shake your head at the shortage of foreign news in all countries.
- You'll also listen with greater interest to a friend's stories about travel.
- The British, you'll see, have a genetic disorder that prevents them from applying suntan lotion properly. Just look at those crazy Rorschach sunburn patterns on the next man who orders a Guinness in the middle of the day.
- Hotels that hoist the world's flags perpetuate falsehoods. The truth is world travelers come from a select few countries. The rest simply can't afford it.
- A traveler from the U.S. who gripes about something petty like bus seats that don't recline will reaffirm the notion of the ugly American.
- If you pay attention to travelers from other countries, you'll realize Americans don't corner the market on ugly.
- If you talk to enough people, you know that "uglies" from the U.S. and elsewhere are far outnumbered by respectful and curious travelers.
- Even if the trip strays from plan, you'll usually long for the next one within twenty-four hours of your return.
- Travel is the only investment with guaranteed returns. Count on it.

25

Dear LaRue:

Anthony Williams is a friend from college who lived in Nigeria after graduation. I told him about our world travels before Kurt and I left California for South Africa.

"You been to all those countries?" he said. "Good. That's enough training. Now you're ready for Africa."

And he was right. Africa is a tough, tough travel. Outside the five-star safaris and secluded beach resorts, that is. It's a swirl of bribes, bad roads, and buses stuffed way beyond capacity. But it's also rewarding, breathtaking, inspiring, and spiritual. Frustrating, confusing, and random. Beautiful, welcoming, and warm.

I'm not a good photographer. I leave that to Kurt. Fortunately, he has more patience and a better eye. He's captured some images during the past couple years that will be forever etched in my mind, photographs that summon a special moment, a random circumstance, a big ole grin.

If I could take just one roll of photographs to record my Africa, here's what I'd like to shoot:

- The effortlessness of the Malawi mother breast-feeding her baby while tending to a field.
- The awe-inspiring resilience of Africans who wake with hope and a smile amid war zones and shantytowns.
- The rocket acceleration and pinball turns of a cheetah closing in on a baby gnu.
- The helpless feeling you get walking past crumbling buildings and potholed roads, knowing that conditions will probably get worse.
- The patience of wet-suited surfers waiting for the perfect wave at Jeffreys Bay, the boarder's Mecca and home of the world's best right-hand break.

- The elation on the face of a child from a small Zambian village after seeing his digital picture for the first time.
- The desperation in the eyes of Zimbabweans whose economy and tourism industry have been devastated thanks to the crimes of their leader, Robert Mugabe. I'd also like to have a shot of Mugabe . . . preferably behind bars.
- Kenyan women in brightly colored wraps, chatting and laughing . . . while walking on the side of a major highway . . . with fifty-pound bundles of sticks on their heads.
- The confusion of the Afrikaner farmer in the twenty-first century, with his wool shorts and high socks, clinging to past eras and wardrobes.
- The jaw-drop beauty of the Serengeti Plain at dawn, lazy Seychelles beaches at noon, and manicured Stellenbosch, South Africa, vineyards at sunset.
- Toothless grins, Masai warrior pretzel ears, and the curious eyes of the veiled women on Zanzibar.

Middle of nowhere, people with nothing, an overflow of curiosity and warmth. That's my Africa.

Love,
Franz

Malawi's economy shriveled along with the crops in 2001, the result of a heartless drought and a heartless government whose corruption relative to its neighbors' may have seemed "standard" to Africa watchers but could be considered nothing less than inhuman to the honest eye. After the crops died, they opened the emergency silos, the ones supposedly stocked with foreign grain, and instead found nothing but excuses and scrunched shoulders from public officials supposed to stand watch.

The over-under wager for developing a deep hatred of elected officials in Africa after traveling the continent is one week, long enough to read a couple news stories about corruption or stray from the pampered safari camps and see the out-stretched hands. Long enough to watch a motorcade of Rolls Royces and black Suburbans race through a shantytown of mud and corrugated steel. I snapped in Zimbabwe, where Robert Mugabe had recently added election theft to his list of crimes. He'd turned tourism havens like Victoria Falls into ghost towns and killed the main source of revenue for most of the population. I think I saw another couple of tourists in our enormous hotel. It was hard to say after being surrounded at all times by locals literally starving to exchange hyper-inflating money or sell wood carvings of giraffes and rhinos. The United Nations said that two-thirds of the region was underfed. On the ground it seemed much more.

But this was also where I fell in love with Africa. Most countries would bow and fold in the face of such natural and political disasters, coupled with the world's highest AIDS populations and malaria mosquitoes that kill millions each year. Not here. Before the trip I thought, Well, they're used to it; but nobody gets comfortable with death. We'd all scrap and fight and claw. Impulses would kick in, and we'd do anything to survive. The difference is, Africans do it with a smile. And an amazing ability to stay human when all humanity crumbles.

Sure, we all know there is extreme poverty in all nations, including ours, but it's hard to grasp its many devastating forms until you walk in the slums and shantytowns, share meals and conversations with people whose belongings could fit into a gym locker. Hunger, illness, crime, and violence. I knew the curses long before our plane landed on the continent. I underestimated the depth and overlooked poverty's more hidden manifestations—like the unemployed miner who's roughed up by corrupt police officers for bribes he can no longer afford to pay or the groups of smart yet bored young boys who sit on street corners all day because their parents can't cover the cost of a book or a bus ride to school. It's not until we settled into Africa that we felt the full, vicious cycle of poverty, a trap from which few escape.

Kurt and I made our way north on worn-down minibuses on which twenty people share ten seats. On a city van in Lilongwe, a two-hundred-pound housewife crammed herself on my seat, placed a large cardboard box on my lap, then rested another on her thigh. The smell attacked before she could close the door. I pried open the box (it was on my lap, after all) and saw the fish, stiff and pungent, leftovers from the outdoor market. She pointed as if to offer one in exchange for the lap rental. I declined, but the man next to me took up the offer. Within a few minutes she was dealing fish from my lap to the entire bus.

We met Millie a few days later in Mzuzu. She swaggered into the bar, sweating, stout, and with cuts on her knees and forehead. Still, she was attractive. A successful inn operator and a mother of three, Millie had earned respect and envy in a country and industry dominated by males. I saw her unloading bags of grain from her rusting Toyota pickup truck. She walked in and bought a beer for the town drunk/high school teacher. I knew he was the town drunk because we'd spent the last couple hours drinking with him. After round eight (six for him, two for us), Kurt asked about accommodations. Millie approached at the same time.

"You should stay with this beautiful woman here," the drunk proclaimed. "Beautiful in face, body, and because she'll always buy me a drink for a finder's fee."

We found space amid Millie's sacks of grain and drove with her to her compound on the banks of Lake Malawi, Africa's third largest. I'd heard about it from an aquarium addict in California who boasted of its colorful cichlids, then proceeded to rattle off a series of names that sounded like strip clubs. Tangerine tiger. Blue orchid. Cobalt zebra #2.

He forgot to tell me the lake is also a prime spot for parasitic worms that spread bilharziasis by penetrating human skin. They get comfy and fat inside blood vessels for months before laying eggs, which are passed back to the water through human urine or stools, beginning the process anew. No, I found that out after we swam in the lake all afternoon.

Millie mentioned it to me on the rocks near her small compound of bungalows. Immediately, I chugged a large bottle of water in sync with her laughs, foolishly hoping to wash any worms out of my system. Don't worry, she said. You're probably fine. And bilharziasis is nothing on the tropical disease spectrum. Try the parasitic worms that grow so big inside the body they look like veins, the kind you have to twist out like a sardine tin or risk splitting them in two. I thought about the color photos in my dad's parasitology books and finished the bottle of water.

With Kurt relaxing on a hammock nearby, Millie talked with pride about the vacation village she'd built with her ex-husband. For most of the year, he resided in London with their kids. Better schools there, she admitted. But isn't this beautiful, she said while pointing to the bungalows, simple yet tidy, and the open-air restaurant with its large rock floor. I noticed the cuts on her forehead and knees had been cleaned. She'd also combed her hair back into a short ponytail. I felt her tentative hand on my thigh.

"You know, all of this can be yours," she said. "Ours. We could run it together."

Seeing her earnestness, I wondered if the "together" stuff was more business proposition or marriage proposal.

"What about your ex-husband?"

"He doesn't come here anymore. This place needs a man."

And for a minute there, I considered the offer.

Not like you've had a ton of others. You could do worse than waking up on the lake every morning, fishing for your meals, cleaning bungalows, and staring at sunrises over Mozambique. Of course the parasites would have to go. But that's nothing a bottle of supersize antibiotics wouldn't kill.

"You don't need a man. Seems like you're doing fine here."

"The business is okay, but it gets lonely."

"Well, I can't say I'm not tempted. It's the best offer I've had in a long time. Then again, it's the only offer I've had in a long time."

She smiled, and I felt the weight lift from the conversation.

"I'll bet that high school teacher in the bar yesterday would be happy to keep you company."

And my arm felt the pain of a playful combination shove-slap from a person who had no problem tossing around fifty-pound bags of grain.

Before leaving Millie's village, I decided to take an afternoon run on the country roads leading to her property, past dozens of shacks made with plywood and tarp.

The air smelled of wild sage thanks to earlier rains; the dulled sun cast everything in sepia-tone. Fishermen spread their nets on tree branches to inspect for holes. I hadn't eaten since breakfast, but still felt energetic and strong. Maybe I'd try for an hour today. I set my Walkman to the band James and steadied my pace.

I was still thinking about Millie's offer and admiring her forwardness. This was Africa, a land often without the luxury of inhibition or choice. Or was it a blessing? There was something healthier about the approach, something Westerners lost as we "matured." Africa seemed more true to nature.

A barefoot man in drawstring shorts pushed an old bicycle out of the bush. He hopped on and decided to ride along in silent partnership, slowing his pedal to match my pace, occasionally yelling words of encouragement in a tongue I could feel but not understand. Then a happy, shirtless boy, no more than seven, legs speckled with clay, ran out of a shack, using all his speed to catch me. I slowed. After a handful of hollers, a few of his playmates joined from compounds along the road. Boys and girls devising entertainment in a world without The Wiggles or Dora the Explorer. Now there were a dozen in the parade, with the man on the bicycle our grand marshal.

The sun cast lengthy shadows across the road. Darkening but still warm. The children's giggles mixed with the music. Down to a fast walk now while they still ran, I stared, trancelike. Oh, those faces, those high-octane, pure-joy faces with teeth bent and noses crusted. The kids yelled and pumped their hands in the air as if they were prizefighters after a TKO, forcing me to stop running because I was laughing so hard.

The smallest of the group, a little girl, pushed through the others. I could see the dress she wore was no more than a bedsheet with some creative stitching. It couldn't hide a bloated belly or limbs that should have been longer. What she didn't have in size, she had in affection and élan. Curiosity pushed her to swipe my leg, then stare at her fingers. I smiled and she reciprocated by hugging my knee with all her body would allow. Soon, too, the others.

A father's voice from a hut pulled them off my leg and forced a trot back to their homes. The man on the bicycle pedalled ahead. I stood in the middle of the dirt road, frozen, and I started to cry. Here was Africa.

Kurt nudged me awake at midnight for a scheduled 10 P.M. bus ride. I rubbed my face and saw a dilapidated bus slow to a stop in front of my bench. A foot-wide fringe of rust circled the bottom like a bed runner. It looked nothing like the photograph hanging above the desk where we purchased tickets. That bus, with its chrome wheels, tinted glass, and televisions glowing inside, appeared to have rolled off a German assembly line and onto a wet highway. This one resembled a war remnant.

When we booked the ride, Kurt and I knew we were getting ripped off. After months and months of haggling with salesmen, we'd honed our street senses enough to know when we were being overpromised and overcharged. Most times, we'd walk away. This time we couldn't. The next bus didn't leave for five days.

A handful of workers jumped from the bus doorway, barking orders to dozens of riders waiting to get out. Two helpers lifted the large baggage door underneath, motioning to us to throw them our backpacks.

"Maybe these people are getting off?" I said to Kurt.

"Nah. Look in the back of the bus. There's no bathroom."

Kurt muscled his way past the crowd of toilet seekers and scrambled to the back of the bus to find the lone empty seat. I tossed our packs in the luggage bin and followed a few minutes later. I couldn't see Kurt through all the people standing, so I yelled to him to save me a place. The aisle was filled with several locals asleep on rope-wrapped boxes and large duffel bags made out of old tarps. An infant, swathed in a filthy red and green cloth sling, suckled on his mother's exposed breast. Etched muscles popped from her arm, the limbs of a life without strollers.

I wonder if she has any idea California socialites pay thousands of dollars to gyms and personal trainers to get those arms.

When I reached him, Kurt said he'd snagged the last seat: "Sorry, dude." I switched course and headed for the front. Several times I tried to sit in vacant seats only to be told they were taken. I lingered for a few minutes next to a man huddled against the window with an orange windbreaker over his face. Another passenger from outside walked straight toward me. Without saying a word, he flicked a finger in the air, ordering me to leave.

"My friend," I said, grabbing a man in grease-stained jeans and a long-sleeve jean shirt, "you work here?"

"Yes. Let's go. Get to your seat."

"Great idea. Except for the fact that I don't have any seat."

"So sit in the aisle."

"The aisle looks pretty full. Plus, look. Here's my ticket. See? Seat 45C. Only thing is, there is no 45C."

The worker looked tired and frustrated.

"Okay, okay. You bought a seat, I'll get you a seat."

The man led me into a small front cabin walled off from the rest of the bus. The stout, stern-looking driver in a retro-style brown leisure suit motioned for us to hurry. Bodies occupied each of the four seats surrounding him. The engine protector, a large mound of steel, rose in the middle of the compartment like a giant boulder. Our helper pulled out a piece of dirty foam rubber and placed it on the metal engine cover.

"Here is your seat."

"You want me to sit on the engine?" I asked.

"Yes. And do it now. Many others will join you soon."

As I folded the piece of foam in half for extra insulation from the heat, the driver in the Freddy Fender garb gave a few blasts of the horn and a stream of young helpers piled into the bus and scrambled for positions around me on the engine. One brought a rolled-up mattress, which he unfolded for five others. They jostled for a space on it, smiling at me the entire time, cautiously moving my legs to one side or the other so they could sprawl out. Finally, the bus pulled out of the depot. Within minutes, a strong diesel and body odor stench filled the cabin. I could feel a headache immediately.

The rains continued, first downward then sideways. More assaulting were the fumes. To help avoid asphyxiation, I stretched over a sleeping man and slid open a shoebox-size window. The road took a sharp bend and the rains poured through the small opening, pelting his face. He reached up without moving his body or opening his eyes and slammed the window shut. "Sorry." The road curved back and the rains resumed their pounding of the windshield while carving larger and larger potholes. A lone wiper fought a losing effort to clear views beyond a few feet.

The diesel and the underarm odor are going to form a front, hit the damp air from outside, and we'll have a toxic typhoon inside this cabin any minute now.

Then a fatal mistake—I shifted back a few inches. Two bus workers sitting next to me noticed I'd ebbed from my precious space and moved quickly to fill the void. One removed his yellow Kaizer Chiefs jersey and reclined across my legs. The other stripped down to his white cotton underwear and rested his sweaty head on my lap. Trapped. Nowhere to move. I looked around the rest of the cabin and saw bodies strewn across one another.

In Newport Beach, California, I could have these guys arrested for indecent exposure and harassment. Here I give them my admiration. In Africa, you take what you can get. There's no such thing as "personal space."

The potholes grew and multiplied. I took advantage of the big bounces to shift the underwear man's head to the side. He didn't seem to notice. Then the bus eased to a stop. Mr. Leisure Suit turned off the motor and reclined in his large chair. Someone dimmed the cabin lights. No one else stirred. It was 4:00 A.M.

"What's going on?" I asked the denim-clad usher after waiting for a half hour.

"We stopped."

"I can see that. Do you know why?"

"The rains."

"I kind of guessed that one, too. Can't we go on these roads?"

"No, the road is bad here."

"So what's our plan?"

"We wait until tomorrow, wait for the rain to stop, wait for the roads to dry, then go."

"Let me get this straight. Our only option is to hope that the rains stop tomorrow, hope that the sun comes out and dries the roads enough so that we can go?"

"Yes?"

"And if the rains don't stop?

"We wait."

"We wait?"

"We wait."

I decided I needed off. So, with care, I moved the nearly naked men around me as not to disturb their sleep, shifting them away from my space though I knew it would be long gone by the time I returned. The storm eased a little as I walked along the side of the bus. A flashlight bounced on the muddy road ahead. I recognized the slim figure with his long, salt-and-pepper hair.

"Fritz," yelled Kurt as he flashed his light in my face. "Great ride, huh? You wouldn't believe the seat I'm in. Some fat dude is stretched out—"

"Don't even start. I'll gladly swap places with you. Whatever you have back there doesn't touch where I'm sitting."

A steady line of passengers disembarked and milled around us as the rains let up some more. They gave me the idea to go back inside and find a vacant seat for a nap. Kurt nodded in agreement and returned with me. We spotted two empty seats, jumped in them, and were asleep moments later. A loud whirring sound and bright sunshine woke us several hours later. The bus was empty save for a few women and their children.

"What's going on?" I asked Kurt.

"I think they're trying to move the bus up this hill."

I stuck my head out the window and looked behind. Half the passengers pushed on the rear of the bus. Spinning tires coated them in red clay. Suddenly, the bus began to fishtail and the group rushed to the right side to prevent it from slipping into a ten-foot ravine. The other half stood on a small hill yelling animated instructions to their friends.

"Uhh, maybe we should be out there pushing?" I asked Kurt.

"Too late now."

After a series of slides, backtracks, gear grinds, and heave-ho's, the rickety bus made it to the top of the hill. The passengers broke into a chorus of applause accentuated with rapid-fire horn blasts from the driver. Quickly they rambled back inside, tracking giant clumps of mud onto the aisles and seats.

Eight hours behind schedule, the bus bounced through the green highlands of northern Malawi. We stopped every half hour to pay bribes to gun-toting soldiers in blue jeans and khaki uniform jackets who had erected roadblocks for "official inspections." Toll roads, Malawi-style. A third of the bus exited before the Tanzania border, freeing up seats. Kurt and I grabbed two in the front row adjacent to the driver. We slept for the next several hours. Jarring brakes snapped us awake.

"What's up?" we asked the driver, still sporting the polyester jacket despite the ninety-degree temperatures.

"No gas."

"I thought we filled up?" Kurt asked.

"Not enough."

We sat on the shadeless, scorching-hot, now-paved road for another hour. The passengers milled around, laughing and talking, taking another setback in stride. Finally, a young boy from a nearby village approached on his bicycle. Several plastic five-gallon tanks hung from the back rim. He carried two more on a wooden pole stretched like a sagging barbell across his shoulders. The underwear man (pants back on now) and his colleague jumped into action, grabbing the tanks from the boy and pouring them into the rig. The bus sputtered on.

Kurt and I reclined in the front seat. Improved roads smoothed the ride. I glanced at him and smiled. His hair fell to his shoulders. He looked thin. But the physical changes in his body were nothing compared with the internal transformation we'd both experienced. He shook his head back at me in mock disgust, as if saying, "Can you believe this?" This was our world. For all the gripes, we were more than content to be there. I looked at Kurt and didn't say a word. I didn't need to. We spoke the same silent language.

A loud crash shattered our peace. Glass shards exploded from the front window, coating Kurt and me. The bus ground to a halt. I grabbed my face to see if I was cut.

"What the . . . ?" Kurt said, staring at the bowling ball–size hole in the driver's window.

I looked down at my feet and saw a gray-and-white-speckled guinea fowl flapping frantically for a few seconds before going still. Blood dripped from its neck. I reached to pick it up, only to have the underwear man snatch it from my grasp. Dinner. Picking glass from my hair and clothes, I managed to convince him to hand me the dead bird for a couple pictures. He relented, then hovered during the photo session, suspicious I'd do something with his evening meal.

The bus continued after the other workers kicked the rest of the broken glass window out to the road. As the driver increased speed, bugs began to stream into the now glassless window. From our front-row seats, we took the brunt of the Technicolor squashes. And then the rains began anew. Slowly at first, then at full storm force. I grabbed a raincoat and a pair of sunglasses from my small bag. Kurt did the same. The driver glanced over and asked Kurt to borrow his sunglasses so he could drive without wiping his face every ten seconds. He obliged and the man smiled for the first time during the journey.

Then it hit me. His smile affirmation, a sage delivering a verdict. This bus ride was a test, one far greater than the passports or the fender bender in Turkey. This was the test of the road. Not so much in terms of difficulty as symbolism. Here at the end of the honeymoon, the ride was our final exam. And we'd passed. Our conquering moment. His smile said so. The rickety bus hadn't arrived, but we had.

We spent the final month of our honeymoon taking more bus rides in eastern Africa and cruising in a rental car through South Africa, reminding each other every half hour to "Stay left!" Before we flew to Cape Town, we camped at a Tanzanian monastery, relived the joys of safari in eastern Kenya, and learned to dive with dilapidated equipment amid flawless underwater panoramas in the Seychelles. We inspected the ornate doors of Zanzibar and the gutted ground where the U.S. embassies in Dar es Salaam and Nairobi once stood.

In Kenya, we decided we needed a movie fix. Kurt opted for *Ali,* while I went to *Training Day,* with a plan to meet in the lobby afterward. After Denzel's downfall, I finished my popcorn by the door and started to chat with a couple of Kenyans who'd seen the film. No way they'd go to the United States, they said. Too dangerous. Too many killings on the streets. Here we were in Nairobi, one of the most crime-ridden cities on the planet, and these guys were petrified about Nebraska, Graceland, Highway 1, and the rest of America, thanks to Hollywood. I tried to explain it wasn't all that bad, but ended up confusing everyone. Including me.

"Sure, we have a lot of crime, but mostly it's centered in certain areas."

"Same as here."

"Here seems much more dangerous."

"How can it be? We have knives. You have expensive guns."

Kurt and I talked about guns and contradictions and Hollywood as we hugged the coast of South Africa along the Great Ocean Road. *Stay left!* Through the sedate Afrikaner farming villages with their white Dutch houses and black farmhands in royal blue coveralls. To the surfing Mecca of Jeffreys Bay, once the desolate end of *Endless Summer,* now more like a year-round spring break packed with boarders, cheap condos, smoothie sellers, and still the best right break on the planet. Past the pay-per-view private game preserves that guaranteed glimpses of the Big Five thanks to electric fences and ATV caravans that kept big game penned as if under a military attack. To Durban, Africa's largest port, the home of Gandhi and an enormous/enormously successful Indian immigrant population. I wondered if Ernst had ever been there.

We turned inland and made our way to the Drakensberg wilderness area, shuttling past forgotten Zulu and Boer War battle sites, shuttered mining towns, and the mountain kingdom of Lesotho. The plan was to spend a few days hiking amid the buttes, plateaus, and waterfalls that slowed to a spire of ice in the winter months. Kurt saw the hitchhiker first. Her hair hid behind a bandanna, her back drooped with two large sacks of belongings. He slowed to a halt, resting the car directly beside her outstretched arm.

"Thank you, thank you," she beamed, stretching the a's as if in midsong.

"No problem," Kurt said. "Move our backpack to the floor and hop in."

"Thank you."

"Where can we take you?"

She clucked two times, sounding like the steps of a horse on a cobblestone road. *Click-cluck.*

"Huh?"

"Up the road. *K'wah, k'wah,*" she seemed to cluck.

"Kwick, kwuck?" Kurt repeated, trying and failing to integrate the clicks into his words.

"Oh, you don't speak Sotho. So sorry."

We handed her the road map and she pointed to a small dot with the name Qwaqwa, well past where we were going. No problem. She'd get off before we veered to the mountains. She explained Qwaqwa means "white-white," named for the alabaster cliffs nearby. For the next couple hours we practiced our Sotho.

"How do you say hello?"

"*Dumela.*"

"I like that. *Dumela.* No clicks. How do you answer?"

She blurters a series of mind-spinning sentences, effortlessly stitching clicks and clucks into consonants.

"Can't we just say *dumela* in return?"

"No, no. You must practice. Then you can come to my village."

"Any time."

"Are either of you married?"

"No."

"Then you must come to my village. We'll find you a bride."

"Serious?" I said.

"Serious."

We gave her a few bags of *biltong* and candy, a couple music tapes we'd bought in Cape Town, and a Nike pullover we guessed would never fit.

Buffet dinners began at five o'clock. They were packed from the beginning. That's because the crowds at The Champagne Castle Inn resembled the ones in the dining room at Eskaton. The old-school resort at the base of the Drakensberg Mountains, known as the Barrier of Spears, had been in operation since 1934. I'd have laid good money that some of the guests in the buffet line we encountered were also at the ribbon cutting. That same mound of potatoes was probably there, too.

"At least it'll be easy to carbo load for a big trek tomorrow," I joked with Kurt.

He looked distracted and maybe even bummed. Sometimes he'd sink into these moods. Never for long. I knew to give him space then. Here, we were stuck at dinner, so I continued.

"You stressing over something?"

"No," he snapped.

I know you're lying.

"End of the trip?"

"Not really."

A slight concession.

"I'm kinda looking forward to getting home," I said. "We've seen a ton. I feel like I need to let it soak in for a bit. Stuff's starting to blur."

"We cheated Africa. Four months isn't even close to enough. We skipped Namibia and Mozambique. I would have dumped the Seychelles for that. And more time in the bush. But that was your call."

Damn, where's this pissy fit coming from?

"Those places aren't going away," I said. "We'll be back."

"How?"

"You don't think we'll travel together again?"

"Dude, you've got plenty of options. Communications, politics. I'm going back to my low-income-housing rentals and hanging with Roy and his girlfriend with the tattoo on her ass."

Ahh.

"Not if you don't want to. Use the rentals as a base, then do whatever you want."

He paused.

"I kinda thought we'd do something together."

"Like what?"

"A business."

"What kind?"

"Something that would keep us on the road. Travel writing, magazines, a book. You do the writing, I'll take care of the business end."

"I don't think that stuff pays too well."

"And I'm going to get serious about my photography."

"Great. Do it."

"Just seems like it would be a waste to spend a couple years out here and go back to the same ole shit."

I looked down at the meat loaf on my plate and lost my appetite. The food was fine, but I had a bad taste in my mouth.

In a room drenched with sun, I woke clear-minded. The sheets were strewn and the pillows sat on the floor, having been punched and shifted continuously. I probably clocked a total of two hours of sleep that night. Regardless, I felt as energized and content as I'd been in months. Our discussion the night before had freed me. I knew that when I opened my eyes.

The Irvine Company would be the safe road, and a prosperous one, the route I'd followed my entire life before the honeymoon. Yes, I could do that job. And I'm sure that, after a few months, I'd be comfortable again with the routine, the images and discussions from around the world becoming fainter and fainter until they were a fuzzy-edged story or a photo album stacked away. But was it my passion? Would I want it to fill the lines of my obituary? Would I want it to fill the lobes of my brain?

I knew the answer as soon as I read the e-mail from Larry. I couldn't go back to the corporate world. Not now. My world was the world. To revert would go against every impulse I'd worked to heighten. I knew the answer, yet still I flirted with the idea, twisting instincts and true feelings in the process. The comments from Kurt made me put an end to it. And I woke with a smile. I didn't know what I would do, but I was beginning to know me.

Kurt and I had shared a lifetime of experiences on the honeymoon—five continents, two years, countless breathtaking vistas and inspiring locals, road prophets and fumbled loves, a handful of speeding tickets and a couple cases of food poisoning. I woke contented because I knew there'd be many lifetimes more. Maybe we would start a business together. His travel journalism suggestion didn't seem like such a bad idea. The job side would sort itself out. Just like the trip. If there was anything I'd learned from Kurt during the journey, it was that. I'd talk to him during the day.

He suggested a horse ride. The woman at the check-in desk praised the idea, handing us a flier with several pictures of muscular beasts: *Our stable boasts a string of seasoned mountain ponies and horses that will take the nature-loving visitor along many winding trails and open plateaus enhancing the perception of Champagne Castle. A well-informed guide in whose care riders will enjoy a truly memorable excursion conducts rides.* Perfect. We threw on some jeans and headed to the barn.

The stable was empty save for a brown mare whose back sagged like the curve of a guitar. Her darkened eyes and long white whiskers jutting from her nose suggested a decade of service. Instead of giving her a gold watch, they gave her to me for the morning ride. Our guide appeared along with a muscled steed a few hands larger than my horse. Without my noticing, Kurt shuffled to take his reins. And we were away.

"Careful with this one," the guide warned Kurt. "A bit stubborn. He does what he wants to do on these trails."

"Hear that, Kurt?" I asked in the worry-tinged tone of a firstborn.

Framed by a semicircular mountain range, on grassy slopes with the occasional flat stretch to run, we kept the horses in line on the mashed trails. An old-fashioned, Wild West romp. Until I saw small herds of zebra, eland, and mountain reedbuck, that is, huddled in small groups, gnawing on tufts of wildflowers and grass.

"My friend," Kurt said to the guide as we reached a valley bottom, "how about we see what these horses can do?"

"Okay. Hold on. Your guy likes to run."

"What?" I said.

"Don't worry. She don't like to run."

Then, *bam!* Kurt's steed sprinted toward a climb, over dips and debris, with more knowledge of a clump of land than a PGA caddy. Every branch and soft spot, every trail twist and bush outcropping. I looked at his chiseled legs from behind and swore he'd continue up the mountain until he reached the three thousand-meter plateau. I also swore at my horse, idle and content to let the others speed away. Maybe we forgot to fill her up with unleaded grain before we left the barn. The heel of my boot, snap of the rein, and a poor man's *heeeeyaaah* did nothing to change gears. If anything, she slowed. We ambled up to the glistening sprinters a mile away.

"Awesome," Kurt beamed. "Man, that was good."

"I told you he like to run."

"Well, let's let him run."

"Ten minutes. At another flat. Now we rest some more."

"Sorry about your horse," Kurt said to me, muffling his enthusiasm.

"No big deal. We're both just enjoying the scenery."

It was impossible not to. Clear skies, freckled by vultures, pulled the distant Lesotho mountain spires in close for a view. Trout fishermen worked a stream in the distance. Hikers attacked peaks from every direction. Without prejudice, cattle herds mixed with antelope and zebra. My stop-along horse and I devoured it all in slow-motion detail.

After a repeat run-walk-gloat-apologize, Kurt offered to switch horses. I declined. And not because I was being polite, or stubborn, or both. I didn't feel the urge to speed anymore. The amble was therapeutic. The previous night's conversation still rumbled in my head, and the peaceful stretches inspired solutions. But after he insisted, I agreed to change mounts for the final stretch home.

Omens. How come we see them only on review? They're just as clear in the present. Always there, right in front, smacking us in the face like white gloves at a duel. In this instance, the first one was when South Africa's Man O' War kicked his front legs as I placed a foot in the metal stirrup, spurring our guide to race over and grab the reins. The constant twitches and tugs of his head were another omen. I know that now. He tugged hard to go off track. He brayed and snorted as if I'd used pepper spray for cologne. His whinny-from-hell sent the zebras scurrying away in terror. Omens all.

We worked our way through a patch of trees and emerged on the side of a paved two-lane road that twisted toward the inn. The horses moved to the ravine alongside, a natural water drain for the winter storms. I saw the stable across a few turns on the far side of a lumpy field. Home free. Then the guide, realizing I'd been atop this speedster for twenty minutes without stepping on the gas, slowed the horses to a halt. We'll run back, he said. Up the ditch until the gate opens for the paddock. Make a hard left turn, cross the road, plow through the field, and we'll be back at the stables.

Wait a minute? That sounded like Kevin Costner barking directions for the buffalo chase in Dances With Wolves. *And I don't have a SAG card.*

My horse understood perfectly. Confident, pissed, he exploded home. He wanted home.

It was at least a mile away, but I saw it clearer than any close-up on the trip. There. Right at the gate opening. On the side of the road before the ravine dipped down. I saw the yellow, diamond-shaped traffic sign with a curvy black arrow to signal turns ahead, held firmly in the ground by a thick wood post. I could see that. A car speeding past threw my focus for a moment, but my eyes immediately re-locked on the road sign.

We were going to hit it, of that I was sure. A fucking road sign a mile away and we were going to plow into it. The only question was how. Graze it? Clip it with my leg? My horse knew. He'd staged every inch of this ride and was now hurling us both toward the explosive finish.

If I had a pistol I'd shoot you without hesitation.

He was the one with the weapon. A hairy, sweaty, two thousand-pound, rocket-propelled grenade with a kamikaze pilot along for the ride. After gaining speed in the ravine he popped up to the side of the road and increased stride beyond anything I'd seen under Kurt.

Forget the pistol. A staple gun will do. One of those industrial-strength ones. Or a letter opener, even. I don't care about the blood anymore.

Our struggles, diplomatic until then, erupted into war. A war I knew he'd win. We are not crashing into that road sign, I told myself *sans* conviction. Using the reins without success earlier had done nothing to deter me from yanking them again. I pulled back hard at first. It felt as if I were attempting to curl a piano.

Nothing. Again. Nothing. My banshee lowered his head and sped with abandon. The pole grew with each stride.

Plan B. If I couldn't stop him, maybe I could redirect him. Use his force to my advantage. That's judo, right? Or maybe just some logic from a Power Rangers cartoon. Whatever. I gave up on pulling back and instead used all my strength to yank his head to one side. I felt his muscles stiffen even more, starting from his ear, shooting to his neck, then pulsing through his body underneath. His head locked, frozen.

I fought to turn him right, onto the road. A couple feet would do. He stiffened toward the left, refusing to slow. I wanted right. He wanted left. Right. Left. We halved the difference.

Running at full stride, he shifted to the side of the pole at the last possible moment and just as I was leaning across his body to the right. My left ribs took the full impact, smacking the wood hard enough to uproot the entire sign and launch it through the air. I saw it sail like a javelin as I flew myself. Out of the saddle, over a fallen tree, and into the bottom of the ravine.

With a deadweight thud, I landed on my back. And yelled like a newborn. Which only made my ribs throb even more. I felt as if I'd just met the firing squad. Only I was still alive. Unbelievable, but I was still operational. I looked up at a vulture flying overhead and, for some twisted reason, thought about my father's questions regarding health insurance. I didn't have any.

I had Kurt. His nag strode up as if bored. Loved that horse.

"Holy shit!" he said.

Thanks for the comforting words.

"Don't move."

"Don't worry. I can't."

"Good. I . . . I mean bad. Can you move your arm?"

He lifted it, and I held it out for a few seconds. Then he did the same with my legs. I still had feeling in them. I could move my head a bit as well. Shocking, considering the piercing, tooth-grinding pain that radiated from my chest throughout every atom of my body. I begged Kurt to let me rest for a long time.

"That was some horrible riding," he said. "What were you trying to do?"

"Stick the base of that sign in the heart of that damn horse."

For the next hour Kurt examined my cuts and bruises while I yelped and fantasized about horse slaughter. Crude, gory horse slaughter. He made a bunch of hokey comparisons to Willie Shoemaker and spouted clichés involving the words *horsing around*. I started to laugh. Then quickly stopped after realizing the battle between the horse and me was nothing compared with the war between laughter and broken ribs.

Slowly, gingerly, Kurt put his arm under mine and helped me to my feet. He'd rescued me before. We made our way to the inn like a trainer and football player after a nasty concussion. The guide was nowhere to be seen. Nor any ambulance, doctor, Band-Aid, or lollipop. Kurt ran a warm bath in our room, then poured me a glass of red wine. You'll need it, he said before giving me the bottle. I was going back to America dinged up.

THIS POOR OLE WORLD OF OURS

The boy entered the bus in Zambia holding his mother's hand. He wore a blue dress shirt, fraying at the cuffs and collar, dusty black shoes with no socks, and ripped black jeans, probably handed down. The other passengers stared out the windows. He stared at his shiny new belt, constantly fidgeting with the buckle.

When he stood, I saw that the belt wrapped once around his waist then almost again. Holes had been punched into the leather to shrink the size to his small frame. This was a belt meant to last many years, and the boy's cherished possession. He was lucky, well off even by Zambian standards. His mother could afford a belt. And a ticket on the bus. Most of his countrymen aren't as fortunate.

We left the upscale hotels and safari lodges in Botswana and South Africa and ventured into Zambia and Malawi overland. They are some of the poorest countries we've seen on the trip. And we've seen many, including Cambodia and Syria, parts of Bulgaria and Indonesia, slums in Brazil, Russia, and Thailand. In fact, if you limited me to just one adjective to describe the world, I'd use *poor*.

A friend e-mailed me during our stop in Cambodia. He wanted to know if the country was suitable for children. "Absolutely," I responded, feeling it would be beneficial for kids to see their counterparts playing happily in front of one-room tin-roof shacks. They could learn a lot from the poor. So could their parents. I know I have.

They'd learn a cold shower is better than no shower.

They'd know what it's like to laugh and cry at the same time after a group of smiling, malnourished kids hug your knee.

They'd understand the world isn't full of double-espresso lattes, but powdered milk and boiled water. Ironic, but ask for a coffee in a country famous for its coffee— Colombia or Indonesia, for example—and you'll probably receive instant. The good beans go straight to Starbucks or Folger's.

They'd see that the toughest stares can usually be melted away with a wave or a thumbs-up sign.

They'd see that in most of the world, children don't tease each other as much about their clothes and adults don't nitpick a friend's wardrobe. Just having clothes far outweighs irrelevancies like color clashes or seasonal choices. That old man with the hole-filled sports coat worn on a ninety-degree day isn't trying to be fashionable. It's probably one of the only pieces he owns.

They'd learn most Third-World citizens view employment as gold, and they'd rarely hear someone say the words *not my job*.

They'd understand why people around the Third World don't become angry when a car breaks down or a village loses power. They know they are privileged to have them.

They'd see that offers of food or drink are rarely refused. Even if the food is half-eaten or removed from its wrapper. It's never considered impolite to offer nourishment.

They'd know what it's like to give away all the money in your pocket during a city stroll and still feel awful after realizing you've forgotten a penniless little girl.

They'd experience a new type of humor. I asked a van driver directions to a hotel in Lusaka, Zambia. "Up there," he said. "I'll take you for one thousand five hundred kwacha." "No thanks," I said. "I want to walk." "Okay," he said. "Only five hundred kwacha to walk."

They'd understand the constant struggle to stay clean in streets without pavement and with feet without shoes.

They'd learn the best auto mechanics in the world are not only in Detroit and Düsseldorf, but also in places like Soweto, where craftsmen work on cars raised on blocks in front of homes. With minimal tools and spare parts, they perform miracles on cars well past factory life expectancy. Ditto for the makeshift scooter-repair shops in Vietnam.

They'd recognize that poverty doesn't automatically equate to unhappiness. Some of the biggest smiles we've seen have been in areas where people have the least.

They'd see our world is packed full of renaissance men and women who can perform multiple tasks to earn a living. In Malawi, every car is a potential cab. The bus station porters in Puerto Montt, Chile, will book you a room at a guesthouse, then walk you there. In Syria, the hummus vendors will also sell you carpets or jewelry if you ask.

They'd learn to be more comfortable seeing global brothers and sisters with heavily calloused feet and soiled clothes, with eyes glazed and bellies misshapen from lack of food, with uncombed hair and in need of a bath. They'd become more comfortable amid poverty, yet hopefully more inspired to tackle it.

They'd see that poor communities aren't all "woe is me." There's an energy, a camaraderie uncommon in Western cities. Ask for a specific cab driver or salesman, and his competitors will know his location and help you track him down.

There is also an amplified spirituality along with packed churches, temples, and mosques. With shorter life spans and fewer material distractions, those of the Third World spend more time focusing on faith. Like the cab driver in Zambia who told us he was Christian before he told us his name, or the carpet salesman in Turkey who came to our inn to drop off a Koran. Mosques, churches, and temples are not only packed on religious days, they serve as town centers and gathering places the rest of the week.

They'd know that their mother was right. There are people starving in Africa. Eat your vegetables.

26

My mother coordinated the birthday party. She'd spent the most time with LaRue of late, sending e-mails after each visit to let Kurt and me know which function was slipping. It's her eyes, she'd say. Or her strength. Never since I'd known LaRue had it been her mind. Lately, it was her mind.

But who cared if she was fading? She'd made it, hadn't she? A century on this planet. Of course we were going to celebrate. We gathered in one of Eskaton's event rooms, all the family: my parents; Lisa and Doug, their wind-up toy daughter Elizabeth, the Chiltons and Hammons, Daniels and Foughts; herds of towheaded cousins whose names floated in my head, unattached to their rightful owners. Eskaton residents sat in wheelchairs and on sofas along the walls. LaRue's constituents. Kurt and I made the rounds, spending extra time with the ones who had followed our journey through postcards and e-mails.

A group of senior barbershoppers launched into melodies recognized only by the Eskaton locals. Songs about canoe rides and flappers and malts. The store-bought cake (*oh, don't tell LaRue that detail*) and nonalcoholic punch, the singers and nurses, overdue conversations about money problems or midlife crises (ones that began with "I'm going to buy a Harley"), our family and the Eskaton crew—we had all the ingredients for the celebration. Except LaRue.

I knew she wouldn't be there. It was something my mom had mentioned in an e-mail a month prior. They'd moved her to another room, this one with IVs and big lights, a space without a trace of home. I asked my mom if they'd moved LaRue's world map with the shiny red pins. No, she said. It wouldn't fit. Did she ask for it? Only her crosses.

I pulled Kurt from a discussion with an elderly couple, clipping his story about a "face-to-face" shark sighting in the Seychelles. At any other time, I would have chided him about the shark's proximity, more like a face-to-twenty-feet-below encounter. Not here, not now. He knew where we were going and excused the interruption. Without words, we walked through the maze of halls until the barbershop harmonies faded to a murmur.

The silence in her room hit me first. No EKG beeps or piped-in Muzak. LaRue had a roommate before, a sour, thin woman who kept the room-dividing curtain pulled at all hours and listened to Montel at uncomfortably loud levels: "WE'RE HERE TO SUPPORT YOU. GO AHEAD AND TELL YOUR HUSBAND THAT IF HE CHEATS ON YOU ONE MORE TIME WITH THE BABYSITTER YOU'RE GOING TO LEAVE HIM. GO ON." She was gone now, so, too, the advice. I didn't ask where. Or why someone with little interest in interaction would spend her days watching shows about improving relationships. LaRue lay curled away from view. Her eighty pounds lifted the sheets no higher than would a small pillow.

Tell me what you're dreaming about, LaRue. Someplace warm and relaxing like a blanket of sand on a distant shore? Maybe someplace far more grand? Tell me it isn't Montel.

Kurt hesitated with a "what-do-we-do," raised-eyebrow stare. I nodded him toward the bed.

"LaRue," he whispered while rubbing her shoulder. "LaRue," he whispered louder. "Wake up a sec."

With surprising fluidity and ease, she rolled onto her back. Someone had given her that haircut she'd long promised. Her hair was matted now but shorter. An improvised job for sure, more of a simple trim than a salon special. The thought of her receiving it made me smile. She reached for her glasses on the metal tray.

"Happy Birthday, gorgeous," I managed to say.

"Happy . . . Birthday," she repeated in a dulled tone.

"LaRue," Kurt said, "we came all the way from Africa for this party. Just like we promised. We're here."

Stony and pursed at first, her lips slowly worked themselves into a grin. I felt her detachment immediately, though it was hard to say how much was from the recent nap, how much from a body shutting down, and how much from reaching the pinnacle she'd long prophesied. Several photos from our trips framed the headboard above. *Elephant Safari* and *My Grandsons,* read my mom's handwriting in the white borders. I smiled at the latter, a shot of the two of us with a group of eight children from a remote Botswana village. *My Grandsons.*

"Great party, LaRue. You know we wouldn't miss this for the world," I said.

A distant smile floated on her face while her head shifted from side to side, stretching to locate us, a slow-motion fan at a tennis match. Her glassy eyes had a purposefulness as if they were recording images for a final time.

"My boys. You . . . made it."

"Of course we made it," Kurt said.

"Did you bring me a postcard?"

"They're right here on the wall."

She turned back toward him, then past. Away from his nervous clutch on the bed's handrail, beyond the insufficient words, past a rain cloud of emotion we fought to contain. She stopped on a space of wall near her pillow. Where she'd hung one cross before, now there were five. A silver one with metal threads rested above the others. Together they captured every existing snippet of her remaining energy. Everyone else, everything else had now become inanimate bystanders.

"There're beautiful, aren't they?" she whispered with a clarity I assumed long gone.

"You're beautiful, LaRue," I said.

The words felt insufficient as soon as I muttered them. There was so much more I wanted to tell her. She'd guided our trip from this hospital bed. I wanted to talk about it some more, to see her point to the pins one last time. I wanted to eat another helping of strawberry shortcake from the cafeteria while she praised the whipped cream and motioned for others to come meet her grandsons, "the world travelers."

Let's go, LaRue. Anywhere. Pick a country. One last time.

By the end of the conversation we were too late. Another nap began to enwrap her. I glanced to Kurt and sensed he was content. His eyes said, "We made it." I knew our journey was over, and that I wanted to be with family. We backed out the door and rejoined the party.

EPILOGUE

Rarely did my mother call me on the cell phone. Such an extravagance, she'd say. I'll just call you in a few days when you're home. I'd remind her that my cell phone was my home phone, but the message never seemed to register.

She called a month after the birthday party. As soon as I recognized her number on the screen, I knew LaRue had died. After the barbershoppers had finished their set and the guests went home, LaRue decided she'd lived enough. The blended meals went untouched. Offers of juice were politely declined. She just drifted off like she'd done more than 36,500 times before. And she was gone.

My parents' phone number leapt on my cell phone display a few weeks later. This one did surprise me. I'd just sat down to dinner with some longtime friends at a Thai restaurant in Washington, D.C., having flown East to see if any publisher was interested in a story about two honeymooning brothers. Sorry to interrupt, Kurt said as I walked away from the table to take the call outside. He told me they were going through LaRue's belongings, boxing clothes to give away, putting furniture in storage, shuttling the plates she decorated with drawings of birds and flowers to family members longing for reminders.

The lawyers, he said, had told him about a small stockpile of blue chips, stocks Ray had bought for her sixty, seventy years ago. Put them in a drawer, he counseled at the time. Forget about them. So that's what she'd done.

How on earth can she have any money? She's been retired, what, since 1955? Eskaton ain't cheap.

"The lawyers say she left it all to you and me."

Before he could explain, a mishmash of images rattled through my brain. Those cheap, powder blue polyester pants that never reached her ankles. The cake-decorating magazines and "bless your soul." Her kindling gaze and the way she strode the halls of Eskaton despite the crafted hips. And of course, the map. Laminated, full of pins marking her walkabouts and ours.

"She wanted us to keep going," Kurt said.

I knew where I'd send the postcards.